STAGE RIGHTS!

Manchester University Press

WOMEN, THEATRE AND PERFORMANCE

SERIES EDITORS
MAGGIE B. GALE AND KATE DORNEY

Already published

Treading the bawds: actresses and playwrights on the late Stuart stage
GILLI BUSH-BAILEY

Performing herself: AutoBiography and Fanny Kelly's Dramatic Recollections
GILLI BUSH-BAILEY

Auto/biography and identity: women, theatre and performance
EDS MAGGIE B. GALE AND VIV GARDNER

Women, theatre and performance: new histories, new historiographies
EDS MAGGIE B. GALE AND VIV GARDNER

Female performance practice on the fin-de-siècle popular stages of London and Paris: Experiment and advertisement
CATHERINE HINDSON

Plays and Performance Texts by Women 1880–1930: An Anthology of Plays by British and American Women of the Modernist Period
EDS MAGGIE B. GALE AND GILLI BUSH BAILEY

STAGE RIGHTS!

The Actresses' Franchise League,
activism and politics 1908–58

NAOMI PAXTON

Manchester University Press

Copyright © Naomi Paxton 2018

The right of Naomi Paxton to be identified as the author of this work has been asserted by her in accordance with the Copyright, Designs and Patents Act 1988.

Published by Manchester University Press
Altrincham Street, Manchester M1 7JA
www.manchesteruniversitypress.co.uk

British Library Cataloguing- in- Publication Data
A catalogue record for this book is available from the British Library

ISBN 978 1 5261 1478 5 hardback
ISBN 978 1 5261 1480 8 paperback

First published 2018

The publisher has no responsibility for the persistence or accuracy of URLs for any external or third-party internet websites referred to in this book, and does not guarantee that any content on such websites is, or will remain, accurate or appropriate.

Typeset by Out of House Publishing

Contents

List of figures	*page* vi
List of abbreviations	viii
Series editors' foreword	ix
Acknowledgements	x
Introduction: re-evaluating the AFL	1
1 Exhibition	17
2 Sisterhood	50
3 Visibility	82
4 Militancy	107
5 Hope	149
6 Legacy	190
Bibliography	205
Index	230

Figures

1.1	The WSPU Drum and Fife Band advertising the 1909 WSPU Women's Exhibition. London School of Economics Library	*page* 19
1.2	Inside the 1909 WSPU Women's Exhibition. This picture appears to have been taken from the bandstand area. © Museum of London	21
1.3	Exterior of the second-division prison cell at the 1909 WSPU Women's Exhibition. There is a notice pinned to the cell that reads, 'In a similar cell PATRICIA WOODLOCK is serving a three months' sentence in complete solitude. She – released – June 16 there will be a Hyde Park Demonstration the same evening at 8 o'clock.' © Museum of London	25
1.4	WSPU member Marie Brackenbury as the 'prisoner' in the second division prison cell at the 1909 WSPU Women's Exhibition. © Museum of London in the second-division prison cell at the 1909 WSPU Women's Exhibition	29
1.5	Detail of the theatre space at the 1909 WSPU Women's Exhibition. From the 1909 WSPU Women's Exhibition Programme, LSE Library	33
2.1	From *How the Vote Was Won* by Cicely Hamilton, 1908. Illustration by C. Hedley Charlton. Author's collection	65
2.2	Decima Moore performing in the Aldwych Rinkeries for the Census Boycott, 1911. © Museum of London	67
3.1	The musicians' section of the AFL marchers in the 1911 Coronation Procession. In the foreground, holding the written sign, are Ethel Smyth and Mrs Pertwee. LSE Library	83
3.2	Decima Moore in the Coronation Procession, 1911. © Museum of London	84
3.3	Lena Ashwell and Gertrude Elliott in the Coronation Procession, 1911. © Museum of London	86

LIST OF FIGURES vii

3.4 Joan Dugdale and her sister Daisy selling *Votes for Women* at the entrance to the Oval Cricket Ground, 1908. © Museum of London   90
4.1 Australian actress Muriel Matters being removed from the Ladies Gallery of the House of Commons. *Illustrated London News*, 7 November 1908, House of Commons Library   116
4.2 Cartoon from *Votes for Women*, with the caption 'THE W.S.P.U.: "One or two more shots and we'll have it down."' Pictured with the AFL are both militant and constitutional suffrage societies including the WFL, Cymric Suffrage Union, MPU, WSPU, Independent Labour Party and New Constitutional Society. *Votes for Women*, 29 December 1911, LSE Library   124
4.3 Costume design for Lewis Sydney as a 'suffragette Maud Allan' for *Pelissier's Follies of 1911* at the Apollo Theatre. Mark Samuels Lasner Collection, University of Delaware Library   136
5.1 Woman's Theatre logo, 1913. University of Bristol Theatre Collection   150
5.2 Leaflet advertising the first season of the Woman's Theatre, 1913. University of Bristol Theatre Collection   156
5.3 'The Enfranchised Waiter'   159
5.4 'The Voteless One'. *Votes for Women*, 23 January 1914, LSE Library   160
5.5 'The Absent Waiter: Wake Me When He Comes'   161
5.6 'The Present Actress'. *Votes for Women*, 30 January 1914, LSE Library   162
5.7 The Woman's Theatre Camps Entertainments logo. University of Bristol Theatre Collection   171
5.8 'Haven'. Poster for British Women's Hospital Fund, 1915, Library of Congress, Prints and Photographs Division, WWI Posters   175
5.9 'How Much More Effective My Work Would Be If My Hands Were Unfettered!'. Detail from front page of *Votes for Women*, 21 August 1914, LSE Library   178
6.1 AFL banner, c. 1911. © Museum of London   197

Abbreviations

AFL	Actresses' Franchise League
MLWS	Men's League for Women's Suffrage
MPU	Men's Political Union for Women's Enfranchisement
NUWSS	National Union of Women's Suffrage Societies
WAB	Women's Adjustment Board
WEC	Women's Emergency Corps
WFL	Women's Freedom League
WSPU	Women's Social and Political Union
WWSL	Women Writers' Suffrage League

Series editors' foreword

The Women, Theatre and Performance series was born out of a desire to bring together research on the many aspects of women's contributions to theatre and performance histories. Historically, the 'Second Wave' women's movement in the 1980s produced research on women in the theatre industry and their work as playwrights, performers, designers, theatre-makers and consumers of theatre and performance. Feminist performance analysis and women's theatre history has now become an established part of performance practice and theatre studies at both a university and a more popular level, although work made by women frequently remains marginal to many educational curricula and within the mainstream repertoire.

In the 1990s, the journal *Women and Theatre Occasional Papers*, from which this series arose, placed an emphasis on history and historiography. Founding series editors Maggie B. Gale and Viv Gardner were concerned to open out women's theatre histories beyond those considered within feminist praxis. Work made by women seen as more mainstream or more commercial was explored alongside more innovative and politically oriented practices. This came from a desire to find a consistent outlet for the retrieval project of women's theatre and performance histories. The emphasis on history does not preclude engagement with contemporary practice, as our edited volumes evidence. Women, Theatre and Performance seeks to make research and debate on women's performance practices available on a more than 'occasional' basis and has so far included edited volumes and single-themed monographs as well as reprints of performance texts by women, all of which share in common the consideration of women's theatre and performance as part of a wider nexus of theatre histories and of social and cultural practices.

Maggie B. Gale and Kate Dorney
The University of Manchester
Editorial Board: Gilli Bush-Bailey, Emeritus Professor of Women's Theatre History at the Royal Central School for Speech and Drama, London; Viv Gardner, Emeritus Professor of Drama, the University of Manchester.

Acknowledgements

With thanks to:

Professor Maggie B. Gale.

My family, my wife and my friends for their support and encouragement.

The many friends and colleagues who first caught my enthusiasm for the Actresses' Franchise League (AFL) and who have been such inspiring collaborators and artists, in particular Shazz Andrew, Samantha Bond, Janie Dee, Louise Gold, David Hall, Jane How, Bruce Guthrie, Kathryn Martin, Andrew Mills, Charlotte Moore and Rebecca Mordan.

The families of AFL members who have been so generous with their time and memories.

Too many academics and historians to mention, but among them: Professor Anna Birch, Professor Katharine Cockin, Irene Cockroft, Dr Barbara Cohen-Stratyner, Beverley Cook, Professor Krista Cowman, Elizabeth Crawford, Dr Susan Croft, Professor Lesley Ferris, Professor Viv Gardner, Dr Ailsa Grant Ferguson, Dr Claire Warden and all the librarians who worked at the Women's Library Reading Room when it was at the London Met.

Matthew Gregory, Encoded Ltd, Martin Levy, Susan Jeffs, Kathryn Martin and Equity Charitable Trust for the financial support which made the Ph.D. possible.

The Society of Theatre Research for an award to help cover image costs for this book.

Mark Dudgeon and Dom O'Hanlon from Bloomsbury for considering and taking on *The Methuen Drama Book of Suffrage Plays* and *The Methuen Drama Book of Suffrage Plays: Taking the Stage*, Sarah Mowat from the National Theatre for programming the 2013 Platform performance of *Suffragettes on Stage*, and Judith Merritt, Perri Blakelock and Emile Chen at the National Theatre for and helping spread the word about the AFL to a new audience through the Dramatic Progress: Votes for Women and the Edwardian Stage exhibition and events.

Introduction: Re-evaluating the AFL

Founded in 1908 as 'a bond of union between all women in the Theatrical profession who are in sympathy with the Woman's Franchise Movement', the Actresses' Franchise League (AFL) was the first such organisation to orient its activities entirely around the politics of suffrage.[1] Neutral in regard to tactics, the League was formed to 'work for women's enfranchisement by educational methods', including 'Propaganda Meetings, Sale of Literature, Propaganda Plays and Lectures', and to 'assist all other Leagues whenever possible'.[2] The League produced and commissioned plays, participated in rallies and exhibitions and was fervently and productively active in the fight for the vote, creating a space in which professional feminist actresses could be, and be seen to be, politically engaged and active. Through the networks and work of the League, performers and writers gained experience of direct action and constitutional campaigning, informing their stance on issues that affected women in the theatre industry by placing their specific experience within a wider socio-cultural framework. Ensuring high-profile members were accessible to the public was a unique feature of the organisation – and through speakers' classes, regular appearances in public and in the suffragist, theatrical and national press, actresses learnt to communicate their political views with authority and confidence on stage and off.

This book was born out of my work primarily as an actress, performer and activist. I knew a little of the AFL but had not realised just how extensive and significant the organisation was. Nor had I realised that their work had carried on through two world wars and beyond, and had direct links to international feminist movements within the theatre. However, my hunch was that the League was more active, innovative and networked within the profession than previous scholarship had acknowledged, and I had many questions – particularly around the diversity of performers and performance genres represented by the membership, and the contribution of theatre professionals to the wider performative aspects of the movement. The answers were startling and exciting. Performers and audiences experienced, through suffrage plays and the theatrical propaganda of the suffrage movement, a different kind of performance – one that directly examined ideas of political participation, representation and spectatorship. These performances played with cultures of display and performative propaganda, manipulating images, text, form and space to find new ways to interact with their audiences and to effectively blur the boundaries between 'acting' and 'being'.

Jacky Bratton's concept of 'intertheatricality', which she notes should not be confined to the female tradition, has been important in forging new appraisals of the known activities of the League and particularly in finding a means of connecting their professional work to the numerous political and social campaigns they espoused.[3] Her intertheatrical model of creativity, in which ideas and acts of collaboration, performance and spectatorship require nuanced interpretation and analysis informed by knowledge of cooperative theatrical and social networks, is extremely valuable in an interrogation into the history of the AFL and its significance in wider histories of British theatre. Micro history – the local and specific used to generate a history of macro culture – is helpful as a means of constructing and considering new histories of the AFL, and the micro details of suffrage meetings, casts, events and even anecdotes evidence a well-established network of active and professionally effective women and men – actresses, actors, dancers, performers, musicians, writers, managers and producers who trained and built their careers together in the 1880s and 1890s. Biographical information also informs the micro, alongside factual data gathered from newspapers and archives forming the basis on which the everyday work of the League can be understood. There has been little consistent historiographically layered research around almost every aspect of the AFL's work – and the weaving together of autobiographical and biographical detail remains vital as a means of building a fuller picture of an organisation whose members operated on many levels of visibility simultaneously. Apart from short pieces in collections of plays, references to individuals and biographies, there is no published comprehensive history of the AFL as an organisation that uses this approach. The intention of this book is to therefore take some steps towards realising this project.

While the book aims to both contribute to a reimagining of the League and to be a first attempt at a full account of the organisation, five areas of the AFL's work are explored in critical detail. Four chapters consider different aspects of the League's work within the context of the suffrage movement before the outbreak of the First World War, and the fifth and sixth chapters examine its contribution to feminist and

INTRODUCTION 3

social campaigns from 1914 to 1958. This introduction reviews material published by and about the League that has shaped the presence of the organisation in existing histories of feminist theatre, political theatre and the suffrage movement. The first chapter, 'Exhibition', looks at the participation of the League in large indoor suffrage exhibitions, fairs and bazaars between 1908 and 1914, contextualising its work within the performative propaganda strategies of the suffrage movement and its interventions in public visually oriented space. Here I consider the representations of women and womanhood in suffrage plays and popular entertainments, the ways in which womanhood was represented and commoditised by suffrage societies and how theatre and performance was used to share experiences of violence, imprisonment and political campaigning. Drawing from accounts of the 1909 Women's Social and Political Union (WSPU) Women's Exhibition, the chapter introduces an examination of the broader scope of performance practices as an integral component of the strategies of suffrage societies. Chapter 2, 'Sisterhood', explores the networks of some League members before 1908 and the support of male theatrical professionals within the organisation. Looking at other social and feminist issues that affected and concerned League members, the chapter considers the impact of the Census Boycott of 1911, includes brief accounts of the work of suffragist actresses in variety and vaudeville and briefly explores the contribution made to the American suffrage campaign by three suffragist actresses allied to the AFL. The third chapter, 'Visibility', looks at how the issue of women's suffrage was portrayed in *The Era* and how information about theatrical support for women's suffrage was circulated in the industry press. Intending to broaden current scholarship, this chapter also focuses on the actresses who were visible as suffragists both in public and in the theatrical profession, through suffrage processions and newspaper-selling in particular, and the plays and journalism integral to that visibility and interaction. The fourth chapter, 'Militancy', investigates activism and direct action by AFL members. Drawing on the stories of actresses who were imprisoned and arrested, the chapter also explores representations of militants and militancy on stage and includes analyses of the conflicts expressed privately and publicly within the League about the issues surrounding militancy. The fifth chapter, 'Hope', begins with an analysis of the AFL's Woman's Theatre project and charts the work of the organisation and its portfolio of wartime projects between 1914 and 1918. This chapter also includes the work of the League after the First World War and the continuing campaign for equal female suffrage.

The final chapter, 'Legacy', charts the work of the organisation from 1930 until 1958. Attempting to draw together what is known about the League post-1928, the chapter details the continuing connections with the theatre industry, introducing research that will hopefully be a springboard for more scholarship. This final chapter reflects upon the story of the League's contribution to the suffrage movement, its many projects and its influence within the theatrical profession over half a century of campaigning. As a whole then, *Stage Rights! The Actresses' Franchise League, Activism and Politics, 1908–58* aims to renew interest in, and suggest more nuanced ways of looking at, the work of the AFL as a unique organisation that revolutionised the ways theatre women operated professionally, socially and politically during the early decades of the twentieth century.

Women, theatre histories and marginalisation

> When I began reading about the Victorian and Edwardian actresses I was presented with a picture of them as handmaidens to the great actor managers, male dramatists and directors of the day; I had no idea they had created their own theatre.[4]

For an influential feminist organisation at the heart of both the Edwardian theatre industry and the campaign for women's suffrage, there is surprisingly little information about the AFL available in the public domain. The first formal study of the AFL, Julie Holledge's *Innocent Flowers* (1981), based on her Ph.D. research, broke new ground in the field of women's theatre history and was an influential component of an emerging feminist awareness and analysis in the 1980s of the history of women's theatre practice in the UK.[5] It is not surprising that Holledge had originally been unaware of the AFL – although mentions of it existed in some autobiographies written by actresses between the wars, the organisation and its work was excluded from academic and popular theatre histories of the twentieth century. Subsequent mainstream theatre histories of the period have sometimes included suffrage theatre but rarely, if at all, explored the significance of the League within the history of theatre and professional practice between 1908 and 1914 and beyond. Therefore, with a few exceptions, the idea of Victorian and Edwardian actresses as 'handmaidens' has been pervasive, and where the League's work is recognised it has been more generally contextualised within histories of the suffrage movement rather than the theatre industry. Prompted by *Innocent Flowers* new accounts of the League's work began to appear through the 1980s and

1990s, with scholars uncovering previously overlooked archival material and using it in combination with Holledge's findings. These discoveries created a framework for the AFL that often seemed to set the story of the League in relation to existing histories of the suffrage movement, rather than to theatre histories, which has meant that it has not been widely or effectively mapped onto, for example, explorations of the socialist and political theatre of the early twentieth century. Writers such as George Bernard Shaw and J. M. Barrie and prominent actor-managers such as Johnston Forbes-Robertson, F. R. Benson and Granville-Barker are not recognised for their support of and collaboration with the AFL or suffragist actresses but are known for their socialist and political interests. Without this political, socialist and feminist context to inform recent literary critiques of suffrage plays and the work of suffragists in the theatre, they have been easily dismissed and judged as amateurish and ephemeral – outside of the mainstream commercial contemporary theatre. When considered merely 'a lively part of the London fringe theatrical scene' the subtlety, wit and intelligence of suffrage plays, full as they are of parody, pastiche, nuance, humour and political commentary, has often been obscured.[6] In reality, the AFL was not on the 'fringe' of its theatrical world but created and performed work in spaces and with performers at the heart of the commercial industry.

Popular or industry-generated theatre histories written immediately after the Edwardian era did not generally champion or detail the work of feminist women and men. Journalists, commentators and critics such as St John Ervine, Max Beerbohm and Walter MacQueen-Pope created a fictionalised theatrical world, relying heavily on anecdote, gossip and critical barbs in their memoirs. Largely written for an amateur readership or fan base, these books are neither expressly analytical, reflective of the wider cultural context of the period nor explicit in their references to individuals or networks. Where women do feature they are invariably portrayed as being without creative agency of their own – much like the 'handmaidens' of Holledge's imagination. MacQueen-Pope's evocative, nostalgic remembrances of the Edwardian theatre milieu mention many actresses who were members of the AFL while avoiding the issue of women's involvement in political theatre and subsequently sidestepping any engagement with feminist campaigning. Although he did mention the 'Suffragettes – or the Wild Women – or the Shrieking Sisterhood', he also asserted that 'Equality did not appeal to the late Victorians or early Edwardians en masse'.[7] Jim Davis, describing MacQueen-Pope as a 'latter day Canute', reflects on his protective presentation of an imagined theatrical Golden Age, seeing his dismissal of women's suffrage as just one among a number of key political and social changes affecting a transition in the theatre that he was reluctant to acknowledge – including socialism, film and 'the inexorable tide of modernity'.[8] These little remembered histories may seem too general to be useful as source material for any scholarly attempt to map the work of the AFL, but their popularity has contributed to a general attitude that assumes the work of the League and of suffragist actresses was insignificant in its own time. Immediately after the First World War, the AFL was written out of popular histories of the theatrical work of the period and consequently later histories based on the earlier works. This is in part to do with a lack of acceptance of particular forms of political theatre – the perception of suffrage plays as realist comedies focused on middle-class issues, as overly commercial or as populist non-'literary' plays – but it is also symptomatic of a more general refusal to embed histories of women's professional theatre work into standard histories of theatre per se.

In their own words: suffrage plays, preservation and publication

In her chronology of plays addressing or supporting suffrage issues, Susan Croft lists 120 plays in all from 1907 to 1914 – not including 'plays from the wider culture on suffrage themes and women's rights, unless they were part of a campaign or reviewed as suffragist in the press'.[9] Edwardian feminists talked to themselves and each other in public space and through the medium of the stage, finding a convention – the theatre – that meant their views could be stated, 'played out' live and be heard with the minimum of disruption. Where verbatim accounts of speeches or accurate documentation of any one individual's involvement may be lost, many of the plays remain, and these can be used as a way to chart changes in style, language and argument over the course of the later suffrage campaign. Part of the impetus behind this book has been to find ways of embellishing existing scholarship through providing a more nuanced approach to the layers of complexity that characterise suffrage drama. The subtleties of the texts produced by the AFL, the Women Writers' Suffrage League (WWSL) and suffragist playwrights cannot be understood without an appreciation of the context in which they were written and performed. For example, for the AFL to maintain its stance on neutrality regarding activist tactics, it could not have published plays that promoted militancy directly or explicitly. Reading these plays through the lens of the research process has revealed them to be more precious and important than I had previously imagined, and even less deserving of the relegated status they still have in the scholarship of this period. With so little written about the movement in the autobiographies and biographies of those involved – where they exist – it is suffrage plays that seem to speak most clearly and freely of the period, employing challenging and complex representations of contemporary women and men in both allegorical and literal settings, drawing on verbatim accounts of the experiences of those within the movement. Plays published by suffrage societies were marketed, sold and designed with the suffragist customer in mind – and, conversely, suffrage plays published by mainstream theatrical publishers may have been less visible on first sight as political propaganda to a general theatre-going public. Some were successful in the UK and internationally, giving a voice to suffragist audiences as well as performers, and allowing them to imagine and create environments and characters that reflected their own lives and ideological interests. Here it is important to note that there were also pro-suffrage songs, operas, music-hall sketches, dances and films that deserve more detailed consideration by scholars working on suffrage and performance histories. These are unfortunately beyond the scope of much of this book.

The idea that 'preservation is linked to publication' is an important one.[10] The print culture in which suffrage plays were first made publicly available was immeasurably different from today. Many of the plays were published either in subscription or weekly journals, or by small and limited clientele publishers – rare in our contemporary corporatised publishing world. The publication context was quick and not necessarily designed for a literary market. Suffrage plays appear to have been relatively free from the pressure of commercial frameworks and have therefore been seen as largely outside of the business model of the industry as a whole. The speed of access now made available by the Internet has meant that many of these plays have only recently become more widely available to more than a limited academic market. Tracing the trajectory of anthologies of plays reveals the different kinds of agendas at play over a number of decades around the politics of women's theatre work and the politics of (re)publication. If the number of British suffrage plays is at least 120, as Croft's research asserts, just over a third have been republished since Holledge's 1981 book. Susan Carlson has acknowledged that, in order 'to understand its full presence and effect', suffrage theatre needs to be broadly defined, while Katherine Cockin has noted that it is hard to create a canon of suffrage plays so early on in the process of scholarship around suffragist theatre: 'Some plays which could be included in the category of women's suffrage drama are not immediately recognisable as such, demanding familiarity with the history of women's suffrage, its arguments and campaign issues'.[11] Therefore almost any piece written from the late nineteenth century onwards and performed at a suffrage meeting, or a piece performed by a suffragist cast, or a play containing a positive suffragist or suffragette character, or work that addresses issues around women's rights or social issues affecting women's lives, or indeed any play written by a known suffragist playwright or a playwright sympathetic to women's suffrage might qualify for inclusion.[12]

The suffrage plays published by scholars since the 1980s have generated a second, limited canon in which some, such as *How the Vote Was Won*, have dominated anthologies come to be representative of the field. Because the plays published have not been organised in any specific way – there are, for example, no volumes of the collected works of individual suffragist women writers – it has been difficult to approach this second canon without generalisation. I have concluded that while it has been vital to republish this body of work, there has often seemed to be little thought for grouping the plays by theme, date, provenance, audience or topic. One might argue that the plays have been published almost haphazardly in an attempt to show the diversity of the genre, but the varying quality of writing, contextual information provided and evidenced performance history has sometimes stifled rather than amplified the communicative potential of the plays. Equally, the politics and economics of the publishing industry impacts on what might be published from this body of work, how it might be published and for what market. In part, then, the project of this book is to bring together informed and integrated contextual research from both suffrage and theatre histories. The ideas the AFL explored through plays, events and activism remain relevant for current campaigners, and it is both heartening and disheartening that despite their very specific language, cultural references and ideas, suffrage plays still speak successfully to audiences today, as issues around the lack of social and political equality for women remain and are in many ways still prevalent in the theatre industry. The work of the League shows that agitation for equality for women at all levels of the theatre industry began long before the women's theatre movement of the 1970s and 1980s. Fortunately, feminist campaigners within the theatrical professions have easier access to the histories of the suffrage movement and the AFL than ever before, which will hopefully create

INTRODUCTION 9

more interest in and awareness of the work of this creative, pragmatic and inspiring organisation.

In their own words: autobiography, archives and ephemera

Remembering has a politics.[13]

One of the most challenging elements of researching the AFL is the lack of detailed archives of the organisation and its members. Annual reports from the pre-First World War period are held in the Women's Library at LSE, and many of the plays published by the League can be found in the Museum of London's collection. However, apart from published press releases, detailed accounts of the work of the organisation are elusive. Where records exist for the years after 1914, they provide a vibrant and evocative glimpse of the diverse work AFL members were engaged in, and evidence of their contacts and networks, and it is to be hoped that raising the public profile of the organisation within the present-day theatre community may prompt the discovery and recognition of further private archives and related materials. The new levels of accessibility provided by the Internet have transformed access to the potential comparative use of data and information. Where there are no autobiographies or known papers, a few details of the lives and careers of the most active and long-serving members of the League can be gleaned from newspaper reports, interviews and obituaries found online. Suffrage newspapers provide invaluable sources of material about meetings and events involving the League and League members, and a significant number of issues of the WSPU paper *Votes for Women*, the Women's Freedom League (WFL) paper *The Vote* and the National Union of Women's Suffrage Societies (NUWSS) paper *The Common Cause* have been scanned and are available for free online, as are hundreds of other contemporary newspapers and journals.[14] Jacky Bratton and Grant Tyler Peterson's notion of a 'digital historian' complements more traditional archival research methodologies – the AFL archives held by the Women's Library and Bristol Theatre Collection have not been fully catalogued or digitised, but the amount of information in online newspaper archives augments the existing papers and allows for a greater appreciation of the networks that League members were part of both in the UK and further afield. As the latest date in the League's papers in the Women's Library is 1916, much of the piecing together of their work after that date carried out for this book was made possible through archival research in person and online. Far from a cognitive lapse induced by the notion that 'if something cannot be found online, it does not exist', this method of research and enquiry means that unexpected connections found through online research create in turn new avenues for paper-based archival exploration.[15] The archive is thus virtual, concrete and fluid – it has become larger, more accessible and, perhaps, more productively interrogated. Concern among feminist theatre historians around the loss of the story of the League reflects the current struggle to maintain the archives of feminist activism and theatre that emerged in the second half of the twentieth century and continue into the twenty-first.

Previous scholarship has relied heavily on autobiography and the limited archives of the AFL. Taking into account problems and questions around authenticity, bias and dates of publishing, there is relatively little in autobiographies that can be used to give an indisputable or full picture of any one period of the League's work. Published autobiographies of League members are rare, particularly those by the most long-standing and active members, meaning that interpretations of the autobiographical writing of a few prominent individuals have come to represent the League in scholarly writing. The existence of the AFL has also been used as a general context for further discussion of these individuals rather than as a direct part of the historian's interest. Of the eight actresses involved in the League who published autobiographies between 1924 and 1948, only three – Lena Ashwell, Cicely Hamilton and Elizabeth Robins – have been the subjects of further biographical scholarship, in addition to the extensive work by Katharine Cockin on the life of Edith Craig (1998, 2001). Eva Moore's *Exits and Entrances* (1924), Lillah McCarthy's *Myself and My Friends* (1933), Gertrude Kingston's *Curtsey While You're Thinking* (1937), Irene Vanbrugh's *To Tell My Story* (1948) and Kitty Marion's memoirs (not published until 2019) are among the autobiographical writing that include mentions of the League, the suffrage campaign and the contribution of the theatre community to the war effort both at home and abroad. None of the autobiographies cited were intended to be *political* memoirs, however, the 'coaxers, coaches and coercers' of the stories being principally fans, theatre aficionados, other industry professionals and a general audience, and therefore attempts to verify dates, names and events with other source material sometimes fail.[16] Material gleaned from contemporary interviews and articles can also be unreliable, and, after 1914, suffrage and suffrage theatre are rarely if ever the focus of journalistic interest. Inevitably narratives around political agency become charged in hindsight, as the act of remembering

INTRODUCTION

is an act of rewriting experience self-reflexively, informed by changed cultural contexts and interpretations. Maggie B. Gale's writing on the autobiographies of actresses working in this period notes the underplaying of some personal and professional relationships in favour of others and the creation of a 'framework of cultural reference points … the public knowledge of which helps the author to create a particular slant on their own life'.[17] Despite this 'slant', for the historian accessibility is key – there are authoritative voices from the AFL in diaries, letters and papers, but they are rarely tempered by later reflection or scholarly analysis and so can be hard to contextualise effectively.

In summer 2014, I made a pilgrimage of sorts to the Suffolk village in which Adeline Bourne, one of the founding members of the AFL, lived during the later period of her life. Knowing her house to be no longer standing, I had not made the journey before, considering it to be of sentimental rather than research interest. Upon reaching the site of her property, now a field, I turned back but was stopped by a woman in a nearby house, understandably curious as to my presence there. To my surprise, she revealed that she knew of Bourne and that her papers had been stored in her garage for some years, rescued from a fire that had destroyed Bourne's home after her death. Having read through the papers, looked at photographs and letters, and found suffrage memorabilia – a 'Votes for Women' armband, for example – among Bourne's belongings, she had tried to look for information online, with no significant result, and kept the items in storage out of a sense of history, hoping that perhaps one day they would be useful to someone. Unfortunately, in 2013, while she was unexpectedly ill, she said that a visiting family member had burnt the papers, letters, photographs and memorabilia without asking her permission, destroying the whole collection. The knowledge of the loss of this archive, however small it may have been in scope in reality, was devastating. If I had visited that spot when I had first learnt of the address a few years earlier, I could perhaps have looked through the archive, and the content of this book might, as a result, be very different, or even differently nuanced. While that knowledge of 'lack' is endlessly frustrating, the existing archives that remain, scattered in libraries, museums and private collections – often where they are not expected – provide significant data that, as yet, has not been fully explored. The original research on the AFL carried out prior to the digitisation of historical materials relied largely on a limited range of materials – papers, autobiographies, programmes and so on – archived somewhat haphazardly. Ironically, additional material such as the lost papers of Bourne in Suffolk might have been similarly 'forgotten' even if it had been in an archive, just as the work of the League and its satellite projects has been. Even though the information about those organisations has been in public and specialist repositories for decades, no one has as yet examined it as part of the story of the AFL. It would not therefore be an excessive overstatement to suggest that the League was and remains embedded in two worlds: as an organisation with a complex matrix of professional and political agendas, articulated in play-texts, performances, in professional practices, in public politics and politics within the theatre industry of the day, but more generally and more significantly than has been previously explored.

New perspectives and a new generation

The work, membership and legacy of the AFL has fallen between suffrage and theatre histories with neither approach providing a broad enough profile of the League that allows for a nuanced analysis of their work. Suffrage historians have focused on the League's contribution to the spectacle and pageantry of the movement at events, particularly processions,[18] whereas theatre historians have attempted to connect the work of individuals in the organisation with existing histories of the late Victorian period and the New Woman movement. As a result, the scale of the League's work and the longevity of its effect as well as its international membership and influence have barely been covered. This has also meant that complexities and ambiguities, particularly around the issue of suffrage militancy, have been largely ignored. With few published analyses of suffrage societies other than the militant WSPU, it is not surprising that the League's work for the WFL and NUWSS, as well as for many other smaller societies, has not been detailed. This in turn has meant that its resolution to remain neutral with regard to tactics and to support all other societies has not been considered to be an integral part of the success and longevity of the organisation. Nor has it created the background for a more nuanced reading of the alliances of the League within the suffrage movement as a whole. The Suffragette Fellowship was founded in 1926 by former WSPU and WFL members 'to perpetuate the memory of the pioneers and outstanding events connected with women's emancipation, especially with the militant suffrage campaign'.[19] Members of the still-active AFL were involved with the organisation and continued to attend and speak at Suffragette Fellowship events as late as 1955,[20] but as many of the most active League members were non-militant, their later connections with specific suffrage organisations

INTRODUCTION   13

apart from the Suffragette Fellowship and the AFL are less well recorded. An example here is the work of Teresa Billington-Greig, a suffragist and vocal critic of the militant movement, who prepared notes for an essay on 'The Theatre and the Suffragettes' that was never completed.[21] If it had been completed and published in the 1940s as intended, or later included in the collection of her writings published posthumously in 1987, it would have informed later scholarship about the League from suffrage historians.[22]

Re-evaluation and renewal

> The action of retrieval and revision ... has to progress and be refreshed through time: it is a fluid and continuous process.[23]

This book has been written in the midst of a renewed awareness of the history of feminism, the suffrage movement and public debate about opportunities for women in the theatre industry. There has been a rebirth of interest in the relationship of suffrage histories and performativity, coinciding with and encouraged by newly accessible research materials and data, developments in theatre historiographic practice and the official release of documents from this period. The AFL had a very specific professional political and ethical standpoint around issues of gender equality in the industry and in society more generally, and a deliberate strategy around professional practice informed by a political agenda. As both performance studies and histories of women in theatre and theatre historiography have developed extensively since the 1980s, there is now perhaps a language within the wider discipline of theatre studies through which the material produced by the League can be read.

The year 2013 saw the public commemoration, particularly in the press and on television, of Emily Wilding Davison's fatal accident at the Derby – probably the most widely publicised act of suffrage militancy and one that has come to represent the movement in the public imagination. This created debate about and tapped into concerns around the freedom of individuals to demonstrate politically on the streets and in public spaces, equal rights, police tactics, the representation of women and the responsibility of government, all of which remain current concerns for feminist campaigners. In 2018 the celebrations and commemorations around the centenary of the passing of the Representation of the People Act 1918 engaged many new audiences and communities in the stories of suffrage activists and activism. Across the UK there were theatre and performance projects that sprang up to share these stories, working with archives and libraries, museums and heritage organisations, the education sector and arts networks to create connections with and raise awareness of current feminist campaigns both in and out of the theatre industry. Despite the fact that there are relatively few original documents available that detail the League's activities, the intellectual and political work the organisation was engaged in resonates very strongly with activists in the theatrical profession today. Genuinely embedded in the theatre industry on a long-term basis, for its members the AFL was the starting point of a lifelong professional network and a strategic politics of practice in an industry that relied on women's labour while awarding women relatively little professional power or agency. The work of the League defies absolute categorisation, spanning as it does fifty years of activity within the worlds of politics, feminism, suffrage, theatre, art, journalism, socialism and literature. The breadth and success of its work from 1908 to 1958 show the unifying threads of collaboration, public visibility and activism as extending further than has been previously recognised. As this book proposes, by provoking, reflecting and exploring the debates surrounding the suffrage movement, the AFL provided opportunities for hundreds of performers and writers to lend their professional names and talents to the cause, forming a new and specifically political theatrical activist group that could draw on and utilise a variety of performance styles and influences in theatre, dance, music and literature. Therefore, further research into the League has the potential to enrich not only the history of the period but debates and scholarship within theatre history and performance studies around performance and performativity, site-specific theatre, political theatre and unionisation, experimental theatre forms, entrepreneurship, audiences, women's writing, gender and networks.

A re-evaluation of the work of the AFL is thus both necessary and timely and places the League at the heart of future scholarship about the histories of political theatre in the UK, encouraging scholars to revisit the theatrical texts created around the agitation for women's suffrage. *Stage Rights! The Actresses' Franchise League, Activism and Politics, 1908–58* reclaims organisation from marginalised histories of theatrical contributions to the suffrage movement and renews and refreshes existing histories of feminist theatre in the UK. My hope is that this book will inspire others to draw together and highlight parallels between the first- and second-wave feminist movements in order to inspire and educate the third, fourth and subsequent waves.

Notes

1. AFL, *Annual Report 1913-14*.
2. A.J.R. (ed.), *The Suffrage Annual and Women's Who's Who 1913* (London: Stanley Paul, 1913), p. 11.
3. J. Bratton, 'Reading the intertheatrical, or, the mysterious disappearance of Susanna Centlivre', in M. B. Gale and V. Gardner (eds.), *Women, Theatre and Performance: New Histories, New Historiographies* (Manchester: Manchester University Press, 2000), pp. 7-24.
4. J. Holledge, *Innocent Flowers: Women in the Edwardian Theatre* (London: Virago Press, 1981), p. 165.
5. J. Holledge, 'Women's theatre – women's rights', Ph.D. thesis, University of Bristol, 1985.
6. M. Sanderson, *From Irving to Olivier: A Social History of the Acting Profession in England, 1880-1983* (London: Athlone Press, 1984), p. 110.
7. W. MacQueen-Pope, *Carriages at Eleven: The Story of the Edwardian Theatre* (London: Robert Hale & Co., 1947), p. 219.
8. J. Davis and V. Emaljanow, '"Wistful remembrancer": the historiographical problem of Macqueen-Popery', *New Theatre Quarterly*, 17 (2001), 299-309.
9. S. Croft, *Votes for Women and Other Plays* (Twickenham: Aurora Metro, 2008), p. 216.
10. K. Cockin, G. Norquay, and S. Park, *Women's Suffrage Literature*, vol. III (London and New York: Routledge, 2007), p. xi.
11. S. Carlson, 'Comic militancy: the politics of suffrage drama', in M. B. Gale and V. Gardner (eds.), *Women, Theatre and Performance: New Histories, New Historiographies* (Manchester: Manchester University Press, 2000), pp. 198-215, at p. 212; K. Cockin, 'Women's suffrage drama', in J. Maroula and J. Purvis (eds.), *The Woman's Suffrage Movement: New Feminist Perspectives* (Manchester: Manchester University Press, 1998), pp. 127-39, at p. 134.
12. B. Friedl, *On to Victory: Propaganda Plays of the Woman Suffrage Movement* (Boston, MA: Northeastern University Press, 1987). Friedl's anthology of American suffrage plays spans the years 1856-1917.
13. S. Smith and J. Watson, *Reading Autobiography: A Guide for Interpreting Life Narratives* (Minneapolis, MN: University of Minnesota Press, 2010), p. 24.
14. These can be found on Google newspapers (www.news.google.com/newspapers).
15. J. Bratton and G. Tyler Peterson, 'The internet: history 2.0?', in D. Wiles and C. Dymkowski (eds.), *Cambridge Companion to Theatre History* (Cambridge: Cambridge University Press, 2012), pp. 299-313, at pp. 306-12.
16. Smith and Watson, *Reading Autobiography*, p. 64.
17. M. B. Gale, 'Lena Ashwell and auto/biographical negotiations of the professional self', in M. B. Gale and V. Gardner (eds.), *Auto/biography and Identity:*

Women, Theatre and Performance (Manchester: Manchester University Press, 2004), pp. 99–125, at p. 114.
18 See L. Tickner, *The Spectacle of Women* (London: Chatto & Windus, 1989); M. Mackenzie, *Shoulder to Shoulder* (New York: Knopf, 1975), and D. Atkinson, *The Suffragettes in Pictures* (London: Museum of London, 1996).
19 J. Purvis, *Emmeline Pankhurst: A Biography* (London and New York: Routledge, 2002), p. 359.
20 Decima Moore spoke at the anniversary of Mrs Pankhurst's birthday, held by the Suffragette Fellowship in 1955.
21 Teresa Billington-Greig Papers, The Women's Library, 7/TBG2/B15.
22 A. FitzGerald and C. McPhee (eds.), *The Non-violent Militant: Selected Writings of Teresa Billington-Greig* (London and New York: Routledge & Kegan Paul), 1987.
23 M. B. Gale, 'Overview', in M. B. Gale and G. Bush-Bailey, *Plays and Performance Texts by Women, 1880–1930* (Manchester: Manchester University Press, 2012), pp. 1–4, at p. 4.

1
Exhibition

In the Victorian and Edwardian period public fairs and exhibitions were enormously popular, showcasing ideas and ideals, political movements, different cultures and the advances being made in technology and science. In every major city there were grand spaces and exhibition halls, and in London large venues such as the Albert Hall, Earl's Court and the Royal Horticultural Hall and smaller spaces such as the Egyptian Hall, St James Hall and Caxton Hall 'hosted an eclectic mix of events', all competing for the attention of the public and each offering a unique social and cultural experience.[1] By 1909, the city was also a regular location for a diverse range of small-scale exhibitions, particularly around industry, the arts and culture, and suffrage societies engaged with the marketing potential of these occasions through their own exhibitions, fetes, fairs and bazaars. Recognising the importance of utilising the persuasive power of visual culture as part of a political agenda, the suffrage movement made itself publicly visible using images and text generated by the movement itself as well as adapting those created in and by the national and international media. Such public occasions frequently offered, in effect, a combination of immersive experience and pageant, with the visitor as audience in constructed, carefully designed presentations of performative feminist propaganda. The presence of the AFL at suffrage exhibitions and bazaars became an integral component of the performative elements of exhibition culture within both militant and non-militant suffrage societies. These were public political spaces in which the League could flourish and where the organisation gained not only opportunities for networking in the profession and among influential suffrage campaigners but also the space for individuals to try out new suffragist material and diversify their professional portfolio. This chapter investigates the AFL's role in and theatrical contributions to suffrage exhibitions beginning with the largest and longest the organisation took part in: the 1909 WSPU Women's Exhibition.

Setting the scene: the 1909 WSPU Women's Exhibition

> What will this Woman's Exhibition be? It will be more than an ordinary exhibition: it will be a rallying ground for all who are interested in women's work, women's aims, women's hopes, and above all in the great, inspiring movement of women towards a fuller and more spacious life.[2]

The WSPU held its Women's Exhibition at the Prince's Skating Rink in Knightsbridge, London, from 13 May to 26 May 1909.[3] Adept at organising marches, deputations, demonstrations and large events on the streets of cities across the UK, the WSPU wanted to make a strong impression on the public and the press and show the government how popular the suffrage cause had become. The Prince's Skating Rink was a large and prestigious venue, well located and easily accessible by London Underground. Home to the Prince's Ice Hockey Club, the rink had been owned since 1903 by Mary Russell, Duchess of Bedford, a suffragist and active member of the Women's Tax Resistance League. The rink had been a site of recent female success, when in October 1908 British figure skater Florence Syers won a gold medal there in the individual ladies skating competition of the London Olympic Games.[4] The aims of the 1909 WSPU Women's Exhibition were to educate, entertain and build support for the movement. The WSPU was growing fast, and the popularity of its newspaper *Votes for Women* had increased substantially from 16,000 copies sold weekly at the beginning of 1909 to nearly 40,000 by 1910.[5] Advertisements for the exhibition appeared in the national press, detailing the specific events and performances to be held each day, and there was regular press coverage of the exhibition in national papers and periodicals including the *Daily Telegraph*, *Morning Post*, *Nursing Times*, *Daily Chronicle*, *Sphere*, *Christian Commonwealth*, *Manchester Guardian*, *Lady's Pictorial* and the *Daily Mirror*. The stalls and decorations at the exhibition were also extensively photographed by Mary Broom, the first female press photographer.[6] Controlled public presentation that presented a positive message was vital for recruitment and fundraising, and the newly formed AFL was a key component of both attracting and entertaining exhibition visitors as well as providing a potential new source of publicity and audience for the WSPU. Many large exhibitions had formal performance spaces, but the Women's Exhibition was unique in having a space dedicated to the professional performance of theatrical propaganda material.

The appeal to visitors began outside the venue with flags and festoons in the purple, white and green of the WSPU, colours which Emmeline

Pethick-Lawrence described in the exhibition programme as having 'become to those who belong to this Movement a new language of which the words are so simple that their meaning can be understood by the most uninstructed and most idle of passers-by in the street'.[7] The exhibition was publicised on the streets of London through the newly formed WSPU Drum and Fife Band, resplendent in purple, white and green uniforms (see Figure 1.1). While the deputations, gatherings and protests organised by the WSPU, WFL, NUWSS and other suffrage groups were not always principally conceived intended as spectacles in their own right, the performativity of such public displays and the media coverage that resulted from them could be as effective in raising public awareness as the protests themselves. The Drum and Fife Band was the first all-female band of its kind, made up of leading professional female brass and woodwind players who 'wanted their support of the suffrage cause to be public and wanted it directly identified with their commitment as artists'.[8] Although

1.1 The WSPU Drum and Fife Band advertising the 1909 WSPU Women's Exhibition

variety acts in the music halls 'made comic use of women brass players in mock-military uniforms', by 1909 the sight of uniformed women musicians on the streets was a visual as well as aural echo of the Salvation Army bands, which had included female musicians since their inception in the 1890s.[9] The allusion to such strict moral and religious proselytising also reflects the fervent religiosity of Sylvia Pankhurst's mural designs inside the exhibition hall, and was also to be seen on the exhibition programme, the front page of which showed an angel with an elongated horn which she was playing 'in a profile view that emphasizes her unflattering, puffed out cheeks', defiantly making noise for the cause.[10]

The band played newly composed music – Ethel Smyth's *March of the Women*, for which Cicely Hamilton had written the lyrics – as well as existing music associated with democracy and freedom and adapted for the suffrage cause, such as *The Women's Marseillaise*.[11] Joan Dugdale, who would become the AFL's organising secretary in 1911, marched behind the band carrying a banner advertising the exhibition, as did Kitty Marion, a member of both the AFL and the WSPU.[12] The number of people that would see and hear the Drum and Fife Band outside the exhibition would be more than the WSPU could ever hope would enter it, but by adopting an aurally dominant and assertive form emblematic of traditionally masculine demonstrations of unity and force, the WSPU showed it did not intend to be silenced.

Sylvia Pankhurst's murals covered the walls of the rink with a repeating triptych of figurative pictures signifying self-sacrifice and triumph through adversity and hope. Drawing on theological images that had been initially designed to educate the illiterate – reminiscent of Pethick-Lawrence's description of the communicative visual power of the WSPU colours – these potent symbols depicted moral right and the dominance of a higher authority than man and men. Two of the three were recognisably biblical in origin: the Pelican in her Piety, a medieval religious allegorical reference to maternal devotion, martyrdom and sacrifice; and a dove and olive tree, signifying hope, peace and fruitfulness. The third symbol was that of a broad arrow, a motif repeated in different areas of the exhibition. Printed on prison uniforms in Britain since 1870, the broad arrow was frequently carried by WSPU members on marches to raise awareness of the punitive treatment suffragettes were subject to as a direct consequence of their political agitation, and it appeared on the medals awarded to those who had been imprisoned for the cause. In Pankhurst's mural designs, each broad arrow was encased in a wreath of victory laurels. These potent images of sacrifice, triumph and hope and the use of the WSPU colours created a backdrop to the hustle and

Exhibition

1.2 Inside the 1909 WSPU Women's Exhibition

bustle on the exhibition floor, a branded environment in which to educate and entertain visitors and facilitate interactions between suffragists and the public (see Figure 1.2). The official title of the 1909 Exhibition was the Women's Exhibition and Sale of Work, and, with the dual purpose of promoting the cause and raising financial support, there were stalls from WSPU branches across England, Scotland and Wales. Visitors were tempted and encouraged to part with their money at every turn, and there were branded mementos of the event and the movement to be bought, won and treasured.

> Every fine piece of embroidery, every baby garment ... represents the woman's answer to the silent centuries in which she has been overworked and underpaid. Here you may find the readjustment of that picture of womanhood so dear to the past ... Here, in the Woman's Exhibition, is the new picture of the woman.[13]

Examples of women's domestic creative expertise used specifically for public political advertisement and sale transformed home-made crafts and their makers into transactions of femininity and feminism for visitors and sellers alike.[14] Suffrage campaigners, and particularly militant societies, were keen to 'offset the negative image created by the opposition of suffrage activists as "the other," genderless creatures who had little or no relation to women's daily lives'.[15] Stall no. 45, which sold and displayed farm and garden produce, held competitions with cash prizes for the 'best Pair of Fowls, drawn and trussed for table' and 'best assortment of Vegetables', encouraging women to visit the exhibition repeatedly and take the idea of the movement into the heart of their domestic lives. Needlework in some form featured on thirty-four out of the fifty-five stalls at the exhibition, and in the same year as the Board of Education issued a publication maintaining that the subject of needlework was essential for a girl 'to reach woman's estate', the WSPU's exhibition was embracing rather than dismissing or diminishing the results of this education.[16] Rather than reinforcing 'concepts of femininity and domesticity that had long been the basis of women's political dependency and social subordination', the WSPU wanted to challenge negative stereotypes of suffrage campaigners.[17] Much of the anti-suffrage campaign focused on the idea that if women became absorbed in national political matters they would neglect their domestic duties and, most dangerous of all, their maternal instincts.[18] The message to women visitors at the exhibition was that however politically naive they might consider themselves to be, every aspect of their lives, skills and experience was of value to the movement. Suffrage plays and literature that both celebrated and criticised the expectation of domesticity were sold at the eight Woman's Press stalls at the 1909 Exhibition, providing opportunities for visitors to learn more about the movement and perhaps question cultural assumptions and expectations of the role of women in society.[19] Half of the Woman's Press stalls sold branded handicrafts and knick-knacks, including handbags, playing cards and address books – ordinary souvenirs that infused day-to-day life with political symbolism. The exhibition also had its own post office, enabling impulse purchases of suffrage commodities to be immediately shared and circulated outside of the exhibition environment.[20] As well as informal interactions, formal communications between visitors and suffragists were a key part of the experience of the exhibition. By creating a space crowded with stallholders selling and exhibiting merchandise, providing regular musical and theatrical performances and encouraging participation in the interactive elements of the exhibition, visitors were given ample opportunity to personalise their experience of suffragists, albeit for a price, becoming audience members as well as visitors. Paying for immersion in this environment provided commercial value as well as political and social currency, with the financial commitment the audience was encouraged to make implicitly and actually supporting the social and political exchange of goods and ideas. Whereas at other large-scale exhibitions visitors might be given a taste of foreign cultures through exotic peoples, displays, food and entertainments, at suffrage exhibitions they were encouraged to see the similarities rather than the differences between themselves and suffragists. In Cicely Hamilton and Christopher St John's popular suffrage play *Pot and Kettle*, Marjorie is shocked to discover that a woman sitting near her at a meeting is a suffragette:

MARJORIE: She had on a fawn coat and a black hat with daises in it; but she was really a suffragette – though I didn't know it. She looked just like anyone else.
NELL: Some of us do.[21]

This sentiment echoes the experience of another woman at a WSPU fair two years later. Mrs Monsell-Moullin reported in *Votes for Women* on 22 December 1911 that she 'overheard a whisper from a lady entering the room, "Are these all Suffragettes? I did not know they were like this."'[22] The immersive world that the WSPU created for their exhibition sought in some cases to counteract negative stereotypes of suffragettes and in other cases clarify or interrogate their meanings and associations – introducing complexity by making information accessible in many different ways and actively encouraging interaction between exhibitors and visitors. The visual propaganda of the movement was communicated constantly, reinforced through the sound and the physical presence of suffragist women.

Constructed representations of women and suffragettes could also be seen in the *Political Peepshows*, twelve models with figures made from wire and Plasticine posed in recreations of popular cartoons from the cover of *Votes for Women* and scenes inspired by the campaign. They were designed and possibly also made by Hilda Brackenbury and her daughters, Mary and Georgina, who had been involved in militant suffrage activity for the WSPU.[23] The *Peepshows* showed images of suffragettes triumphing over cabinet ministers in various ways: at by-elections, outside the Houses of Parliament, in the dock and police court and on Downing Street. Recognisable figures representing particular ministers or policemen – such as the prime minister, Herbert Asquith, and Inspector Jarvis, responsible for the arrests of many WSPU members – appeared alongside depictions of suffrage campaigners in both literal and fantastical scenarios.[24] One of the most symbolic was entitled *Captive Womanhood: 'Release'* and portrayed a figure of a woman approximately 12 inches high, barefoot, with a covered head and one hand raised protectively to her face. The figure was trapped under a net held down 'by pegs typifying the various forces at work blocking Woman's Enfranchisement, viz: H.M. Government … Prejudice, Masculine Domination, Mrs. Grundy, Blind Chivalry &c.' and the suffragettes were depicted as mice, working hard to free the woman from her oppressors by gnawing at the net holding her down.[25] The simplicity of the image reinforced the message the WSPU wanted to convey: womanhood was literally trapped by institutional, political and social discrimination, and suffragists had to use their own bodies in a collective and individual effort for freedom.

A lived experience: the performance of prisoners at the exhibition

'HOLLOWAY CELLS, LIVING SUFFRAGETTE PRISONERS' ran the line of the advertisement for the 1909 Exhibition in *The Times*.[26] Representations of two prison cells were constructed inside the exhibition to show the comparison between a 'second-division' cell occupied by a suffragette prisoner and a 'first-division' cell as allocated to a male political offender.[27] By recreating the cells, the WSPU invited the public to reconsider its assumptions about the status of female political prisoners and the punishment given to them by the justice system. Although reporting that the government would not lend any authentic prison articles for use in the second-division cell, the WSPU advertised it as having been made to the exact size as the cells in Holloway prison, recreated with 'absolute fidelity, even down to the number of panes in the window, the nails in the door, and the coconut fibre with which the pillow is stuffed'.[28] The first-division political prisoner's cell, by contrast, included a sprung mattress on the bed, books and writing materials and a comfortable armchair. Examples of the food provided for both divisions showed the contrast in diet as well as environment. Ex-prisoners took turns acting out the roles of prisoner and wardress, and, for a fee of 6d, explained to their audience the daily routine of life in prison (see Figure 1.3). Three times daily the 'prisoner' could be seen performing her duties: washing the floor and pans, making the bed, sewing stockings, shirts and mailbags. Pictures of the interior of both cells were printed in the *Illustrated London News* on 22 May 1909, halfway through the run of the exhibition. In the first-division cell, the picture shows the figure of a man sat in an armchair reading a newspaper. At the exhibition this figure was a waxwork. The cell is full of objects and decoration, and it is initially hard to see the indications of the prison-cell

1.3 Exterior of the second-division prison cell at the 1909 WSPU Women's Exhibition

structure containing it all. The male political prisoner is dressed in his own clothes and is shown as having free access to writing and reading materials. Although his political views and politically motivated actions have obviously been contentious, he maintains his individuality and is able to keep up to date with current affairs and to communicate with the outside world. By contrast, the female political prisoner is pictured in the prison uniform with its broad-arrow design, sitting in a submissive position with her head down and her hands in her lap. The plank bed is against the wall, with bedding and the few objects she has been allocated from prison supplies packed away in the corner of the cell. She is presented as depersonalised and institutionalised and appears to have been given no means of communication or intellectual stimulation, completely controlled and contained by the prison environment and authorities.

The reality of the size of the second-division cell and the bleak, claustrophobic interior must have been shocking yet perhaps also thrilling to voyeuristic visitors, a vicarious glimpse into an experience that the majority of them would not have had and would hope never to have. The cell gave audiences a sense of the physical restrictions experienced by prisoners without being exposed to the realities of isolation, fear, noise, smell and temperature that would have accompanied visiting a real cell. This controlled public voicing of a hidden world would be a powerful one for suffragists and suffragettes, many of whom had had no negative direct contact with policemen or the law before their involvement in the movement. As Elizabeth Crawford has noted, it was 'the incongruity of middle-class women coming into close physical contact with the police that gave the WSPU so much publicity', and middle-class suffrage prisoners who found themselves alongside working-class female prisoners in custody and prison seized the opportunity to bring attention to their stories.[29] AFL member Sybil Thorndike, whose father was a prison chaplain, had experience of visiting prisons and prisoners although she was never imprisoned for her role in the suffrage campaign. She noted, 'None of us who know the insides of prisons can ever be too pleased with themselves, because we know how many chances and opportunities may have helped us which have been missing in the lives of our less fortunate brothers and sisters.'[30] Female suffrage prisoners, for the most part literate, politically educated and confident, were in a unique position to highlight the social and economic inequalities faced by disadvantaged women whose voices were rarely heard or represented. These interactions raised social awareness of the status of working-class women – particularly those imprisoned for prostitution, theft and infanticide.

Some scholars have been fairly dismissive of the prison cells at the exhibitions, describing them as sensationalist sideshows rather than immersive environments,[31] but more than a staged picture that the audience could passively observe, the cells forced and facilitated interaction and personal contact between suffrage prisoners and the public. Of course there is no way of knowing how each 'prisoner' presented her story or interacted with visitors, or if there was any unifying script or direction for the demonstrators to follow. For at least one female journalist during a subsequent exhibition in Glasgow, in 1910, the most distressing element of the whole 'great if gruesome attraction' was the 'rough and unlovely garments' on show, which implies that either she was not moved by the testimony of the 'prisoner' or that she didn't think her readers would be.[32] It is easy to assume that it must have been almost impossible for visitors to the cells not to be moved by some aspect of their presentation, but that is maybe to read too much into the experience, armed with the knowledge of how later testimonies of suffrage prisoners who had undergone forcible feeding would be presented to the public. At the time of the 1909 Women's Exhibition, hunger-striking by suffragette prisoners had not yet begun, with the first WSPU medals for hunger-striking given in August 1909. There are records of the prison-cell exhibits at suffrage exhibitions before and after this date – the WFL had a Holloway prison cell at their sale of suffragist work in the spring of 1908 and the WSPU exhibitions in Glasgow and Southport in 1910 featured the two cells seen at the 1909 Exhibition.[33] The Glasgow event included within the exhibit a small modelled group to illustrate force-feeding of suffrage prisoners although it is not made clear what form that model took.[34] There was also a quilt on display embroidered with the names of all the hunger-strikers 'in their own handwriting', an object that made explicit the complicated connections between domesticity, militancy, protest and politics.[35] However, as suffragette prisoners began to regularly use hunger-striking to protest against the government's policy of not granting them political prisoner status, there is little indication that any live representation of hunger-striking and/or forcible feeding was presented in public as a propaganda tool, although detailed accounts of the process later inspired American artist and writer Djuna Barnes to wonder whether she had 'as much nerve' as 'her English sisters' and deliberately undergo forcible feeding in 1914 'to describe the process and its attendant sensations' in an article for a New York magazine.[36] Testimonies by suffrage prisoners of the physical and psychological toll of forcible feeding were and are incredibly moving, and the WSPU used them for propaganda purposes throughout the campaign to protest to the government, prison authorities and medical profession and to demonstrate the risks campaigners were prepared to take. The voices of suffragette prisoners, damaged by oral and nasal feeding tubes, described the horror of forcible feeding to the public – and the telling and retelling of prison experiences at meetings and breakfast receptions for released prisoners became increasingly common. The WSPU circulated pictures of critically ill hunger-strikers alongside printed testimonies of the force-feeding process, and Scotland Yard began to make and distribute covert surveillance photographs of militant prisoners. Suffrage newspapers published detailed accounts of the trials of arrested suffrage campaigners, providing a fascinating glimpse for contemporary readers and scholarly researchers into the motivations of individual women for undertaking direct action. Short stories and poems were also frequently published in the newspapers of the WSPU and WFL, alongside accounts of conversations with 'ordinary' second-division prisoners, and in 1912 the Glasgow branch of the WSPU published a collection of poems, *Holloway Jingles*, written by suffragette prisoners.[37] As the 'Cat and Mouse Act' (The Prisoners (Temporary Discharge for Ill Health) Act 1913) came into force, photographs of, appearances by and reports of daring escapes by released 'mice' were retold and repackaged within the movement, in the suffrage press and at public meetings across the country.

The fear of incarceration for daring to express political views or thoughts that were against the prevailing authority might have been a troubling one for some visitors to the prison cells. Women who wanted to break out of the strict social conventions were often inhibited from doing so as they were perceived to be rejecting their inevitable domestic responsibilities. Elaine Showalter posits that hysteria and feminism in this period exist on a 'kind of continuum', with the outward physical and vocal expression of suffragette protest as 'the alternative to hysterical silence'.[38] Given the intellectual tools with which to articulate their experiences and the fellowship of other suffragists, through print, images and in person, as in the exhibition, women could challenge both Darwinian and Freudian ideas of biological determinism. At the exhibition, the female prisoner was able to share her story of political dissent, protest and punishment and to invite the audience to question the fairness of the government's treatment of suffragette prisoners. Both demonstrators, the 'prisoner' and the 'wardress' were on hand to voice and interpret their experience through and with the vocabulary of the suffrage movement, with the intention of ensuring the empathy of visitors was with all suffragette prisoners. It is interesting to speculate about the impact of the display for ex-prisoners in their roles of prisoner and wardress as well as its impact on visitors (see Figure 1.4). Reliving their prison experiences day after day may have been a cathartic experience for some as it is easy to imagine that there would have been questions from visitors about their emotional experience of prison life and the impact of the absence and incarceration on family and friends as well as the physical toll.

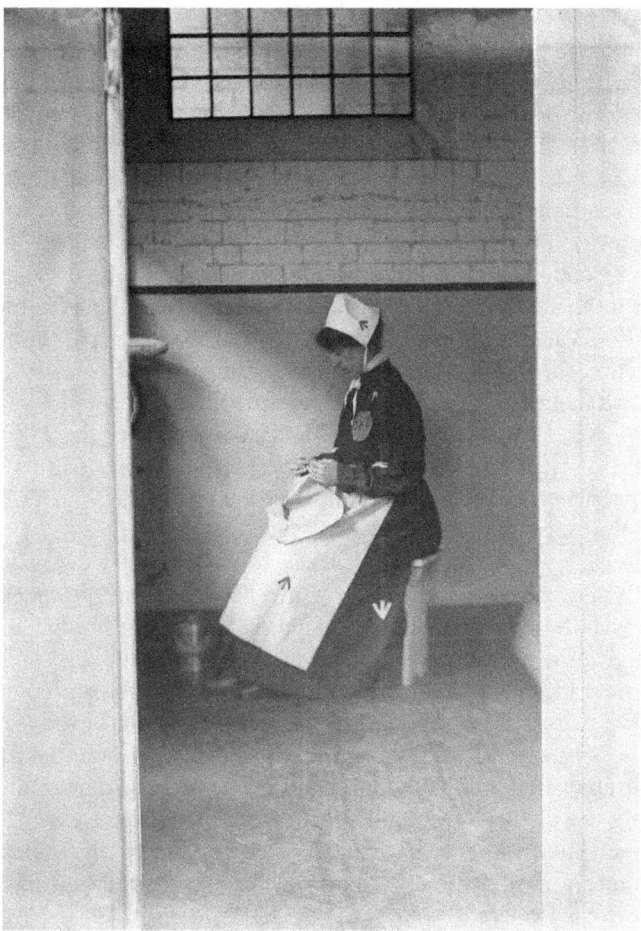

1.4 WSPU member Marie Brackenbury as the 'prisoner'

As opposed to the more polished skills of the actresses, the playing out of lived experience by the female demonstrators would have been a powerful reminder of the consequences of the public political agitation for Votes for Women. It's not known if professional actresses took part as demonstrators in the cell installations, although League members had been imprisoned for militant actions by May 1909. While in Holloway prison in the spring of 1910, League member Sime Seruya continued to help organise the entertainments for the WFL's Green, White and Gold Fair. Smuggling out a letter addressed to Edith Craig written on toilet paper and hidden in the shoe of a fellow prisoner, she suggested improvements to the prison-cell installations that had proved so popular at the 1909 Women's Exhibition, ironically in the perfect environment to make sure the replica cells would be as accurate as possible: 'I think 3 cell doors (one practicable) & lavatory would be most effective & would be a great attraction ... if added to this way it will bring last year's visitors again ... the improvement since Suffragists complained should be on view'.[39] As Seruya intimates in her letter, the cells were a successful part of the 1909 Exhibition. Part sideshow, part installation, part role play, part immersive experience, the prison cells are an interesting example of suffrage performativity and were clearly a popular attraction, taking £24 19s (equivalent to over £2,300 in 2015 values) over the course of the exhibition, which at 6d (just over £2 in 2015 values) per person means that nearly 1,000 people visited the prison cells over the twelve days, an average of eighty-three people per day.

The cells were strategically placed to provide easy access to two exhibits of persuasive visual propaganda about suffrage prisoners. The first was a display of statistics 'by the use of carved or modelled figure which give the eye an instant sense of contrasted numbers' including differences in income and conviction rates – the latter represented by figures in prison dress 'representing so many hundreds or thousands of convicted prisoners'.[40] The second was the YHB or 'Young Hot Blood' photographs, 800 pictures mounted in over 70 feet of space and documenting the history of the movement from 1906. There were pictures of women speaking and debating at meetings and by-elections across the country, mass demonstrations and the arrest, trial and release of suffragette prisoners. Opposite the cells were two stalls of the Women's Press, and the polling booth. Announcing that the Prince's Skating Rink would be a special constituency for the duration of the exhibition, the WSPU's polling booth was open to all visitors, regardless of gender or nationality.[41] Playfully subversive as well as educational and interactive, the booth was open each day from 2.30 p.m. to 10.30 p.m., with the results of each poll announced at the bandstand at 3.30 p.m. the following day. Subjects for the polls had been sent in by the readers of *Votes for Women* with the unusually cautious stipulation that 'no question which enters into party politics will be selected'.[42] Topics ranged from the arts ('Should the nation find £74,000 to purchase Holbein's *Duchess of Milan*?' For: 112; against: 589; 'Should the state subsidise the opera?' Yes: 233; no: 130) to the role of women as workers ('Should women serve on juries?' For: 622; against: 62; and 'Should women be policemen?' For: 196; against: 197). On Tuesday, 14 May, the poll was 'Should censorship of plays be abolished?', a timely question as the select committee of the House of Lords and House of Commons was preparing to discuss that very topic. The results at the exhibition favoured the censor with 312 votes counted against the abolition versus 286 in favour. The select committee went on to call at least ten members and supporters of the AFL as witnesses in July and August 1909, including Johnston Forbes-Robertson, Lena Ashwell and Laurence Housman.[43] By far the largest recorded vote was on the question proposed on Saturday 15 May: 'Does the propaganda of the Anti-Suffragists help or hinder the Votes for Women movement?' with the results given as 'Helps: 1,037; Hinders: 72'.[44] This result, totalling 1,109 votes, gives an indication of visitor numbers by accounting at least for the number of individuals who voted over an eight-hour period if not the number attending the exhibition that day as a whole. While the polling booth was a chance for visitors to give their opinions, the theatre space provided opportunities to hear the issues raised debated on stage within the context of all the interactive representations of women and womanhood present at the exhibition.

The AFL at the exhibition

Formed just six months before the exhibition, the AFL was responsible for organising five performances of entertainments in the theatre space each day, an enormous task for such a newly formed group. Currently there are no known archival holdings of the printed individual programmes produced by the League for the daily performances, but they can be pieced together from information given in the exhibition programme and from the reports published in *Votes for Women*. The variety of plays, sketches, music recitals, recitations and dance produced in the theatre and the sheer number of performers involved is indicative of the breadth of support for the suffrage movement and the League across the theatrical professions. Edith Craig remembered in her diaries that:

> Just before the exhibition opened, Eva Moore ... rang me up to know if I would take over the theatrical department as Adeline Bourne, who had being doing it, had to give it up ... All I remember now is having loads of hatboxes full of letters handed over to me. I had no idea what

the programmes were to be as there were letters for people unknown to me, saying 'Darling, I will be with you at four but I must get away by six' and loads with no addresses at the head and signed only by either their Christian names or nicknames.[45]

The success of the theatre at the exhibition is a testament to Craig's organisational abilities and her recollection of hatboxes full of letters is significant – only somebody at the heart of the theatre profession, like her, would be able to identify the performers who had responded with such informality to Bourne's original call for support. The performances in the theatre space in the exhibition and at subsequent similar events were a mixture of recently written propaganda plays and a variety of other entertainments: there was an improvisational quality to the working practice and a willingness to respond to the immediacy of the exhibition context. Craig recalled that 'we had to make up our programmes every day and never knew until then what we were going to have'.[46] Not all the work on display to the audience was suffragist in origin or design, but the performers openly expressed their support for the cause and for the League through their participation, adding and in some cases overlaying a suffragist context to the recitals, songs, plays or sketches they performed. All the pieces performed in the theatre space would need to have been both easy to set up and to strike. Performers were used to being on tour and working in different venues, adjusting their moves, sightlines and business where necessary to accommodate the size and layout of each performance space. The plays and pieces chosen or accepted by the League for performance at the exhibition were interspersed with programmes of music and dance and so the experience of the audiences in the theatre would have varied enormously from day to day. The theatre space in the Prince's Skating Rink was a separate space situated to the right of the main entrance (see Figure 1.5). The plan of the exhibition shows an auditorium approximately three times the size of the stage, although as no scale is given it is not known how large the auditorium was or how many seats were available for each performance. There was a green room accessible from the stage and three unmarked rooms near an emergency exit, presumably also a useful entrance and possible stage door for the musicians and performers. The unmarked rooms may have been used variously as stores for costumes, props and musical instruments or perhaps functioned as dressing rooms if necessary, making the transition between scenes or plays and the quick rotation of performers and sets more efficient. A small area at the back of the auditorium

Exhibition

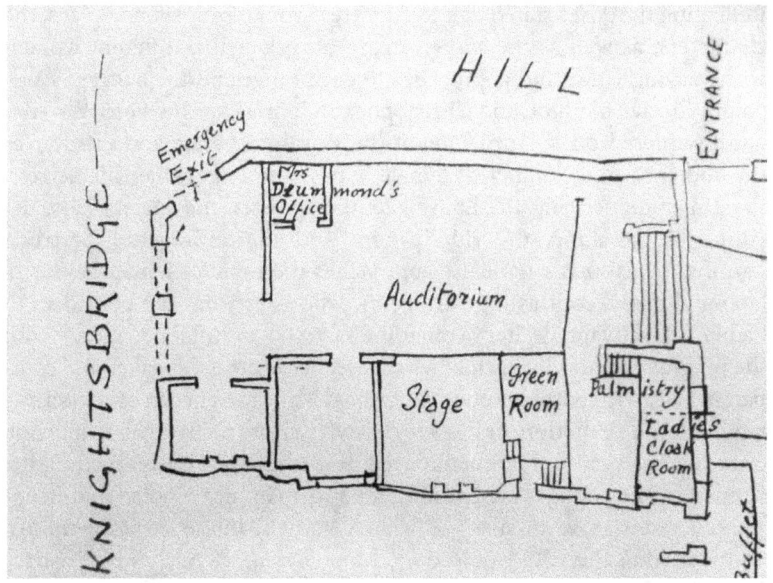

1.5 Detail of the theatre space at the 1909 WSPU Women's Exhibition

labelled 'Mrs. Drummond's Office' can be reasonably presumed to be the space where Kitty Marion notes in her unpublished autobiography that Flora Drummond, known in the WSPU as 'The General', asked her to 'look after the telephone'.[47] Perhaps Drummond thought that Marion, as a professional performer herself, might be better placed to discreetly answer the telephone than someone who did not have an awareness of how disruptive sound and movement could be during a performance.

The most popular propaganda plays performed in the theatre over the course of the exhibition were *How the Vote Was Won*, *A Woman's Influence* and *Lady Geraldine's Speech*. These three plays were, according to *Votes for Women*, the most interesting because 'in every one of them is seen the passing away of the old conventional woman'.[48] Each was written and first performed in 1909 and so therefore can perhaps be taken as an accurate indication of the contemporary concerns of League members regarding the suffrage and the women's societal role as well as presenting contemporary feminist issues other than those directly connected to the suffrage cause – so, for example, the issue of 'sweated' labour, female education and work and the concepts of 'woman's sphere' and 'womanliness'.

Reflecting the AFL's stated aim to educate through propaganda plays, the characters, as well as the audience, are introduced to different women with varying views and approaches to each other and the suffrage campaign. Cicely Hamilton and Christopher St. John's *How the Vote Was Won* had premiered on 13 April 1909 at the Royalty Theatre and introduces the audience to a number of female 'types': the larger-than-life actress, the put-upon servant, the housewife, the spinster, the society lady, the young bluestocking, the elderly aunt and the suffragette. Gertrude Jennings' *A Woman's Influence* approaches the topic of female 'sweated' labour directly, contrasting Mrs Perry, who uses what she considers to be her only advantage, her 'womanliness', to try to influence men – with the pragmatic, morally upright Mrs Lawrence. Actress, speaker and campaigner Beatrice Forbes-Robertson played Mrs Lawrence in every performance at the exhibition and was reviewed by *Votes for Women* in glowing terms as 'the very embodiment of the new spirit which is pervading the women of the younger generation, not anti-man, not bigoted, but deep-sighted and wise, who know just what a woman's influence really means, and just what the vote would do'.[49] *Lady Geraldine's Speech* by Beatrice Harraden features a gathering of women representing different professions and female experiences including a doctor, an artist, a musician, an academic and a shorthand typist – confident, educated, professional women who are not afraid to state their views about the issue of Votes for Women in public. This play also features the most overt caricature of an anti-suffragist – a frequent tactic used in suffrage theatre and sketches to highlight the absurdities of the arguments against the enfranchisement of women. Suffrage plays employing this theme include Cicely Hamilton and Christopher St John's *Pot and Kettle* (1909), Mary Cholmondeley's *Votes for Men* (1909), Evelyn Glover's *Miss Appleyard's Awakening* (1911), H. M. Paull's *An Anti-Suffragist or The Other Side* (1910) and Mrs Harlow Phibbs' *The Mother's Meeting* (1913).

Another popular piece in this genre was Cicely Hamilton's *Anti-Suffrage Waxworks*, performed twice in the theatre at the exhibition and 'designed to personify every argument against the suffrage, so as to render future Anti-Suffrage meetings superfluous'.[50] The 'waxworks' were presented to the audience by the show-woman, a role taken by Hamilton herself at the exhibition, and were played by people.[51] Inspired by the character of Mrs Jarley, the proprietor of a travelling waxwork show in Charles Dickens's 1841 novel *The Old Curiosity Shop*, this style of presenting people as waxworks or automata was based on a popular series of scripts published by Samuel French between 1883 and 1889 called

Mrs Jarley's Far-Famed Collection of Waxworks.[52] The character of Mrs Jarley – the original script states that she can be played by either a man or a woman – moves the figures around, pretending to wind them up as if they were mechanical. The figures then present a repetitive movement, usually to demonstrate or comically punctuate a fact or character trait mentioned. *Mrs Jarley's Waxworks* was a popular late Victorian and early Edwardian amateur entertainment throughout the United Kingdom and America, often performed at special occasions and for fundraisers and charity nights. The flexibility and accessibility of the *Waxworks* made them ideal for both educating and entertaining, and the combination of monologue and *tableaux vivants* ensured that performances could be simply staged, with characters and themes easily added in or taken out at short notice. They could also be adapted to reflect, highlight, exploit and spread contemporary cultural memes. *Mrs Jarley's Waxworks* was popular among theatre professionals as well as their audiences and was regularly performed between 1910 and 1918 at the annual theatrical garden party held in aid of the Actors' Orphanage Fund in London.[53]

Hamilton's *Anti-Suffrage Waxworks* featured six figures presented by the show-woman:

> The Truly Womanly Woman (who, among other domestic occupations, is reading a novel by Mrs Humphrey Ward); the Early Victorian Lady (who faints at the mention of the atrocities committed by the Suffragette);[54] Queen Elizabeth; The Suffragette in quaint dress, and self-imposed heavy chain; The Objector, with more or less manly chest, and a phonograph inside him, who says 'all there is to say' against woman suffrage; and The Policeman, who directs the traffic and is 'easily managed'.[55]

Hamilton pokes fun at the domestic ideal in 'The Truly Womanly Woman', who rocks a cradle with her foot, stirs a saucepan and reads a novel by Mrs Humphrey Ward, an author and playwright who financially supported her family through her professional work as a writer, campaigned for the education of girls and yet remained a prominent and influential anti-suffragist. The early Victorian lady, sometimes called early Victorian maiden, is so appalled by the militant campaign that she can only resort to a traditionally feminine form of protest, 'swooning at intervals'.[56] Here, as before, Hamilton herself mocks the perceived innate weakness of the female sex while also reproving women for colluding in their belittlement in society by perpetuating 'feminine' modes of behaviour. Although the early Victorian maiden could also be a positive stereotype to be celebrated – symbolising the earliest female university students and the higher education of women – she was in the *Waxworks* presented as a means of typifying physical frailty, small-mindedness and lack of independence. Queen Elizabeth I, displayed as one of the anti-suffrage figures, was described as 'a salient figure of whose character, as the show-woman remarked, was her feminine deference to the opinion of her ministers'.[57] In contrast, Hamilton's suffrage play *A Pageant of Great Women* (1910) champions Queen Elizabeth I's sovereignty, power and right to the throne. The *Anti-Suffrage Waxworks* and *Pageant of Great Women* were often played together – for example at the Swansea WFL event of May 1910, thereby including this contradictory representation in the same performance and encouraging the audience to consider and question historical portrayals of female role models. In the *Anti-Suffrage Waxworks*, the figures are clear stereotypes, echoing in some cases the characters in suffrage plays and the popular press and yet, like Queen Elizabeth, often used by both sides of the debate. The presentation of the Suffragette conforms to anti-suffrage propaganda with her quaint dress and heavy chain, a self-imposed yoke of protest intended to show her to be humourless, serious and desperate for attention. In one of the most popular suffrage plays performed by the AFL at the exhibition, this character was made the source rather than the target of the joke. *How the Vote Was Won* features Winifred, determined, good-humoured and sardonic, dedicated entirely to the cause, full of relaxed confidence in her own independence, vocal and unconcerned about attracting the male gaze. Outside the theatre space, the exhibition teemed with militant women reinforcing the message that the Suffragette waxwork was a negative construct based on prejudice, ignorance and fear of women and their potential political agency. For a production of the *Waxworks* in Sheffield in 1910, this character was presented as 'rowdy, ill-dressed, and wearing football boots', a less austere and more playful portrayal that celebrated women's physicality.[58] The Objector was apparently the only speaking figure of the *Waxworks*, although whether he actually spoke or the voice was 'heard' to come out of the phonograph is unknown. The final character of the Policeman is presented as a figure of fun, his power manifest over traffic rather than people and posing no real intellectual or physical threat to the show-woman or to the movement. At a performance of the *Anti-Suffrage Waxworks* for the International Suffrage Congress earlier in 1909, the show climaxed in some militancy-inspired broad comic physical action when the Suffragette 'waxwork' attacked the Policeman and 'was arrested with jerky vigour, much to the indignation of Queen Elizabeth who ... at once rose and battered him intermittently on the head with her sceptre'.[59] Policemen were being mocked elsewhere in the exhibition, not only through the plays and the peepshows but also through demonstrations of physical force.

Stage-struck: violence as entertainment at the exhibition

The theatre space at the exhibition was used by Edith Garrud to give dramatic demonstrations of her martial-arts skills on 15 and 21 May. Edith and her husband were among the first professional English ju-jitsu instructors, having first learnt the martial art in 1899 at the Bartitsu School of Arms and Physical Culture on Shaftesbury Avenue. Garrud was a member of the WSPU and taught self-defence classes to members of the WFL and WSPU on Tuesday and Thursday nights at her dojo on Golden Square near Oxford Circus.[60] The performance of violent acts for entertainment purposes seems an unusual feature of the exhibition, but it demonstrated 'the capabilities of women to physically challenge men using strategy, skill and tactics, rather than brute force'.[61] At the exhibition Garrud staged a one-on-one confrontation between a suffragette and a policeman:

> The demonstration took the form of a new two-minute drama without words ... a three-round contest between the policeman and the Suffragette. The little woman, despite overwhelmingly adverse odds as regards height and weight, made the policeman lose his dignity, his balance, and his helmet, whereat militant members of the audience shrieked with delight.[62]

The use of caricature – the small suffragette, seemingly the certain underdog, making the best advantage of her stature and skills to triumph over the apparently overwhelming physical force of the law – created suspense and engaged the emotions of the audience, as well as exciting their admiration towards the winning combatant and exposing the loser to ridicule. This ridicule was all the more potent, of course, because of the high status of the policeman character at the beginning of the contest. As in the *Anti-Suffrage Waxworks* the policeman is there to be outsmarted and overcome, and when the expected outcome is turned on its head the audience's sympathies are with the winner, who of course in this case is representing suffrage campaigners. The depiction of the woman in the jujitsuffragette demonstration as reactive and defensive is appealing not only to supporters of the militant campaign but also to the constitutional suffragists. She does not initiate the violence but, if forced to engage, shows her inner strength outwardly and decisively. This bloodless combat is easy to engage with, however, and the woman's role is defensive throughout, responding to the attacks of the male character and using his momentum and strength against him. By showing herself to be vulnerable, receiving rather than initiating the violence and exaggerating this vulnerability through the visual difference in stature – Mrs Garrud was 5 foot tall – it would be unlikely, within this context, for the audience to disapprove of such 'an exotic yet superior spectacle of grace and artistry capable of defeating the strongest masculine force'.[63] Garrud went on to co-write a play featuring ju-jitsu called *Physical Force* that was performed in the theatre space at the WSPU's Christmas Fair in 1911,[64] and later became the trainer for 'The Bodyguard', a group of militant women who protected Emmeline Pankhurst in 1913.[65] It appears that the AFL was instrumental in programming the ju-jitsu demonstrations and that Garrud had trained other female demonstrators to accommodate the interest of the suffrage societies. Sime Seruya's smuggled letter in 1910 asked Edith Craig to write to Garrud at her Golden Square dojo to 'fix up the J.J. turns so that Mrs. Garrud can book them as quickly as possible'.[66]

The AFL at other suffrage exhibitions

> Everybody who is anybody in the theatrical world is to help. There will be a perfect galaxy of stars – singing, dancing, playing – for the delectation of the public.[67]

The AFL took part in many suffrage events and exhibitions from 1909 onwards. The League was also responsible for the entertainments (all in London unless otherwise stated) at the WFL's Old World Fair in April 1909; the WFL's Yuletide Fair in December 1909; the WSPU Grand Suffrage Bazaar and Exhibition in Glasgow in April 1910; the WSPU Christmas Fair and Fete in December 1911; the WWSL and Men's League for Women's Suffrage (MLWS) Sweated Labour Exhibition in May 1913, the WSPU Summer Festival in June 1913, the NUWSS Woman's Kingdom Exhibition in April 1914, and the United Suffragists Christmas Sale in December 1914. Members of the League also took part in the NUWSS Oriental Fete in December 1912 and the Women and Army Work Exhibition in May 1915, and the organisation had its own stall at the Anglo-American Exhibition in 1914 and the United Suffragists Woman's Christmas Sale in 1915. While this list is not exhaustive, it shows how networked the League remained within both militant and constitutional suffrage societies. Although most of these later events ran for a much shorter time than the 1909 Exhibition, the League's contribution appears to have been certainly as varied. At the Yuletide Festival held by the WFL in the Albert Hall later in 1909, *The Vote* reported that the League's banner joined others on the platform alongside a banner with the WFL's motto 'Dare to be Free' in their colours of green and gold, and 'prisoners' bannerets and Suffrage texts' decorated the walls.[68] The AFL presented four short plays, including Shaw's *Press Cuttings*, and individual members also contributed to the speeches and other entertainments in the main space. *The Vote* recorded that 'Miss Sime Seruya's Christmas-tree, with its gifts and "brights" was well patronized by the youngsters', and that 'the Actresses' Franchise League ... proved, as they always do, a tower of strength.'[69]

The WSPU Scottish Exhibition ran from 28 to 30 April 1910 at the Charing Cross Halls in Glasgow. WSPU members from branches across Scotland held various fundraising events, including jumble sales, dances and whist drives, to contribute to the mounting of the exhibition.[70] The AFL again provided the entertainments, this time officially under the direction of Edith Craig.[71] Actresses advertised as travelling up from London were Edith Craig, Decima Moore, Mrs Brown Potter, Cicely Hamilton and Winifred Mayo.[72] Plays presented there included the *Anti-Suffrage Waxworks*, *How the Vote Was Won* and *The Tableaux of Famous Women*. There was local support from well-known Glaswegian performers including Laurence Hanray, Muriel Pope and Milton Rosmer of the newly formed Glasgow Repertory Theatre, and Graham Moffat, founder member of the Glasgow MLWS and author of the suffrage play *The Maid and the Magistrate*. Press coverage included the *Glasgow Herald*, *Glasgow Evening Times*, *Glasgow Evening News* and the *Daily Record and Daily Mail*.[73]

By 1913, perhaps because the increasing visibility and notoriety of the militant campaign meant a public-relations strategy built around its success had become problematic, the WSPU's Suffragette Summer Festival, held in Kensington in June 1913, transformed the Empress Rooms into an idealised summer garden, with 'everything calculated to make people entirely forget the heat and rush and bustle of June in London'.[74] Seemingly a world away from the religious imagery used in the 1909 Exhibition, the design for the Summer Festival employed different visual propaganda to create a sense of peace. The entrance represented a country barn in a meadow, the stalls were situated in a walled garden, with sellers dressed in 'flowered muslin frocks', and visitors exhausted from walking under the pergolas could rest on rustic benches. The AFL performed twice daily in a room dubbed the Café Chantant, producing forty half-hour concerts during the ten days of the fair.⁷⁵ The Summer Festival is notable for its use of children as part of the visual and consumer propaganda of the movement – framing their role as innocents within the stylised pastoral setting of the event. Children had previously been an important part of the experience of suffrage exhibitions and events, as consumers, participants, and audiences. In exhibitions and bazaars held by the WSPU, WFL and NUWSS, children were catered for through fairground rides, lucky dips and presents on a Christmas tree – all in the colours of each society. For the 1913 WSPU Summer Fair and Fete, for example, children were overtly used to sell propaganda – dressed as brownies, elves and gnomes they roamed the constructed space of a 'Suffrage Meadow' in the Empress Rooms in Kensington, selling copies of the WSPU's paper, *The Suffragette*.⁷⁶ Constantly blurring the boundaries between the personal and political, and the private and public, the WSPU used the branded bodies of their supporters, including children, as well as their deeds and words to advertise for the cause. Entertainments for children at the 1911 WSPU Christmas Fair and Fete included conjurors and suffrage-themed Punch and Judy shows. The event was a theatrical spectacle in all areas, being presented as an eighteenth-century fair complete with market-sellers dressed in 'quaint old world costumes' who opened the event every day with a choral performance of traditional street and market cries.⁷⁷

The visible, active and audible presence of male supporters of the movement to entertain and amuse the crowds is an interesting feature of the 1911 Christmas Fair. A beadle walked around the space, 'announcing the entertainments in the theatre and various other events of the day', and three magicians took part over the course of the fair, including Herbert J. Collings, one of the founder members of the Magic Circle, who presented his 'Drawing Room Séance' as well as conjuring tricks.⁷⁸ The Men's Political Union for Women's Enfranchisement (MPU) ran the 'Fun of the Fair' section of the event, which included a roundabout, hoopla, shooting gallery and specially designed suffrage shies.⁷⁹ The exhibition programme encouraged both women and men to take part in the shooting gallery and to prove that 'muscular force is not the basis of all Government … skill and determination have to be taken into account', announced that members of the WSPU and MPU would keep account of the success of both sexes and post the results up each day. The suffrage shies consisted of five paintings hung on a screen, with a hole at the centre of each painting. If the visitor could throw a ball directly through the hole, a mechanism was released that replaced the image. The pictures depicted two sets of ideas: 'Life as it is to-day, and Life as it should be and will be when women are able to improve their own conditions in their own way and on their own more expert knowledge'.[80] Therefore, for just two balls a penny, or seven for 3d (just over £1 in 2015 values), visitors with good aim and honest intentions could turn injustice to justice, jealousy to comradeship, prejudice to common sense, bondage to freedom and ignorance to wisdom.[81]

Suffrage Punch and Judy shows, written by Inez Bensusan, were performed on the bandstand twice daily by MPU member Mr E. J. W. Warren.[82] Traditionally, the character of Judy dies, along with her baby, beaten to death by Punch in the first act of the show, only to appear later as a ghost, but it is hard to imagine that the suffragette Judy would have fallen victim to Punch's slapstick at the fair. It is also possible that the Edith Garrud's crowd-pleasing combat between a suffragette and a policeman would have been imitated and heightened for comic effect in the puppet show. The opportunity to explore other issues concerning suffrage campaigners – especially in front of a captive audience of children and adults – must have been a delightful one for Bensusan. AFL members championed campaigns including rights for working women, parental rights for mothers, and longer sentences for men convicted of violence against and sexual assault of women and girls. With its familiar characters, settings and convoluted storylines which allowed for the introduction of new characters and scenes to augment the basic plot, Punch and Judy was an accessible medium for propaganda and allowed serious topics to be presented with humour, satire, irreverence and fun. Many of the most successful suffrage plays performed by the AFL were comedies – their lightness of touch and charm acting as a foil to the serious political message underneath. A suffragette Judy, representing the women of the WSPU to the children of the women of the WSPU, could have physical dominance over Punch and the policeman if necessary, could protect her baby from attack, could speak and be heard, demanding attention, her share in the story and her chance to change the outcome for the better. A suffragette Judy might try to convert Punch to the cause, perhaps try and steal some 'Votes for Women' sausages away from a government crocodile, outwit a policeman and escape a prison cell, use her fearsome reputation as a militant to trick or tease and most of all invite the audience to see her as having political agency in a previously male-dominated story. Having a second performance each day at 8 p.m. might also have allowed for some less child-centred material. However, it was not only to audiences with militant sympathies that Suffrage Punch and Judy was performed. At an AFL tea dance, held in Kensington in January 1914 to raise funds, Inez Bensusan wrote and performed a 'Political Punch and Judy' in which there were fourteen characters, including Winston Churchill and Lloyd George.[83] With ample opportunities for improvisation and audience interaction, suffrage Punch and Judy shows seem to have been a clever, fun and accessible medium for performing propaganda. Ever quick to respond to topics and tropes, it would have been easy to subvert the violence of the traditional presentation of Punch by exploiting the mediatised stereotypes of suffragists and suffragettes to comic effect. The world of Punch and Judy, in which anything implausible might happen at any moment is a world in which, perhaps, the possibilities of change can be explored, joked about, played with and enjoyed.

> In feminist tragedy women are the victims of male power and violence, in feminist comedy the men are stripped of their power and are incapable of violence. They are buffoons, dogs with bark but no bite, who can be insulted or humiliated by women but will never retaliate.[84]

The portrayal of men at the 1909 Exhibition was largely as figures of fun, steeped in privilege and benefiting from traditional gendered roles. Their interactions with women and suffragists are represented as amusing scenarios in which the women have the upper hand, and their voices were rarely heard outside of the theatre space. The only real waxwork at the exhibition was that of the male political prisoner, vilified for his comfortable surroundings and privilege but, unlike the female political prisoner, not given a voice with which to explain his story or even express his views about the way the suffragette prisoners were treated. In the theatre, men could demonstrate their support for the movement by giving their time and talents to entertain the public, as well as showing their support for their female colleagues. Men helped to organise and decorate the exhibition and performed not only in the theatre but also as supporters and representatives in their own right. The contradictions between the constant presentation of men as anti-suffragists and the actual presence of men as suffragists and sympathisers must have been an uncomfortable one for both male and female visitors to the exhibition. The prominent presence of the militant MPU at the 1911 Christmas fair showing they 'could entertain as well as fight' helped to present a more realistic picture of the campaign and allowed for a more nuanced, representative and gender-balanced visitor experience than that of the 1909 Exhibition.[85]

The whole exhibition of suffrage

At all the suffrage exhibitions women and 'woman' were performed and portrayed through carefully constructed representational frameworks that tried to negotiate and balance the boundaries between education, propaganda, politics, entertainment and commerce. Through the allegorical figures in Sylvia Pankhurst's artwork that adorned the vast walls, the still images of protest and triumph captured by the Young Hot Blood photography, the stylised, uniformed musicians in the Drum and Fife Band and the ex-prisoner demonstrators clad in replica prison garb, the images of women were used variously to attract, inform and manipulate visitors and exhibitors. At the 1909 Exhibition, individual women were active, powerful and vocal, signifying that the WSPU wanted to be seen as an overwhelming and irresistible force for change. The sounds of performing women were heard throughout the space, as singers, actors, speakers, demonstrators, stallholders and entertainers. The voice of the political prisoner was heard through the prison-cell installations, and the political voice of the visitor was also sought, and expressed, through the polling booth. Actual and acted appearances of famous and influential women formed an important part of the presentation of the event – and famous performers donated their time and talents in the theatre and bandstand and on stalls, selling products endorsed first by the WSPU and, second, by themselves. It is easy to imagine the potential effect that this propaganda might have had on the performers themselves – and also perhaps on performers who were not League members but who came once or twice to the exhibition to perform. If they chose to slip out via the emergency exit near the auditorium they might miss much of the experience, but it is more than probable that many performers would have been curious about the rest of the exhibition space and would have taken the opportunity to look around. Marketing suffrage at the exhibition included embracing problematic and potentially negative perceptions of women and their labour and challenging anti-suffrage rhetoric that women were somehow inherently unfit to participate in national politics. As working women in a profession that was very much located in the public domain, however, the suffragist writers and actresses of the AFL and WWSL did not seem to have been as keen to as the WSPU to prioritise traditional female domestic roles. Suffrage plays certainly acknowledged them but with a focus on issues of class and inequality and most frequently through the characters of female domestic servants better educated about the constitutional aspects of the movement than their mistresses. Plays such as Evelyn Glover's *A Chat with Mrs Chicky* (1912) and *Miss Appleyard's Awakening* (1911) follow this pattern, although the political agency of middle-class women can be seen to benefit working-class women in plays such as Joan Dugdale's *10 Clowning Street* (1913) and Gertrude Jennings' *A Woman's Influence* (1909) where the character of Margaret attempts to improve the working conditions for women in a nearby factory. In other pieces, humour is based around critiques of gender, class and economic structures in relationship to domestic work. In plays such Henry Arncliffe-Sennett's *An Englishwoman's Home* (1910) and L. S. Phibbs' *Jim's Leg* (1911), the male characters are unable and unwilling to manage domestic chores, and the resulting chaos is left for the capable female characters to deal with. Plays written by suffragist actresses and playwrights where women are constrained by their domestic obligations and long to be free of them include Helen Margaret Nightingale's *A Change of Tenant* (1908) and Margaret Wynne Nevinson's *In the Workhouse* (1911), which feature female protagonists who are economically disadvantaged due to circumstances beyond their control. Their lack of economic agency is directly related to their powerless position in a dysfunctional domestic and political environment: they have no prospects of being able to independently and legally support themselves and/or their children.

Suffragist playwrights more frequently wrote female characters who wanted to break out of conventional roles and assert their independence. Happily unmarried and childless women, such as Hamilton, found little comfort in celebrations of domesticity and modernity as the ultimate purpose for women, and she and others like her chose to focus much of their writing for the stage around the value of female friendships and relationships, creative and intellectual pursuits and political and social agency outside of the domestic sphere. Hamilton's *Beware! A Warning – to Suffragists*, published by the Artists' Suffrage League c. 1909, portrayed women in the home as trapped and prohibited from participating in any activity other than those traditionally confined to the domestic sphere. Her polemic book *Marriage as a Trade*, also published in 1909, detailed her view that marriage was an unavoidable economic arrangement in which women had to 'conform to the expectations of their "employers" and were therefore unable to develop their intellectual potential'.[86] Plays such as Inez Bensusan's *The Apple* (1909), Graham Moffat's *The Maid and the*

Magistrate (1912) and Cicely Hamilton's *Jack and Jill and a Friend* (1911) and *Just to Get Married* (1914) include female characters openly stating that they don't want to be limited to a gendered domestic role before or after marriage.

Within six months of their first year in existence, the AFL had performed at two large-scale events: the WFL's Green and Gold Fair and the WSPU Exhibition. They had commissioned and presented new writing that directly responded to the political struggles of the suffrage campaign and had used their extensive professional contacts and support within the theatrical industry to present a huge variety of entertainment. Having a space in which performers could try out and develop their work in front of an audience was invaluable in terms of professional development in an industry driven by commercial viability, and the League initiated some of its most famous and popular pieces at suffrage exhibitions as well as creating a network of performers and allies who understood their contribution as being part of the visual propaganda at the heart of the campaign. Audiences for the theatre at the 1909 Exhibition were not coming to the work 'cold' – they themselves were seeing the performances in the context of a heightened awareness of the movement and specifically of the exhibition. With five performances a day, the audiences coming into the theatre space had had ample opportunity to visit and interact with the many other performative elements and brought those experiences to their interpretation and appreciation of the AFL's work. Craig recalled that 'the little theatre ... was always full and made a great deal of money' – in fact, the theatre took £261 (nearly £25,000 in 2015 values) over the course of the exhibition, which, at 1 shilling a ticket, equates to 5,220 tickets sold.[87] The League also made over £10 (nearly £1,000 in 2015 values) on sales of programmes at the exhibition.[88] By being so heavily involved and providing such a variety of entertainments, the AFL built trust within the movement as a whole, creating more employment opportunities for themselves as individuals and as a networked group. This also helped to develop audiences for their non-suffrage professional work, increasing their professional profile in both the suffrage world and the theatre industry. It also removed performers from the conventions of their theatrical training and working lives. At the exhibition, they discovered that the space in which suffrage plays could be performed was not just physical but intellectual and social too, something which would become an important part of their future plans. The next chapter will explore this idea in more detail and consider the professional networks within which the AFL worked and was formed.

Notes

1 R. Dee, *Sweet Peas, Suffragettes and Showmen* (Andover: Phillimore & Co., 2011).
2 *Votes for Women* 16 April 1909, p. 550.
3 The WSPU exhibition ran concurrently with five other exhibitions taking place in the major spaces of London. The *Daily Mirror* lists the Golden West Exhibition at Earl's Court; the International Sports and Territorial Exhibition at the Agricultural Hall in Islington; the Royal Navy and Military Tournament at Olympia; the Imperial International Exhibition at White City and the Pharmaceutical Exhibition at the Horticultural Hall. *Daily Mirror*, 8 May 1900, p. 4.
4 *The Fourth Olympiad Official Report of the Olympic Games of 1908* (London: British Olympic Association, 1909).
5 J. Mercer, 'Media and militancy: propaganda in the Women's Social and Political Union's campaign', *Women's History Review*, 14:3-4 (2005), 471-86, at p. 474.
6 D. Atkinson, *Mrs. Broom's Suffragette Photographs* (London: Nishen Photography, 1989), p. 2.
7 Exhibition programme, 1909, p. 14.
8 P. Gillett, *Musical Women in England, 1870-1914: 'Encroaching on All Man's Privileges'* (New York: St Martin's Press, 2000), p. 222.
9 Gillett, *Musical Women*, p. 200.
10 Gillett, *Musical Women*, p. 200.
11 *Votes for Women*, 28 January 1909, p. 294.
12 Brian Harrison, taped interview with George Dugdale, Women's Library, 8/SUF/B/156; Kitty Marion's unpublished autobiography, Manuscripts and Archives Division, Schwarzman Building, New York Public Library.
13 *Votes for Women*, 21 May 1909, p. 688.
14 *Votes for Women*, 8 December 1911, p. 155.
15 K. Florey, *Women's Suffrage Memorabilia: An Illustrated Historical Study* (Jefferson, NC: McFarland & Co., 2013), p. 137.
16 Board of Education, *Suggestions for the Teaching of Needlework*, Circular 750, p. 3.
17 M. Finnegan, *Selling Suffrage: Consumer Culture and Votes for Women* (New York: Columbia University Press, 1999), p. 112. These negative stereotypes affected all the militant societies. In 1910, the WFL issued a series of postcards called *Suffragettes at Home* that showed members doing traditionally female chores and domestic work themselves, with captions that read, for example, 'Mrs. Joseph McCabe Bathing Her Baby', 'Alison Neilans Cleans the Stove' and 'Mrs. How Martyn Makes Jam'.
18 J. Bush, *Women Against the Vote: Female Anti-suffragism in Britain* (Oxford: Oxford University Press, 2007).
19 *Votes for Women*, 28 May 1909, p. 722.

20 *Votes for Women*, 28 May 1909, p. 722.
21 C. Hamilton and C. St John, *Pot and Kettle*, in N. Paxton, *The Methuen Drama Book of Suffrage Plays* (London: Bloomsbury, 2013), p. 59.
22 *Votes for Women*, 22 December 1911, p. 193.
23 S. Pankhurst, *The Suffragette Movement* (London: Longmans, 1932).
24 Inspector Jarvis appears to have had some sympathy with or respect for the militants. He attended a Suffragette Fellowship reunion dinner in 1936. See E. Crawford, *The Women's Suffrage Movement: A Reference Guide, 1866–1928* (London and New York: Routledge, 2001), p. 561.
25 Political Peepshows Programme, London: Women's Social and Political Union, 1909.
26 *The Times*, 25 May 1909, p. 2.
27 Suffrage prisoners wanted to be awarded the status of political prisoners and kept in the 'first division' rather than treated as ordinary criminals and placed in the 'second or third division'.
28 Exhibition Programme, 1909, p. 39.
29 E. Crawford, 'Police, prisons and prisoners: the view from the Home Office', *Women's History Review*, 14:3–4 (2005), 487–506, at p. 488.
30 Lady Carter, *A Living Soul in Holloway* (London: F. Miller, 1938), p. 12.
31 See B. Green, *Spectacular Confessions: Autobiography, Performance Activism and the Sites of Suffrage* (New York: St Martin's Press, 1997), and K. Cockin, *Edith Craig and the Theatres of Art* (London: Bloomsbury Methuen Drama, 2017).
32 *The Evening Times*, 29 April 1910, p. 7.
33 Women's Freedom League advertisement in the Glasgow and West of Scotland Association for Women's Suffrage Scrapbook, Mitchell Library.
34 *Glasgow Herald*, 29 April 1910.
35 *Votes for Women*, 6 May 1910, p. 521.
36 J. Purvis, 'A lost dimension? The political education of women in the suffragette movement in Edwardian Britain', *Gender and Education*, 6:3 (1994), 319–27, at p. 323; D. Barnes, 'How it feels to be forcibly fed', *New World Magazine*, 6 September 1914.
37 N. A. John, *Holloway Jingles: Written in Holloway Prison during March and April 1912* (Glasgow: Glasgow WSPU, c. 1912).
38 E. Showalter, *The Female Malady: Women, Madness and English Culture, 1830–1980* (London: Virago, 1985), p. 161.
39 Letter from Holloway Prison from Sime Seruya to Edith Craig, 1910, Women's Library.
40 Exhibition Programme, 1909, p. 40.
41 Exhibition Programme, 1909, p. 37.
42 *Votes for Women*, 23 April 1909, p. 581.
43 *Report from the Joint Select Committee of the House of Lords and the House of Commons on the Stage Plays (Censorship)* (London: Wyman & Sons, 1909).
44 *Votes for Women*, 21 May 1909, p. 690.

45 A. Rachlin, *Edy Was a Lady* (London: Matador, 2011), p. 160.
46 Rachlin, *Edy Was a Lady*, p. 160.
47 Kitty Marion's unpublished autobiography, Manuscripts and Archive Division, Schwarzman Building, New York Public Library. p. 12½.
48 *Votes for Women*, 28 May 1909, p. 724.
49 *Votes for Women*, 28 May 1909, p. 724.
50 *The Common Cause*, 11 November 1909, p. 404.
51 For a more detailed analysis of Hamilton's *Waxworks*, see S. Moran, *The Stage Career of Cicely Hamilton (1895–1914)* (Frankfurt: Peter Lang, 2017).
52 G. Bradford Bartlett and W. Gurney Benham, *Mrs. Jarley's Far-Famed Collection of Waxworks*, 4 vols. (London and New York: Samuel French, 1873).
53 *Advertiser* [Adelaide], 6 August 1910, p. 18; *Stage Yearbook*, 1911; *London Standard*, 29 June 1912, p. 5; *The Era*, 7 June 1913, p. 11; N. Coward, *Present Indicative* (London: Heinemann, 1974), p. 80.
54 *The Common Cause*, 11 November 1909, p. 404.
55 *Swansea Herald of Wales*, 14 May 1910.
56 *Sheffield Daily Telegraph*, 17 October 1910.
57 *The Common Cause*, 11 November 1909, p. 404.
58 *Sheffield Daily Telegraph*, 17 October 1910.
59 *Manchester Guardian*, 29 April 1909, p. 8.
60 T. Wolf, *Edith Garrud: The Suffragette Who Knew Jujutsu* (Raleigh, NC: Lulu, 2009), p. 25.
61 E. Godfrey, *Femininity, Crime and Self-Defence in Victorian Literature and Society: From Dagger-Fans to Suffragettes* (London: Palgrave Macmillan, 2012), p. 105.
62 *Evening Post*, 7 August 1909.
63 D. Looser, 'Radical bodies and dangerous ladies: martial arts and women's performance, 1900–1918', *Theatre Research International*, 36:1 (2011), 3–19, at p. 5.
64 Exhibition Programme for WSPU Christmas Fair and Fete (London: The Woman's Press, 1911).
65 Godfrey, *Femininity*, p. 99.
66 Letter from Holloway Prison from Sime Seruya to Edith Craig, 1910, Women's Library.
67 *The Common Cause*, 15 April 1909.
68 *The Vote*, 16 December 1909, p. 86.
69 *The Vote*, 16 December 1909, p. 86.
70 *Votes for Women*, 4 March 1910, p. 353.
71 *Votes for Women*, 15 April 1910, p. 455.
72 *Glasgow Herald*, 30 April 1910. In fact, Mrs Brown Potter was already in Glasgow performing in *Madame X* by Alexandre Bisson at the Kings Theatre.
73 *Votes for Women*, 6 May 1910, p. 521.
74 *Suffragette*, 16 May 1913, p. 518.
75 AFL, *Secretary's Report, June 1912–June 1913*, p. 11.

76 *Suffragette*, 16 May 1913, p. 518.
77 Exhibition Programme for WSPU Christmas Fair, p. 11.
78 Exhibition Programme for WSPU Christmas Fair, pp. 13, 19.
79 Exhibition Programme for WSPU Christmas Fair, p. 17.
80 Exhibition Programme for WSPU Christmas Fair, p. 17.
81 Exhibition Programme for WSPU Christmas Fair, p. 17.
82 Exhibition Programme for WSPU Christmas Fair, p. 19.
83 *Daily News and Leader*, 30 January 1914, p. 2.
84 J. Holledge, 'Women's theatre – women's rights', Ph.D. thesis, University of Bristol, 1985, p. 283–4.
85 Men's Political Union for Women's Enfranchisement, *Second Annual Report*, 1911.
86 L. Whitelaw, *The Life and Rebellious Times of Cicely Hamilton* (London: The Women's Press, 1990), p. 96.
87 Whitelaw, *Cicely Hamilton*, p. 96.
88 AFL, *Accounts*, June 1909.

2
SISTERHOOD

> I founded my first Friday meetings at the Criterion, Piccadilly Circus – I couldn't have anything more central – and we were crowded ... I got all the big stars of the London stage.[1]

Members of the AFL were participants in a variety of 'sisterhoods' through their shared experiences as working women, professional performers, and activists.[2] The actresses who founded the League had spent many years building their public and professional profiles and reputations, and their suffragist work helped to open up new creative possibilities, as well as theatrical and political networks. For Claire Hirshfield, 'because many of its earliest members enjoyed celebrity status and public esteem, the AFL was perhaps the most successful of all "professional" women's organizations in drawing popular attention and sympathy to the cause of female enfranchisement'.[3] Many of the original members of the AFL were established artists and well known to the theatre-going public long before the founding of the League in 1908. Useful here in terms of providing a context for understanding professional practice is a newspaper clipping, dated 2 August 1890 and kept by May Whitty in her papers, showing the results of a competition for the 'most promising young actresses on the London stage'.[4] Marked only as 'The London' among her papers, it is difficult to ascertain exactly which paper the cutting originates from, but the results of the competition, gathered from some 16,000 voters of both sexes, included the names of many future AFL members, suggesting that networks of performers were being formed in the 1880s and 1890s that would prove instrumental in the success of the organisation. This piece of ephemera, clearly important to Whitty as a means of archiving her career, was printed when she was already an established performer. She had made her London stage debut at the age of seventeen in April 1882 and by 1890 was an established actress, performing in Mrs Musgrave's *Our Flat* at the Opera Comique in which she initially understudied and then took over the lead role from Fanny Brough, another future AFL member.[5] The clipping is a helpful starting point for a brief exploration of the existing connections between actresses mentioned who would later form the League. Some had trained together – for example, Gertrude Kingston, Violet and Irene Vanburgh and Adeline Bourne all began their careers with Sarah Thorne's company at the Theatre Royal, Margate in the late 1880s.[6] Sarah Thorne, who managed the Theatre Royal in Margate from 1867 to 1874 and again from 1879 to her death in 1899, opened her school of acting in 1885 after a successful career as an actress.[7] Although she did not believe that acting could be taught – 'one can only develop a talent that is already there – one cannot create it' – her training included classes in voice, gesture, accents, make-up and, crucially, the chance for all her students to perform weekly rep.[8] Adeline Bourne remembered the rigour of her year-long training in Margate with fondness,[9] and after leaving Thorne's stock company, Bourne went on two American tours with Mrs Patrick Campbell and subsequently worked for J. E. Vedrenne and Harley Granville-Barker at the Court Theatre, and for Olga Nethersole, also mentioned in 'The London' clipping, who had made her London debut in 1888. Gertrude Kingston also made her London debut in 1888, while Violet Vanburgh sought formal training from Thorne after she had first appeared on the London stage in 1886 at the age of nineteen.

Not what you know but who you know?

Influential and well-connected relatives, then, as now, could provide opportunities to appear before the public on professional stages that less fortunate, if no less ambitious, performers did not have access to. Whitty acknowledged this in an interview in 1922, saying that unless there was 'interest or personal knowledge', it was 'terribly difficult' for young performers to get their first professional job.[10] Her own daughter, Margaret Webster, was fortunate in growing up surrounded by actors, managers and writers, and so already had significant contacts within the industry when she began her career. Sydney Fairbrother made her professional debut in 1890, aged eighteen, after an interview with future League president, Madge Kendal, secured by her actress mother who had been part of the Kendal company on their first American tour.[11] Part of a theatrical family, all six of the Moore sisters were theatre professionals, and Eva and Decima, both mentioned in 'The London' clipping, had been appearing in the West End since the 1880s. Eva had made her London stage debut aged nineteen, in 1887 at Toole's Theatre in *The Cricket on the Hearth*,[12] while Decima had made hers in December 1889, aged seventeen, in Gilbert and Sullivan's *The Gondoliers* at the Savoy Theatre.[13] Three of their sisters, Bertha, Ada and Emily, all professional musicians, would later be involved in the League, with Emily becoming the AFL's musical organiser.[14] Bertha programmed musical entertainments for the theatre space at the 1909 Exhibition, which included her daughter Marjorie singing and reciting, and later that year gave a matinee at the Court Theatre 'primarily with the object of allowing of the debut of her daughter, Miss Marjorie Moore, both as a vocalist and actress'.[15] Jane Comfort, the niece of Madeleine Lucette Ryley, was fortunate in also having family connections that secured her League membership in 1909:

> 'I had just left school and I was studying for the stage ... and how I wished I could join the Actresses Franchise League. My aunt said, 'You're not eligible to join; you're not an actress!' But Gertrude [Elliott], who was always ready to help, said, 'Why don't you come and walk on in The High Bid at Her Majesty's Theatre.' And so I went on in one of the crowd scenes ... that was my first appearance on the London stage and as soon as I could say I was an actress I became a member of the League.[16]

Comfort gained not only a West End credit, highly desirable for any aspiring performer, from Gertrude Elliott's generosity, but a valuable starting point with which to begin to create her own professional network in the industry. Her role in *The High Bid* placed her within an ensemble of ambitious actors and actresses, and from this position she was able to see the fringes of a professional world in which her existing familial associations counted for much and gain at first hand an understanding of the hierarchies at work.[17] Michael Sanderson's detailed analysis of the numbers of performers in the Victorian and Edwardian periods shows that nearly 29 per cent of actresses beginning their careers in the 1880s came from theatrical families, a figure which fell to nearly 18 per cent for actresses entering the profession after 1890. Sanderson attributes this to the 'increasing respectability' of the profession, partially influenced by the number of aspiring performers and playwrights from middle-class families, implying that the new generation of educated women and men entering the business around the turn of the century was attracted to it in part because of the move towards naturalism in European theatre.[18] Tracy C. Davis, while criticising Sanderson's conclusions as drawn from a narrow field of data and therefore 'deeply flawed', supports the broader idea that the stage was 'well suited' to the education of middle-class women and 'stood to benefit enormously by certain aspects of their socialization'.[19] It is therefore not surprising that educated women within the theatre were also attracted to the suffrage movement: they were aware of the political and social context of the campaign and sought to use theatre to extend and explore these thoughts from a female perspective. For ambitious and politicised actresses, the League provided a chance to form close working alliances and friendships with influential employers and writers and to be part of the production of new, female-led writing for the stage.

No duel but a duet

> Men are also human, and if met frankly and straightforwardly in work, or for that matter, out of it, are as capable of honest, helpful good fellowship as any woman.[20]

Current academic research has not revealed an equivalent contemporary organisation to either the AFL or the WWSL for suffragist men in the theatre, but male support for both organisations from inside the theatrical community included many prominent actor-managers, journalists and playwrights.[21] *A Declaration of Representative Men in Favour of Women's Suffrage*, published in 1909 by the MLWS, recorded male supporters for the equal franchise across many different industries and professionals, with ninety-nine names listed under the headings 'Literature and Drama', 'The Stage' and 'Music and Arts'.[22] The AFL worked with the MLWS, the MPU and the Northern Men's Federation for Women's Suffrage among others, and League committee member Maud Arncliffe Sennett was the chairman of the Northern Men's Federation. AFL member Gertrude Jennings' suffrage play *A Woman's Influence*, first performed in 1909, ends with a call for recognition of the importance of men and women working together for the vote. The final lines of the play unite the female and male characters in solidarity: 'that's the key to the whole Woman's Movement. We can do so much more if we work together'.[23] It is unfortunate that the men who lent their practical and professional support to the League through performing, writing, patronage and publicity are little remembered or celebrated for their suffragist work, because they were an incredibly important part of the success of the organisation. The female membership of the AFL provided the framework for the participation of male writers, and, by commissioning and publishing plays, the League not only created, defined and dominated their chosen genre but also gave space for male members of the profession to experiment and contribute. George Bernard Shaw, Henry Nevinson, Harley Granville-Barker, H. V. Esmond and Israel Zangwill were among the writers associated with the League through their spouses: Charlotte Shaw, Margaret Wynne Nevinson, Lillah McCarthy, Eva Moore and Edith Ayrton Zangwill respectively. Drawn into the work of the League by their partners, families, friends and colleagues, men who wished to contribute could easily do so, finding themselves directly engaged in the immediate propaganda of the movement. Initially only able to make a formal contribution to the organisation as patrons, the later development of an affiliated AFL men's group shows not only how widespread and popular the work and message of the League had become but also the desire among male actors and playwrights to publicly support the campaign. Eva Moore, interviewed by the WFL newspaper *The Vote* in 1910, recalled her experience of collecting support for a suffrage petition from influential male theatre professionals.

> I went round in a 'taxi' one evening from 7.30 to 11.30, from theatre to theatre, with a petition, getting signatures; and to the credit of our well-known actors and actor-managers, be it said, there were very few refusals. Sir Charles Wyndham was one of the first to sign, and everywhere I met with the greatest sympathy.[24]

Eva Moore's account of her journey around the West End shows how she was able to capitalise on her influence within the industry: gaining access to each theatre, finding her way around the various backstage areas and speaking to performers and managers during show time. The professional friendships and acquaintances made in the early years of her career as well as her established reputation meant that Moore, and therefore the League, could gain access to individuals at every level of the profession. The suffrage movement had infiltrated the industry through the League, gaining physical as well as discursive access to the stage. While there is not room here to include biographical detail about every male supporter of the League, I would like to highlight three of the men who regularly and publicly supported the organisation: Johnston Forbes-Robertson, Israel Zangwill and Laurence Housman.

An actor-manager who had made his first stage appearances in the 1870s, Forbes-Robertson had been in Henry Irving's company and had first worked with American actress, playwright and later WWSL and AFL member Elizabeth Robins in 1889 in *The Profligate* by Pinero – also a later supporter of the AFL – at the Garrick Theatre. His wife, future president of the League, Gertrude Elliott, made her New York debut in 1894 and first appeared in the West End in 1899, marrying Forbes-Robertson a year later.[25] Elliott and Forbes-Robertson were a successful, powerful and well-connected couple and frequently spoke in public of their support for Votes for Women. Their status as employers and leading performers meant that the prospect of making a favourable impression on them must have been a tantalising one for new as well as established performers.[26] Actress Adeline Bourne, who was a member of Forbes-Robertson's company for two transatlantic tours, is cited as the catalyst for the foundation of the AFL in the few accounts given by League members, although Bourne herself gave the initial credit for the idea to actress and WSPU member Winifred Mayo. Pragmatic and ambitious, Bourne recognised that public visibility was key to gaining support and publicity and that if Elliott and Forbes-Robertson were prepared to be open about their support for women's suffrage, others would speak up and out in the knowledge that they had influential allies within the industry. A dedicated suffragist, Forbes-Robertson chaired the inaugural meeting of the AFL on 26 November 1908 at the Criterion restaurant, and for an AFL meeting held at the Theatre Royal, Drury Lane, during his 'Farewell Season' in 1913 many of his company, both female and male, volunteered their time as stewards or literature sellers.[27] This show of support from company members indicates their desire not only to impress their manager but also to follow his lead in openly demonstrating suffragist sympathies. Forbes-Robertson addressed audiences in venues across the UK and in the USA on behalf of militant as well as constitutional societies, and regularly spoke for the MLWS, of which he was a vice president.[28] In a speech given at the Queen's Hall on 1 February 1909, he announced his desire for the day for women when 'every calling, every trade, every profession that they can follow is open to them' and encouraged the audience to strive for a better society, one in which 'all the bars in front of women are swept away'.[29] At a speech made later that month in Dublin, he conceded to the audience of Irish Women's Franchise League members that 'our own view of things, men's view, is ever unconsciously warped by self-interest', and remains one of the few Edwardian actor-managers to have not only openly expressed his support for suffrage but to have made a point of emphasising the equality of pay for actors and actresses in his own company.[30] League member Sybil Thorndike recalled that Forbes-Robertson and fellow actor-manager Lewis Casson talked 'about Women's Suffrage every place they went to' and credited Casson, who she would later marry, with awakening her own interest in the movement.[31]

Writer and playwright Israel Zangwill, like Forbes-Robertson, was a vice president of the MLWS.[32] His wife Edith was in the AFL and WWSL, and both were members of the WSPU, also helping to form, with Inez Bensusan, the Jewish League for Woman Suffrage in 1912. Zangwill spoke at both WWSL and AFL 'at homes' and meetings, often alongside other male supporters whose wives were in the League, including actors

Ben Webster, the husband of May Whitty, and Henry Ainley, Suzanne Sheldon's husband. In 1911, Zangwill wrote *Prologue for a Women's Theatre* to be performed for the AFL's Grand Matinee at the Lyceum Theatre. The piece makes a clear call for the sexes to work together:

> 'The time is out of joint?' Then what's the cure?
> Joint work of men and women to be sure:
> Joint work to foster every noble growth,
> Joint work to make a better world for both.[33]

Zangwill was confident that the vote would give actresses the chance to have more agency in choosing future roles and that the campaign had already changed the way women behaved in the profession, writing in *Votes for Women* that the 'nature of their profession tends to turn them into other people's passions, other people's ideas and ideals. In this movement they can express an idea, an ideal, and a passion of their own'.[34] Laurence Housman, co-founder with his sister Clemence of the Suffrage Atelier, was also part of the MLWS. He wrote plays and speeches for the AFL, articles for both the WSPU and WFL, and was an honorary male associate of the WWSL.[35] Housman was not afraid of publicly supporting the suffrage movement – in 1912, he attended the International Suffrage Alliance conference, representing the WWSL and the Women's Tax Resistance League, and in 1913 he was excused from serving on a London jury because he wanted to 'not conscientiously be a party to trying women while they are not on an equal footing with men'.[36] Housman wrote many poems in support of the cause, and his translation of Aristophanes' *Lysistrata*, which included contemporary suffrage jokes and references, was chosen by Gertrude Kingston to open her Little Theatre in 1910 and was subsequently published by the Woman's Press in 1911.[37]

While many prominent actor-managers and theatre producers were supportive of the campaign, a few equally powerful individuals were not, although I have found none to have specifically spoken in public on an anti-suffragist platform or as representatives of anti-suffragist societies. Privately, however, their views were expressed without ambiguity. Lena Ashwell recalled:

> the scorn which women who thought that they should be recognized as citizens drew upon themselves from otherwise quite polite and sensible people. Managers, authors, pressmen became quite passionate in their resentment ... Once when I went to see Tree I had in my hand a book called 'The Soul of a Suffragette,' by W.L. Courteney. Tree picked it up

and with a magnificent gesture of contempt flung it into the far corner of the room.[38]

Adeline Bourne had written to Lady Tree in 1909, having apparently been told by actor manager Herbert Beerbohm Tree that his wife was not interested in the movement. Bourne's letter reassured Lady Tree that the League was formally unconnected with the militant societies, mentioned the names of other prominent actresses members and, having made a strong and succinct political case, finally attempted to flatter Lady Tree, writing that her 'name & influence would be such a help because actresses ... like other people and sheep require to be lead'.[39] Despite the invitation to lend her influence to both the campaign and the League, Lady Tree did not join, presumably much to the relief of her husband, although she later became part of the League's wartime projects and committees after 1914.

Other theatrically influential anti-suffragists included the actor husband of League member Irene Vanbrugh, who seems to have been worried about her being openly supportive of the campaign – 'Dot [Dion Boucicault Jnr] was very much against my associating myself so definitely with them.'[40] The boundaries between personal relationships, theatrical alliances and political activism were constantly blurred – but, unlike Tree, Boucicault's opinion appears not to have swayed his female relatives away from supporting the League as his wife, sister-in-law and younger sister were all members of the AFL. Family frictions aside, the danger for openly suffragist actresses was that of the potential loss of employment due to their political allegiance to the cause. Music-hall performer, variety actress and militant member of the WSPU Kitty Marion wrote that not only did some of her friends abandon her when they discovered she was campaigning but that her career suffered. However much her account was written for an audience she assumed would have had sympathy for the cause, it is likely that the individuals she mentions were not alone in negatively affecting the careers of other performers who they considered had blurred the lines between their political and professional activities.

> Mr. Henri Gros, who had booked me several times, told me I need not ask him for any more work. A girl ... told me ... when she mentioned my name, he said, 'Oh, that bloody Suffragette, she'd better not come here for anything.' A Music Hall agent laughed when he saw me wearing the 'colors' ... 'If you'll take off those colors, I'll see that you get booked up for life,' he said. And I said 'No, you should have booked me before I put them on, it's too late to take them off now.'[41]

Support for suffragist women could not be guaranteed in the theatre, despite strong personal relationships and robust constitutional arguments, and the men who actively supported the League also did so from within their own potentially precarious positions of power and influence and their existing networks of patronage and authority. Men remained at the centre of the power structures and hierarchies within the industry, and while the actress-managers within the AFL were encouraging other women into production, administration and backstage work, there is still more research to be done to find evidence that more than a few suffragist actor-managers created practical transformations in the ways women could participate in all areas of the business.

More than just the vote: actresses, labour and the stage

> Of all the women workers in the world the actress should be the greatest helper in this vital cause.[42]
>
> I am a suffragist. What woman who has been out in the world and has had to take care of herself is not a suffragist?[43]

Female sweated labour, economic and legal inequality and male violence against women and girls were among the issues League members believed female suffrage would tackle. The unique position of actresses in the labour economy and their ability to support themselves financially gave them an awareness of the difficulties faced by other women in and out of the home. At political odds perhaps with their aspirational middle-class theatre-going audiences, there was also frustration expressed at those who, through lack of direct experience, had no appreciation of the urgent need for legislative change. Actress and playwright Bessie Hatton told an interviewer from *The Vote* that, in her opinion, 'the real enemies of the Suffrage … are the lazy rich, bridge-playing, fashionable set', and Eva Moore stressed to the same paper that her financial independence had been gained through her own hard work, railing against what she perceived to be the comfortable apathy of the moneyed classes: 'I began to earn my own living at fifteen, and I think the woman who has to do this knows a good deal more about life … and she realizes that she is handicapped as against her male competitors.'[44] AFL members, by virtue of stepping out of the traditional female role and seeking paid employment on the stage, allied themselves with other working women rather than middle-class women who did not work. The League had marched directly behind a contingent of women workers from the East End in June 1910,[45] and in a petition to the House of Commons in 1913 described themselves as part of a self-supporting and working sisterhood:

> Representing a very large and important faction of working women ... this meeting of actresses calls upon the Government immediately to extend the franchise to women: that all women claim the franchise as a necessary protection for workers under modern industrial conditions, and maintain that by their labour they have earned the right to this defence.[46]

Campaigning by the League included holding meetings and putting on performances for audiences at both ends of the social and socioeconomic spectrum – from the Criterion restaurant in Piccadilly to workman's halls in the East End. By 1911, the AFL had branched out 'with the help of Mr. George Lansbury', and held meetings in Bow and Poplar consisting of 'suffrage plays, songs and recitations, [and] good converting speeches'.[47] The League was present in the East End's Victoria Park for a number of suffrage demonstrations and meetings – including speaking from its own platform for an event organised by Sylvia Pankhurst's East London Federation of Suffragettes.[48] Playwright and WSPU member Beatrice Harraden accompanied Emmeline Pankhurst to an election in Bow and Bromley in 1912 and was moved by her interactions with the working women there, and the potential of the vote to change their lives.[49] The practical experience of interacting with and performing for a wide range of audiences provided League members with up-to-date knowledge about the lives of other working women, as well as opportunities to disseminate this knowledge to a wider public audience through the medium of suffrage theatre.

AFL member Joan Dugdale's 1913 play *10 Clowning Street* is set in the office of a fictional prime minister who sends his daughters out to work under assumed names – one to a laundry, one to a shop and one to work as a parlour maid for a Labour MP.[50] All anti-suffragists when they leave, the three return in horror at the working conditions of ordinary women, convinced of the urgent need for women's enfranchisement. Judith, the eldest, comes home from the laundry radicalised, defiant and determined to join a militant suffrage society. She is alarmed by her previous lack of awareness of the lives of the women she had been working with:

> JUDITH: It's opened my eyes; taught me what women have to go through when they're not sheltered behind padded front doors like ours ... To see those women having all the life taken out of them ... wrung out, mangled, and sweated, at three and four shillings a week! Do you know they go there

at seven, and don't come out till eight or nine in the evening sometimes, and then they are so tired, they hardly have the energy to crawl home ... I never knew such things existed.[51]

The second sister, Isabella, trudges home exhausted from overwork and bemoans the hypocrisy of politicians who advocate for the working class and then treat their servants poorly, and when Enid, the third sister, returns, she, like Judith, announces that she has been converted to militancy: 'I feel so roused up at the way they've neglected shop-girls that I could blow up the House of Commons without a qualm!'[52] Their father is appalled: 'I ought never to have let you out of the house. I might have known you'd go and make a mess of it. Women can't do a thing alone. You're all fools, damned fools, every one of you!'[53] Many characters in suffrage plays undergo a transformation from anti-suffragists to fervent supporters of the cause by the end of the play, but in *10 Clowning Street* the conversion of the most powerful character is not heartfelt and is obtained by duress rather than reason.[54] Earlier in the piece the prime minister admits to Marchmount, the editor of 'The Daily Discriminator, a leading London paper' that 'The Opposition are voting with us. We're all one at bottom on Women Suffrage, you know; don't want it at any price ... it's an open secret.'[55] He eventually agrees to support the votes-for-women campaign – not because he has been moved by his daughters' experiences or opinions but by the threat of their turning to militancy and the bad publicity that would accompany it.

> JUDITH: Now then, Papa – 'Yes' or 'No'? A Woman Suffrage Bill this session, introduced as a Government measure, and to pass through all its stages ... Or – your three daughters in Holloway Gaol? Choose![56]

10 Clowning Street is humorous, but real experience of the consequences of militant action informed both the writing and the playing of the piece. The portrayal of policemen and politicians in the play is certainly not as kindly figures of fun but rather as aggressive and misogynistic anti-suffragists with a corrupt grip on power.[57] Joan Dugdale had been a WSPU member since 1907 and had been imprisoned for militancy, as had her sister Una, who produced the play.[58] Una's husband, Victor Duval, who appeared in the original cast of the play, had himself been arrested and imprisoned in Pentonville Prison for his support for the cause.[59] Duval founded the MPU and was from a family of suffragists – his father was a member of the MLWS, and his sister was a WSPU member, who, like Victor's wife and sister-in-law, had been imprisoned for militant actions. The play was published in full in *Votes for Women* a week after it was produced, and Joan Dugdale's evident understanding of the journey of a bill through the Houses of Parliament and her exposure of the private machinations between anti-suffragist politicians and journalists make *10 Clowning Street* an interesting piece to both read and perform, as well as an example of her nuanced and empathetic attitude towards everyday working women.

The problems created by economic inequalities affecting women were certainly a popular and provocative topic in the theatre, and in suffrage theatre in particular. That poorly paid women might be forced to supplement their income through prostitution was one of the fears of feminist campaigners. Sensationalist journalism helped to keep the issue current by focusing on stories about innocent girls being kidnapped and forced into prostitution, but this picture was misleading, as some suffragists were all too aware. *Downward Paths, an Inquiry into the Causes Which Contribute to the Making of the Prostitute* by suffragist Maude Royden firmly asserted that scenarios involving the kidnap and deception of young girls were very rare, citing suffragist Teresa Billington-Greig's article *The Truth about the White Slave Traffic*, published in the *English Review* in June 1913. Billington-Greig had investigated a 'crop of sensational stories of procurers' and found not only that none of the stories could be substantiated but also that neither 'the National Vigilance Associations of England or Scotland had ever come across such a case'.[60] Royden highlighted the lack of opportunities and frameworks of support for married women, particularly those with children, those who had been widowed or deserted, escaped domestic violence or lived with husbands who were unable to work. Low-paid and sweated labour were condemned in Royden's inquiry, as were seasonal trades that employed women on low freelance wages: 'The victims of the procurer do not need to be drugged: they have been made helpless enough by poverty and misfortune.'[61] Royden acknowledged the powerlessness of women in the theatrical professions seeking employment from male managers, writing that 'an actress's failure or success depends very often not on the verdict of the public but on the gossip of a small circle of managers'.[62] She reported that eight of the 830 prostitutes interviewed for her book had previously been professionally on the stage, although she gave no details of their former careers.

Steve Nicholson notes within his extensive examination of theatrical censorship that 'one of the most talked about social and political issues in the years before 1914 was the so-called white slave trade'.[63] Plays that dealt overtly with the issue of prostitution and sex within a socio-economic context were not licensed for performance by the censor and so could not be performed for a public audience on the commercial or 'legitimate' stages. Famous examples include Ibsen's *Ghosts*, submitted in 1891 but unlicensed until 1914; Maeterlinck's *Monna Vanna*, refused in 1902 and 1908 but also licensed in 1914; and Bernard Shaw's *Mrs Warren's Profession*, refused a licence in 1898 and not passed until 1926.[64] The debates over *Mrs Warren's Profession* directly affected the prospects of production for Cicely Hamilton's adaptation of Elizabeth Robins' 1913 novel *Where Are You Going To?* which Robins had been prompted to write after the passing of the Criminal Law Amendment Act in 1912 that prevented the arrest of known brothel-keepers or pimps on suspicion alone.[65] Hamilton's play was refused a licence, with representatives from the Lord Chamberlain's office directly citing Shaw's play in their communications. Suffragist actresses in the UK and the USA had long been championing Shaw's piece – and there had been private productions of it in both countries, including one by Mary Shaw in New York in October 1905 and another by Edith Craig's Pioneer Players in London in June 1912. Playwright Christopher St John, described the piece as 'very near the hearts of all women fighting the battle for civic freedom' and attributed the 'fuss and commotion' surrounding it to the fact that the character of Mrs Warren baldly gave 'her reasons for having adopted her ghastly trade', therefore forcing audiences to confront the socio-economic realities for women who were unable to support themselves in any other way.[66] Sos Eltis has described Shaw's play as 'providing the template for all subsequent feminist theatrical engagements with prostitution', seeing a connection with the work of other suffragist dramatists, such as Elizabeth Robins' 1907 play *Votes for Women* in which 'social and class divisions ... cut across the shared interests of gender'.[67]

Among the many examples of feminist plays including this theme is H. M. Harwood's play *Honour Thy Father*, produced by the Pioneer Players at the Little Theatre on 15 December 1912, in which a middle-class woman, Claire, is revealed to have been supporting herself and her parents through prostitution, after losing her job as a shop-girl for refusing to sleep with her male superiors. Her father, Morgan, whose gambling debts she has been paying, is morally outraged.

> MORGAN: If you'd been a good girl – a decent girl –
> CLAIRE: Oh, what have decency and goodness got to do with it? People can't live on that sort of thing. You can't save money to send to your family out of decency and goodness.
> MORGAN: *(bewildered)* But – I understand that you *did* get a position – something in a shop.

CLAIRE: Yes, fifteen shillings a week – living 'in'. You don't know what that means, do you? Even then I couldn't keep my place – unless I was prepared to be 'accommodating' ...

With no income apart from that provided by his daughter, Morgan cannot afford not to accept her support. Admitting his ignorance of the lives of independent working women, he attempts to punish her for her moral 'fall':

MORGAN: I utterly disapprove of your associating with your sister – I shouldn't dream of allowing it.
CLAIRE: You will have to allow it.
MORGAN: What? Are you to dictate to me?
CLAIRE: *(quietly)* Haven't I the right?
MORGAN: The right? The right?
CLAIRE: The person who pays the piper – calls the tune – I've learnt *that* in my profession.

Sos Eltis describes the playwright's intention as seeking to 'separate disgust at prostitution from condemnation of the prostitute', with Claire refusing to indulge in 'the conventional self-disgust of the theatrical fallen woman'.[68] Through the medium of suffrage theatre and in the contexts of suffragist debates around the lives and experiences of women of all backgrounds and classes, female and male writers attempted to explore, unpack and examine the conventional moral hypocrisies around class, virtue and female labour that perpetuated political and social inequalities.

Sisterhood in suffragist theatre

Suffrage plays that acknowledged and explored the connections between sexism, politics, poverty and sexual exploitation were predicated on an understanding of sisterhood within the movement and a deep interest in the shared experiences, aspirations and fears between different communities and between one class of woman and another. Although not professional actresses, the performances of the role-playing prisoners in the prison cells at the 1909 Women's Exhibition engaged in a dramatisation of authenticity, encouraging spectators to engage in a multilayered reading of the event. Invited into an imaginative as well as, literally, constructed space, the audience could see the women's costumes, hear their stories, interact with them as individuals and, crucially, know that these performative verbatim elements and personal interactions were based on lived experience. Audiences watching members of the AFL performing in suffrage plays were perhaps confronted with similarly layered complexities of meaning, interpretation and knowledge. Lesley Ferris has referred to this as 'the politics of living performance'.[69] In other words, seeing openly suffragist actresses in suffrage plays blurred the lines between performance and reality and added a poignancy to their fervour, resonances that are all but lost to researchers and performers today when engaging with these texts. Gathering many famous names together to present a theatrical picture of female solidarity and strength that would motivate, educate and move the audience is a feature of one of the most performed suffrage plays, Cicely Hamilton's *Pageant of Great Women*. Claire Eustance, in her writing on militancy and the WFL, suggests that performances of the piece were 'creating environments where an interest in challenging the barriers to women's equality could be reinforced and refined'.[70] In the *Pageant*, Woman presents an impressive display of female intellectual and physical might throughout history, attempting by force of sheer numbers to overwhelm the character of Prejudice, and by the end of the piece there are forty-four Great Women on stage. Members of the AFL usually played the three main characters of Woman, Justice and Prejudice, while local supporters took the roles of the Great Women. As Katherine Cockin suggests, 'the diversity of women was emphasized by the collective acting out of greatness by local suffragists. Greatness seemed to be within reach of every woman.'[71] The fellowship of suffragists and the sisterhood of women combined to create a powerful collective experience that used storytelling and role play to bind individuals together in support of one voice, that of Woman, and one main theme, that of women's right to be treated equally. The *Pageant* is an evocative and moving mass experience with two audiences: one watching the piece from the auditorium and one made up of those representing the Great Women onstage. Both look at each other across the staged debate, simultaneously and tacitly hearing, representing and supporting the ideas through and with their physical presence.

The First Actress, written by Christopher St John, also takes the idea of solidarity among women as a challenge directly into theatricality and the theatrical space. First performed in May 1911 with a cast that included Ellen Terry, May Whitty and Lena Ashwell, the play is set backstage at the New Theatre, Drury Lane, in 1661 and takes place before and after the first-ever performance of a woman playing a female part. After a negative assessment of her performance by one of the men of

Sisterhood

2.1 From *How the Vote Was Won* by Cicely Hamilton, 1908

the King's Players Company, Margaret Hughes, the *First Actress* of the title, retires to bed in her dressing room in despair. As she sleeps, the piece becomes a pageant play, with actresses entering to play famous actresses from the future, praising Hughes, thanking her for her courage and reassuring her that her pioneering role forever changed the stage. Although Hughes does not wake to see them, the audience is presented with a tableau of theatrical sisterhood both past and present that proves her struggle was not in vain.

One of the most well known and popular suffrage plays embraces the idea of collective action by women. *How the Vote Was Won* is based on an original short story by Cicely Hamilton, a spoof history described as 'Some short Extracts from Prof. Dryasdust's "Political History of the Twentieth Century," published in the year 2008 A.D.' (see Figure 2.1).[72] The play imagines a general women's strike, called by suffrage campaigners to take the government's argument that women do not need votes as they are all supported by men to its logical conclusion. All the women who have previously worked and supported themselves leave their jobs on the same day to go to their nearest male relative and demand to be supported. It soon becomes clear that this action built on sisterly solidarity has been effective and that the women of the theatre have wholeheartedly taken part. Among the group of women gathering in one house in Brixton is a music-hall-actress character, Maudie Spark, who describes herself as the 'Queen of Comediennes' and reveals that the theatres and music halls in London are closed because 'the actresses have gone on strike – resting indefinitely'.[73] As in *10 Clowning Street*, while some men are apparently converted to the cause, the economic prospect of half the population ceasing to work forces others to support women's suffrage. The end of the play reports a procession of men, wearing badges and sashes in the colours of the constitutional and the militant societies, marching to Westminster to demand Votes for Women. *How the Vote Was Won* provided a fantastical glimpse of how of women working and protesting together en masse might create change. Two years after the first performance of the play, an opportunity arose for women all over the country to do just that.

Census: protest and performance

> Never in the wildest dreams of youth did I picture myself skating with a celebrated actress in the Strand at five o'clock on an April morning.[74]

The 1911 Census Boycott was initiated by the WFL and supported by the WSPU. Intended to cause disruption to the process of government, suffragists were urged not to participate in the census process by refusing to give information. The boycott was widely advertised in the suffrage press, and there were gatherings of boycotters across the UK. In London, the event that sought and gained the most publicity was held at the Aldwych Rinkeries, a rollerskating rink close to the WSPU headquarters. When the doors to the rink opened at 1 a.m. on Monday, 3 April, enumerators working for the Census Office and standing outside estimated 500 women and seventy men had entered the building.[75] Articles published by reporters from the *Evening Standard and St James's Gazette* and the *Daily Telegraph* report that nine members of the AFL either sang or recited and were followed on stage by WSPU leaders Emmeline Pethick-Lawrence and Emmeline and Christabel Pankhurst.[76] Cellist May Mukle had been going to play, but, because the Rinkeries did not have a music licence, she was unable to. The pieces chosen by the League were mostly comic and included Decima Moore reciting 'Woman This and Woman That', Laurence Housman's suffrage-themed pastiche of Kipling's 1890 poem, 'Tommy' (see Figure 2.2). Another of Housman's poems, 'Woman's Cause', which had first been performed at the joint AFL and WWSL matinee in November 1909 and subsequently published by the WWSL in 1912, was also performed. The tone of the piece is solemn and uplifting, full of the heroic propaganda of the movement. It begins:

Sisterhood

2.2 Decima Moore performing in the Aldwych Rinkeries for the Census Boycott, 1911

> No Cause is great that is not hard to gain,
> No right so clear as not to be denied:
> Else, in the past, no martyrs had been slain,
> No prophets stoned, no saints by torture tried.
> Backward we look, and see the wrong confessed –
> Forward – and lo, to other wrongs are blind:
> And at our doors new wrongs stand unredressed,
> Needing the martyr's faith, the prophet's mind.[77]

By the end of the third and final stanza, Housman's writing becomes full of patriotic fervour, invoking the might of Justice, England and Faith to the cause. At 3 a.m., a large number of those at the Rinkeries left the building for a breakfast at the Gardenia, a vegetarian restaurant next to the Theatre Royal Drury Lane on Catherine Street, after which they went back to the rink, where the skating continued until 6 a.m.

Scholars of both the suffrage movement and the census were able to explore a limited number of individual census returns in 2009, when the information for some counties was released, and have had full access since January 2012.[78] Many League members and supporters appear to have boycotted. Decima Moore's house was listed as uninhabited, as was

Maud Arncliffe Sennett's. Both were at the Rinkeries, with Inez Bensusan, Emily Pertwee, Winifred Mayo, Adeline Bourne and Rosa Leo. Winifred Mayo, along with her mother, aunt, sister and two female servants, made her protest before joining her colleagues at the rink – their census form is marked 'Suffragettes. refused [sic] all information and wrote across census form no vote no census. Information obtained from neighbours.' Kitty Marion also refused to give information, and Australian actress Muriel Matters wrote 'No Vote No Census' over her form, adding 'As I am not a <u>person</u> under the franchise laws I am not a person for Census purposes.' Harley Granville-Barker made a note on the census form that his wife, Lillah McCarthy, 'for reasons connected with Woman's Suffrage objected to fill in the paper', and dramatist Henry Nevinson made a similar amendment to his census form: 'Other women were staying in the house but they refused consent to the Census on the ground that Women have no representation in the Countrys [sic] Government.' Israel Zangwill was not at home, and his form reads, 'The rest of the household is not entered as we feel that until women have the political rights of citizens, they should not perform the duties of citizens.'[79]

Jill Liddington, in *Vanishing for the Vote*, notes that economic circumstances seemed to have affected the participations of active resisters, with professional women doctors and teachers well represented. Her assertion that 'financial self-confidence allowed women to cock their snook at the census' rings true among the known boycotters from the League, but other prominent individuals to whom it might also apply complied with the census – notably Gertrude Jennings, May Whitty, Edith Craig, Irene Vanburgh and Lena Ashwell.[80] In fact, it appears that the majority of the League's membership complied with the census. There are many reasons as to why this might be the case, given the arguments for and against the boycott. Some may have felt strongly that it was important for women to be counted in order to contribute to the statistics that campaigners for welfare reforms relied on, while those with young families may not have wanted to leave them overnight. Actresses might not have wanted to break the law, fearing the £5 fine – equivalent to nearly £450 pounds in 2015 – and many actresses who did not own their own homes, lived in boarding houses or were away in digs on tour may not have had a sympathetic landlord, family or partner willing to accommodate their protest on the census form or incur the fine on their behalf. As Jill Liddington has noted, the 'tantalizing absences and silences' of evaders can only provoke speculation – perhaps League members and supporters for whom no information exists – such as the Forbes-Robertsons, Eva Moore and Cicely Hamilton – were part of the anonymous 500 women and seventy men at the Aldwych Rink or perhaps they had chosen to evade the enumerators in another way.

> To judge the 1911 census rebellion merely by its arithmetic is to miss the boycott's compelling symbolism and its historic significance … it was the first time women had been faced on census night with a political dilemma; and the first time a sizeable group of the disenfranchised had defied a government and refused to be counted – all without one single arrest.[81]

The Census Boycott is an example of a political action for women's suffrage that invaded private as well as public spaces, forcing suffragist actresses to think in detail about their representation as citizens. It is impossible to tell how many actresses might have taken an active part had the threat of a fine not hindered them, or if concerns had not been raised about the damage such a boycott might do to public-health statistics in the long term.

Sisterhood on other stages

> First the concert, then drama, musical comedy, and to-night the music hall![82]

Far from being limited to the 'legitimate' theatres, members of the AFL performed to and engaged with a variety of audiences and spectators across all classes of society. The development of suffragist performance party pieces, including pastiches, poems, songs and monologues, created an accessible and mostly comic repertoire of material more reminiscent of the versatility of the variety stage than the formality of the dramas in which so many of the League's members had begun. The adaptability of these shorter, more topical pieces allowed the actresses to demonstrate their support in non-theatrical settings and impromptu performance spaces. The growth in specially written suffragist party pieces also coincided with the crossover of 'legitimate' theatre performers to the variety stage. *The Era* reported on 23 January 1909 that,

> One of the most interesting music-hall debuts made for some time was that of Miss Decima Moore, which took place at the Manchester Tivoli last night … At the second house she gave a very varied 'turn' … the audience must benefit by an entertainment that is not only diverting but educative in good taste.[83]

Moore's Tivoli debut was also mentioned in the American entertainment paper *Variety*, and Decima Moore's advert in *The Era* on 30 January 1909 shows that she had a vaudeville agent as well as an agent for 'Dramatic work'.[84] Moore was not the only AFL member to move into variety and vaudeville. Others included Olga Nethersole, who admitted to the *New York Press* on 10 October 1913 that she 'was scared to death at first' but had 'been happily disappointed. My dressing room is commodious. My audiences are as appreciative as I could possibly wish ... After all, vaudeville is really not half bad.'[85] Not all Nethersole's attempts at bringing feminist issues to the vaudeville stage were successful: the *New York Dramatic Mirror* reported in November 1913 that Nethersole's sketch about divorce laws, *The Last Scene of the Play*, 'was taken off after a single performance', but she seems to have persisted – by June 1914 the same paper reported that 'from Coast to Coast ... Day in and night out on her tour, Miss Nethersole has preached the ballot for women'.[86] AFL member Lillie Langtry also appeared in American vaudeville in 1906 and subsequently on the British music-hall stage in 1911. In her second American vaudeville tour in 1912–13 she included two pro-suffrage pieces.[87] The crossover could also work the other way. Music-hall star and AFL member Marie Lloyd, no stranger to campaigning for the rights of performers within the theatrical profession, lent her support to suffrage societies by singing at the WFL's Old World Fair at Caxton Hall in 1909 as part of a series of concerts to raise funds, and appearing in *How the Vote Was Won* in the same year, presumably as the character of Maudie Spark, the music-hall comedienne.[88] As an influential, wealthy and famous performer, she was able to support the sisterhood of suffragists in unique ways. One such gesture involved her allowing her theatrical hamper to be used to smuggle a militant speaker into a meeting at the London Pavilion in 1913. Marked 'Marie Lloyd, Pavilion. Luggage in advance', the hamper contained the WSPU speaker Annie Kenney, who was out of prison on licence after a period of hunger-striking and subject to immediate rearrest under the 'Cat and Mouse' Act if she appeared in public. Kenney wrote about the incident in her autobiography, *Memories of a Militant*, recalling the workmen who unknowingly delivered her to the theatre in the hamper making 'growls ... about the weight, about actresses having no consideration for the poor men who had to carry their baggage, and so on. I was turned, toppled, banged, dropped, before one of them got me (in my hamper, of course) on to his back.'[89] When she emerged from the hamper and appeared on stage, Kenney was immediately arrested.

WSPU member Mary Richardson, who had been in the audience at the Pavilion, was detained for puncturing the tyres of the detectives' taxi outside the theatre in an attempt to hinder Kenney's arrest. 'As I sat in my cell ... I thought of Marie Lloyd's sporting gesture in allowing her hamper to be used to get Annie into the theatre and onto the stage. I laughed and laughed again at the thought of it.'[90] Perhaps unable or unwilling to risk her position and status, Lloyd seems not to have openly participated in suffrage events after 1910, although gestures like the one involving Kenney indicate that she remained strongly in favour of the movement. While there is not room within this book to explore the stories of suffragist performers in the music hall, there are many examples of individuals and groups who openly supported the cause. One such can be found in the unpublished autobiography of League member Kitty Marion, who recorded being pleasantly surprised to meet other suffragist performers during a period of work in April 1909, with her copy of *Votes for Women* initiating the contact:

> I was playing the Chelsea Palace ... with Harry Lauder topping the bill. I shared a dressing room with Joan Rees-Webbe ... On Monday night when we met in the dressing room, her younger sister, Audrey, who mostly accompanied and understudied her, craned her neck towards a paper on my dressing table and enquired 'Is that an evening paper?' No, that is 'Votes for Women' I challenged, quite expecting to shock these two apparent little innocents on the subject. To my surprise Audrey gave a joyous gasp, 'Are you a Suffragette?' 'I am.' I replied. 'So am I!' proudly proclaimed Audrey and a priceless suffrage friendship was cemented. Joan was an 'anti' but their parents the Rev Rees-Webbe and Mrs. Rees-Webbe as well as Dolly, their older sister were ardent 'believers' and took me to their hearts with open arms.[91]

The AFL had a musical division, headed by Emily Pertwee, and many professional musicians and singers as members. These members represented a wide range of genres, including French cabaret star Yvette Guilbert, opera singers Marie Brema and Alice Esty, classical singer Clara Butt, musical comedy singers Marie Tempest and Decima Moore and singer and composers Liza Lehmann and Elvira Gambogi. League members who worked primarily as dancers and dance teachers also embraced many different traditional and emerging styles, and include Italia Conti, dance pioneer Margaret Morris and Hilda Bewicke, who was part of Diaghilev's Ballets Russes. Boundaries between different genres of theatre were broken down by suffragist actresses, musicians and performers, with the popular stage allowing members of the League to experiment with different styles of performance, extending their skills and bringing the suffrage message to new audiences. In 1911, the AFL were part of making a pro-suffrage film, *True Womanhood*, produced by Barker Motion Photography Limited. *True Womanhood* was based on a story by Inez Bensusan, who also appeared in the film alongside Decima Moore, Auriol Lee and Ben Webster.[92] The plot was described in *The Bioscope* as follows:

> It sets forth the trials of a 'sweated' woman worker, for whom, owing to the drunken habits of her husband, there is nothing left but the workhouse. She is saved, however, by a Suffragette, who comes as a fairy godmother to the unhappy woman, and brings about a reconciliation between the husband and wife, and helps them to make a fresh start in life.[93]

True Womanhood also included two scenes representing a poster parade and a suffragette being thrown out of a meeting for interrupting a politician's speech. Unfortunately no copy of the film appears to have survived in archives, but it is another example of the League embracing new audiences and harnessing innovative methods of telling and representing stories for the cause.

Transatlantic links: a sisterhood overseas

> That fight for the Suffrage ... was a great fight and taught many virtues, courage, endurance, patience and above all things established a great unity among women of all nations ... and always they found there were so many reasons for agreement – rather than disagreement – that there were common interests, common sympathies and understanding.[94]

Performers, writers and producers from many different countries, including Australia, France, Germany, Italy, Portugal, Russia, Germany and the USA were part of the AFL membership and the sharing of songs, plays and music created an international sisterhood of suffragist performers.[95] American suffragists had contributed to the British campaign since its inception and were an established part of the propaganda of the movement – as Chapman and Mills have noted, 'autobiographical works about Americans' hawking *Votes for Women* on London streets ... fostered empathy between U.S. suffragists and their British "sisters"'.[96] One such account, *The Diary of a Newsy* (1911) by Jessie Anthony, contains an entry for 28 July 1911 that details her experiences selling the paper outside Charing Cross Station and includes an encounter with an unnamed AFL member who bought a copy.[97] Although there appears to have been no equivalent national organisation to the AFL among suffragists in Australia and the USA, there was activism for the vote within the theatre communities, and suffragist actresses and writers used their professional networks to create and promote work that supported the cause. Susan Pfisterer and Carolyn Pickett have noted the influence of expatriate Australian suffragists such as Inez Bensusan, Katharine Susanna Prichard and Muriel Matters in the AFL, and scholars of American suffrage theatre – among them Bettina Friedl in her anthology of American suffrage plays, *On To Victory* (1987) and Albert Auster in *Actresses and Suffragists* (1984) – have acknowledged the impact of the AFL on suffragist theatrical networks in the USA.[98] Mary Chapman and Angela Mills explored the influence of Elizabeth Robins' 1907 play *Votes for Women* on the American campaign in their anthology *Treacherous Texts*, citing it as 'one of the most frequently performed suffrage dramas in the United States during the 1910s'.[99]

Rather than attempt a comprehensive account of the American suffrage theatre, this chapter aims to briefly introduce three performers who were associated directly with the AFL and active in promoting their work in the USA but who have not as yet been the subject of particular scholarship around suffragist theatres. Beatrice Forbes-Robertson, Fola La Follette and Maxine Elliott worked together and as individuals, and their work helps to provide an insight into the AFL's professional influence, networks and interests abroad. Beatrice Forbes-Robertson, the niece of Johnston Forbes-Robertson, was on the first committee of the AFL, had been in the original cast of *How the Vote Was Won* at the Royalty Theatre in 1909 and appeared regularly at the 1909 Women's Exhibition in *A Woman's Influence* and *Lady Geraldine's Speech*. Her experiences as an actress and a suffragist had made her a versatile, passionate and resourceful advocate for the suffrage movement. In 1910, after her marriage to American lawyer Swinburne Hale, she retired from the stage, moved to the USA and began lecturing and speaking for women's suffrage. Beatrice Forbes-Robertson spoke alongside Lena Ashwell, Constance Collier, Mary Shaw and Marie Tempest at a meeting held by the New York Equal Suffrage Association at the Hotel Astor in January 1911 and helped to organise a production of Cicely Hamilton's *Pageant of Great Women* at the Broadway Theatre as a benefit matinee for the Woman Suffrage Party in March of that year.[100] She spoke regularly for suffrage societies across the USA and Canada, produced suffrage plays at fundraisers across the country and came briefly out of retirement to perform in a benefit performance of Shaw's *Press Cuttings* for the Woman Suffrage Party at the Broadway Theatre in March 1912.[101]

A vocal supporter of the campaign for the vote, Fola La Follette was the daughter of Wisconsin senator Robert M. La Follette and Belle Case La Follette, a lawyer and suffragist activist. Fola La Follette spoke and lectured frequently in support of the vote and was keen to attract the public support of other actresses for a suffrage parade through New York City on 3 May 1913. Sandra Adickes' research suggests that there was interest from the theatrical community, with a Women's Political Union-sponsored 'cabaret burlesque' in which Ruth St Denis danced and Sarah Bernhardt sang.[102] June 1914 saw La Follette in Spring Valley, Minnesota, lecturing on 'The Democracy of Woman Suffrage', and her biography in the programme included an endorsement from Carrie Chapman Catt, the president of the International Suffrage Alliance.[103] A 1915 publicity leaflet stated that she had 'completed a tour of sixty-five consecutive dates throughout ten states' and would 'devote the winter of 1915–16 exclusively to the platform'.[104] Offering readings from a number of plays, La Follette also spoke about her experiences as an actress and the role of theatre in public life.[105] She wrote an article, *Suffragetting on the Chautauqua Circuit* for *Ladies Home Journal*, in January 1916, detailing her experiences and the difficulties she faced in being visibly and vocally pro-suffrage during her travels. Fola La Follette's husband, playwright George Middleton, was also a campaigner and speaker for women's suffrage. He wrote about his participation in the 1912 and 1913 suffrage parade, noting how much support the movement had won in the intervening year: 'This year the cause had grown so that over a thousand men stood up and were not afraid to be counted.'[106] His suffrage plays include *Back of the Ballot* (1915) which he described as a farce, written 'frankly for propaganda and fun', and *Tradition* (1914) a quietly moving piece about family life, female aspiration and women's work.[107] Middleton, encouraged by the English critic and AFL supporter William Archer to develop *Tradition* more fully, wrote a three-act play, *Nowadays* (1913), which was described by the paper of the Woman Suffrage Party of New York, the *Woman Voter*, as 'the first attempt by an American author to treat radically the economic phase of the woman question.'[108]

Sister of the AFL's president, Gertrude Elliott, actress and manager Maxine Elliott moved between the worlds of theatre in America and society in England. Openly suffragist, she hosted an AFL 'at home' at the Criterion in May 1909 and appeared with many other members of the League in a benefit matinee for the NUWSS at the Kingsway Theatre in June 1910. She also had her own theatre in New York. Built in 1908, Maxine Elliott's Theatre was on West 39th Street and Broadway and seated over 900. Like her sister, she was confident about sharing her views with the press:

> Miss Maxine Elliott, in a recent interview in New York, was accused of being a suffragette. 'Of course I am', she retorted. 'Isn't every woman who earns her living. This is a woman's age'.[109]

Elliott was determined that her theatre 'would be dedicated to the production of plays presented by herself or other leading actresses ... This was one theatre, she said, where the actress was not going to be treated as a second class citizen',[110] and she frequently lent the building to suffrage groups for performances. Beatrice Forbes-Robertson and Fola La Follette appeared together in *How the Vote Was Won* at Maxine Elliott's Theatre on 31 March 1910 in aid of the Equality League of Self-Supporting Women. Maxine Elliott recited a piece by feminist writer Charlotte Perkins Gilman, Johnston Forbes-Robertson gave an address, and Beatrice Forbes-Robertson produced the performances and also appeared in *A Woman's Influence*.[111] In an interview promoting the matinee, La Follette declared that it was 'distinctly fashionable to be a suffragist nowadays'.[112] Reviews of the performance mentioned the famous faces there, noting the overt support for the cause from influential women, with one paper reporting that the audience were 'earnest, fashionable and intelligent' and that Mrs Frederick Vanderbilt had become 'openly allied' merely by being seen to purchase eighteen tickets for the performance.[113] There was support from Broadway producers too – in September 1912, Oscar Hammerstein offered his Victoria Theatre, a vaudeville house, gratis to suffrage campaigners for a week. Each day a different suffrage society took responsibility for two performances.[114] There is not space within this book to explore the international connections of the League further, but there are many areas of mutual interest and suffragist work within the US and UK theatre communities that deserve further scholarship and attention.

Sisterhoods

> The League has done good work in other directions than the one for which it was originally formed. It has shown that women, and actresses especially, are able to stand by each other and work together for the common good.[115]

Underpinned by connection and sociality, members of the AFL regularly appeared in public as a collective of suffragists, operating through the kinds of networks and allegiances broadly definable as being based on an ideal of sisterhood. Actors, musicians, dancers and performers connected professionally through their work at home and abroad, in London and on tour in the UK and internationally, exchanging intellectual and theatrical ideas through their practice and praxis. The professional lives of suffragist actresses operated through a series of connected networks that crossed over each other through family associations as well as theatrical traditions and political connections. Such associations are often lost in the formalising of theatre histories, unless they are foregrounded in the narratives created around the established and recollected careers of 'star' players, but when exposed they show the breadth and complexities of the campaign for suffrage and for other issues concerning women's social role as played out through theatre and the women for whom it was their profession. The men who supported the League did so based on their own political convictions and their desire to support their wives and female colleagues. It is notable how many married couples were involved in the League and that, in contrast to their spouses, suffragist actors seem to have been less visible outside of the theatre environment than their female colleagues, engaging with theatrical networks as employers and employees rather than activists. They predominantly demonstrated their support for the cause by writing and participating in performances of propaganda plays; chairing and speaking at formal meetings; and writing letters to suffragist, national and international newspapers and journals. The camaraderie of suffragists was an important and highly visible public and private strategy, encouraging collective action and activism that took suffragist actresses off the stage and onto the streets in their support of the suffrage cause, and the next chapter will explore how the actresses of the League embraced public visibility, appearing on the streets of London en masse in demonstrations and marches and selling suffragist newspapers and literature on the streets of cities across the UK.

Notes

1. Adeline Bourne interviewed in *Home This Afternoon*, BBC Radio, 13 May 1964.
2. 'Sisterhood: A concept central to the women's movement, which places stress on female solidarity and co-operation … the implicit assumption that all women have certain areas of experience in common on which a sense

of identification can be founded.' S. Gamble, *Routledge Critical Dictionary of Feminism and Postfeminism* (London and New York: Routledge, 2000), pp. 315–16.
3   C. Hirshfield, 'The Actresses' Franchise League and the campaign for women's suffrage, 1908–1914', *Theatre Research International*, 10:2 (1985), 129–53, at pp. 129–30.
4   May Whitty's papers are held in the Library of Congress.
5   M. Webster, *The Same Only Different* (London: Victor Gollancz, 1969), p. 122.
6   M. Morley, *Margate and Its Theatres, 1730–1965* (London: Museum Press, 1966), p. 113.
7   C. M. P. Taylor, 'Thorne, Sarah (1836–1899)', *Oxford Dictionary of National Biography* (Oxford: Oxford University Press, 2004). Available at www.oxforddnb.com/index/51/101051460/ (accessed on 12 July 2017).
8   *The Sketch*, 9 October 1895. Transcribed by the Theatre Royal Margate archive.
9   Harry Morgan, 'A chat with Adeline Bourne', *Lady's World*, 1911, Vandamm papers, New York Public Library Performing Arts Library.
10 Dame May Whitty, 'The stage as a profession for women', *Good Housekeeping*, c. 1922, p. 102.
11 S. Fairbrother, *Through an Old Stage Door* (London: Frederick Muller Ltd., 1939), pp. 55–7.
12 E. Moore, *Exits and Entrances* (London: Chapman & Hall, 1923), p. 16.
13 M. Ainger, *Gilbert and Sullivan: A Dual Biography* (Oxford: Oxford University Press, 2002), p. 302.
14 A.J.R. (ed.), *The Suffrage Annual and Women's Who's Who 1913* (London: Stanley Paul, 1913), p. 333.
15 *The Era*, 12 June 1909, p. 14.
16 J. Holledge, 'Women's theatre – women's rights', Ph.D. thesis, University of Bristol, 1985, p. 69.
17 Gertrude Elliott and Johnston Forbes-Robertson produced and performed in experimental matinees of *The High Bid* by Henry James at Her Majesty's Theatre from 18 February 1909. T. Bosanquet, *Henry James at Work* (London: L. and V. Woolf, 1924), p. 69.
18 M. Sanderson, *From Irving to Olivier: A Social History of the Acting Profession in England, 1880–1983* (London: Athlone Press, 1984), pp. 15–17.
19 T. C. Davis, *Actresses as Working Women: Their Social Identity in Victorian Culture* (London and New York: Routledge, 1991), p. 15.
20 L. Ashwell, 'Acting as a profession for women', in Edith J. Morley (ed.), *Women Workers in Seven Professions: A Survey of Their Economic Conditions and Prospects* (London: George Routledge & Sons, 1914), pp. 298–313, at p. 309.
21 A. V. John and C. Eustance (eds.), *The Men's Share? Masculinities, Male Support and Women's Suffrage in Britain, 1890–1920* (London and New York: Routledge,

1997), Appendix 2. John and Eustance list eleven known societies with male-only membership, four societies with religious affiliations known to have male support and a further eighteen predominantly female-only societies with known male involvement. *The Suffrage Annual and Woman's Who's Who*, published in 1913, lists a total of forty-six suffrage societies in the UK and Ireland.

22   *A Declaration of Representative Men in Favour of Women's Suffrage*, Men's League for Women's Suffrage, 1909. This pamphlet is held in the Women's Library at LSE.
23   G. Jennings, 'A woman's influence', in V. Gardner, *Sketches from the Actresses' Franchise League* (Nottingham: University of Nottingham, 1985), pp. 69–74, at p. 74.
24   Eva Moore interviewed in *The Vote*, 3 December 1910, p. 64.
25   It was in Nat Goodwin's production of *The Cowboy and the Lady* at the Duke of York's Theatre.
26   Hirshfield, 'The Actresses' Franchise League', p. 132.
27   The actors included S. A. Cookson, Grendon Bentley, J. H. Ryley, Richard Andean, E. A. Ross and Robert Aitken and the actresses Dorothy Browne, Maud Buchanan and Olive Richardson.
28   Men's League for Women's Suffrage, *Third Annual Report*, 1910, p. 6; *Fifth Annual Report*, 1912.
29   *Votes for Women*, 11 February 1909, pp. 326–7.
30   C. Tylee, '"A better world for both": men, cultural transformation and the suffragettes', in M. Joannou and J. Purvis (eds.), *The Women's Suffrage Movement: New Feminist Perspectives* (Manchester: Manchester University Press, 2009), pp. 140–56, at p. 147.
31   Brian Harrison, taped interview with Sybil Thorndike, Women's Library, reference 8SUF/B/063.
32   Men's League for Women's Suffrage, *Fifth Annual Report*, 1912.
33   I. Zangwill, 'Prologue for a women's theatre', in V. Gardner (ed.), *Sketches from the Actresses' Franchise League* (Nottingham: University of Nottingham, 1985), p. 7.
34   *Votes for Women*, 5 December 1913, p. 142.
35   A.J.R., *The Suffrage Annual*, p. 137.
36   *The Era*, 28 June 1913, p. 12.
37   L. Housman, *The Unexpected Years* (London: Jonathan Cape, 1937), p. 247; *Votes for Women*, 17 March 1911, p. 386.
38   L. Ashwell, *Myself a Player* (London: Michael Joseph, 1936), p. 164.
39   S. Cory-Wright, *Lady Tree: A Theatrical Life in Letters* (Raleigh, NC: Lulu, 2012), pp. 186–7.
40   I. Vanbrugh, *To Tell My Story* (London: Hutchinson & Co., 1949), p. 83.
41   Kitty Marion, unpublished autobiography, New York Public Library, p. 7.
42   Letter from Madeleine Lucette Ryley, *The Era*, 28 August 1909, p. 19.
43   *New York Press*, 10 October 1913.

44 *The Vote*, 23 December 1909, p. 100; Eva Moore, interviewed in *The Vote*, 3 December 1910, p. 64.
45 *Daily Mail*, 20 June 1910, p. 7.
46 Draft Petition to the House of Commons, AFL Papers, Women's Library.
47 AFL, *Secretary's Report June 1910-1911*; *The Common Cause*, 9 March 1911.
48 AFL, *Secretary's Report 1912-13*.
49 *The Suffragette*, 29 November 1912, pp. 100-1.
50 The play was performed at an entertainment for the MPU at the Cosmopolis Hall in Holborn on 16 December 1913.
51 Joan S. Dugdale, '10 Clowning Street', in N.Paxton, *The Methuen Drama Book of Suffrage Plays: Taking the Stage* (London: Methuen Drama, 2018), pp. 215-36, at p. 229.
52 Dugdale, '10 Clowning Street', p. 234.
53 Dugdale, '10 Clowning Street', p. 231.
54 Examples of popular suffrage plays following this structure include *Miss Appleyard's Awakening*, *Lady Geraldine's Speech*, *Pot and Kettle* and *How the Vote Was Won*.
55 Dugdale, '10 Clowning Street', p. 225.
56 Dugdale, '10 Clowning Street', p. 235.
57 Brian Harrison, taped interview with George Dugdale, Women's Library.
58 A.J.R., *The Suffrage Annual*, 1913, p. 231.
59 MPU, *Second Annual Report*, 1911, p. 6.
60 M. Royden, *Downward Paths: An Inquiry into the Causes Which Contribute to the Making of the Prostitute* (London: G. Bell & Sons, 1916), pp. 110-11.
61 Royden, *Downward Paths*, p. 114.
62 Royden, *Downward Paths*, p. 181.
63 S. Nicholson, *The Censorship of British Drama, 1900-1968* (Exeter: Exeter University Press, 2003), p. 105.
64 Nicholson, *The Censorship of British Drama*, pp. 27-9.
65 For a detailed explanation of Robins' work in this area, see S. Thomas, 'Crying "the horror" of prostitution: Elizabeth Robins's "Where Are You Going To...?" and the moral crusade of the Women's Social and Political Union', *Women: A Cultural Review*, 16:2 (2005), 203-21.
66 *Votes for Women*, 7 June 1912, p. 583; St John was born Christabel Gertrude Marshall and changed her name upon converting to Catholicism. See Katherine Cockin, 'St John, Christopher Marie', *Oxford Dictionary of National Biography* (Oxford: Oxford University Press, 2004). Available at www.oxforddnb.com/index/57/101057057/ (accessed on 12 July 2017).
67 S. Eltis, *Acts of Desire: Women and Sex on Stage, 1800-1930* (Oxford: Oxford University Press, 2013), pp. 163, 171.
68 Eltis, *Acts of Desire*, p. 173.
69 L. Ferris, 'The female self and performance: the case of *The First Actress*', in K. Laughlin and C. Schuler (eds.), *Theatre and Feminist Aesthetics* (Madison, WI: Fairleigh Dickinson University Press, 1995), pp. 242-57, at p. 255.

70 C. Eustance, 'Meanings of militancy: the ideas and practice of political resistance in the Women's Freedom League, 1907–14', in M. Joannou and June Purvis (eds.), *The Women's Suffrage Movement: New Feminist Perspectives* (Manchester: Manchester University Press, 1998), pp. 51–64, p. 57.
71 K. Cockin, *Edith Craig (1869–1947)* (London: Cassell, 1998), p. 105.
72 C. Hamilton, *How the Vote Was Won* (London: Women Writers' Suffrage League, 1908), p. 1.
73 C. Hamilton and C. St John, *How the Vote Was Won*, in N. Paxton, *The Methuen Drama Book of Suffrage Plays* (London: Bloomsbury 2013), pp. 5–28, at p. 21.
74 *Votes for Women*, 7 April 1911, p. 440.
75 J. Liddington, *Vanishing for the Vote: Suffrage, Citizenship and the Battle for the Census* (Manchester: Manchester University Press, 2014), p. 141.
76 *Evening Standard and St James's Gazette*, 3 April 1911; *Daily Telegraph*, 4 April 1911.
77 Arncliffe Sennett papers, British Library.
78 Liddington, *Vanishing for the Vote*, p. 3.
79 Census forms, National Archives.
80 Liddington, *Vanishing for the Vote*, p. 227.
81 Liddington, *Vanishing for the Vote*, p. 233.
82 Decima Moore, quoted in *The Era*, 23 January 1909, p. 44.
83 *The Era*, 23 January 1909, p. 44.
84 *London Notes* in *Variety*, January 1909, p. 11; *The Era*, 30 January 1909, p. 39.
85 *New York Press*, 10 October 1913.
86 *New York Dramatic Mirror*, 12 November 1913, p. 22; 3 June 1914, p. 19.
87 L. Woods, '"The golden calf": noted English actresses in American vaudeville, 1904–1916', *Journal of American Culture*, 15:3 (1992), 61–71, at p. 65.
88 *Common Cause*, 15 April 1909, p. 12; Holledge, 'Women's theatre – women's rights', p. 89.
89 A. Kenney, *Memories of a Militant* (London: E. Arnold & Co., 1924), p. 238.
90 M. R. Richardson, *Laugh a Defiance* (London: George Weidenfield & Nicolson, 1953), p. 73.
91 Kitty Marion, unpublished autobiography, New York Public Library, p. 12.
92 E. Crawford, *The Women's Suffrage Movement: A Reference Guide, 1866–1928* (London and New York: Routledge, 2001), pp. 220–1.
93 *The Bioscope*, 8 June 1911, p. 455.
94 May Whitty, Handwritten speech, c. 1942, Margaret Webster Papers, Library of Congress.
95 Danny O. Crew's reference guide gives examples of a number of popular songs which were used in the US and UK campaigns, including those originally published in suffrage newspapers. See D. O. Crew, *Suffragist Sheet Music* (Jefferson, NC: McFarland, 2002).

96 M. Chapman and A. Mills, *Treacherous Texts: US Suffrage Literature, 1846–1946* (New Brunswick, NJ: Rutgers University Press, 2011), p. 116.
 97 Chapman and Mills, *Treacherous Texts*, p. 136.
 98 S. Pfisterer and C. Pickett, *Playing with Ideas: Australian Women Playwrights from the Suffragettes to the Sixties* (Sydney: Currency Press, 1999), pp. 37–42; B. Friedl, *On to Victory*; A. Auster, *Actresses and Suffragists: Women in the American Theatre, 1890–1920* (New York: Praeger, 1984).
 99 Chapman and Mills, *Treacherous Texts*, p. 120.
100 *Woman Voter*, January 1911 pp. 6, 3. LaFollette Family Papers, Library of Congress.
101 *Woman Voter*, February 1912, p. 26, LaFollette Family Papers, Library of Congress.
102 S. Adickes, 'Sisters, not demons: the influence of British suffragists on the American suffrage movement', *Women's History Review*, 11:4 (2002), 675–90, at p. 680.
103 Souvenir program for Chautauqua, Spring Valley, MN, June 1914, p. 19, LaFollette Family Papers, Library of Congress.
104 LaFollette Family Papers, Library of Congress.
105 Publicity leaflet, 1915, LaFollette Family Papers, Library of Congress.
106 George Middleton, 'Snap shots', *La Follette's Magazine*, May 1913.
107 Friedl, *On to Victory*, p. 326.
108 G. Middleton, *These Things Are Mine: The Autobiography of a Journeyman Playwright* (New York: The Macmillan Company, 1947).
109 *The Era*, 27 February 1909, p. 16.
110 D. Forbes-Robertson, *My Aunt Maxine: The Story of Maxine Elliott* (New York: Viking Press, 1964), p. 206.
111 Programme for matinee, 31 March 1910, Robinson Locke Collection, New York Public Library.
112 *Cleveland News*, 11 March 1910, LaFollette Family Papers, Library of Congress.
113 *New York Telegraph*, 1 April 1910.
114 *New York Times*, 2 September 1912.
115 Harry Morgan, 'A chat with Adeline Bourne', *Lady's World*, 1911, Vandamm Papers, New York Public Library Performing Arts Library.

3
Visibility

> The ordinary man in the crowd, whether he confesses it or no, is impressed by the sight of some well-known stage favourite exquisitely dressed, belying every Suffrage caricature and poster, and bravely carrying her own banner, with the rose and green ensigns of the A.F.L., from Cleopatra's Needle to the Albert Hall.[1]

The League participated in mass marches, processions and demonstrations for and with all the suffrage societies, becoming part of what Barbara Green has referred to as 'the decorative performances of street theater'.[2] The largest of these was the Coronation Procession of 1911, in which militant and constitutional suffrage societies marched together. Also known as the Great Procession of Women, it took place on 17 June 1911, two months after the Census Boycott, and was 'the most spectacular, the largest and most triumphant, the most harmonious and representative of all the demonstrations in the campaign'.[3] Between 40,000 and 60,000 women from over forty suffrage societies walked five abreast through London from Temple to the Albert Hall. The AFL was the thirteenth society in the procession, and the position of the organisation is an indication of their usefulness to the movement as figures of interest for the general public as well as the press. While not participating in the directly performative and representative elements of the procession – in particular the Historical Pageant and the Pageant of Queens that preceded them on the march – their placing meant that while they followed the WSPU and prisoners' sections, they were ahead of the main contingents from the WFL, the NUWSS, and their sister organisation, the WWSL. The League's presence featured prominently in press accounts of the event:

> The members of the Actresses' Franchise League, carrying tall staves, bound with roses and green ribbons, and elegantly gowned and walking under archways of pink roses and greenery, were loudly cheered on their way as the crowd recognized one after another footlight favourite.[4]

Although nearly each individual in the AFL section of the procession was mentioned by name in the press reports, the impression sought by the organisers was one of uniformity in appearance, dress, movement and behaviour. Participating members were required to make their

Visibility

own staves for the procession, decorated with a variety of rose called 'Dorothy Perkins', as well as to purchase scarves at the league offices in Robert Street: 'Everyone to wear the colours, pink and green, as an order, from left shoulder to right hip, the pink next the face'.[5] The instructions to League members were very specific about the dress and deportment required of marchers, with apparently no concession made to levels of public fame or hierarchy within the theatrical profession.

> Every member is requested to assist the general colour scheme by wearing White, which includes cream, ecru, or tussore shades. Failing white, black and white, grey or black dresses to be worn. Very pale pink, or very pale green not barred, but members are particularly asked not to wear any sort of shade of blue or heliotrope, or any red or yellow. Hats worn should be white, or black, or hats trimmed with pink roses.[6]

The actresses marched in four sections, managed by members Joan Dugdale, Decima Moore, Maud Hoffman and Mrs Pertwee as marshals. Winifred Mayo was the League's chief marshal, Sydney Keith was the banner marshal and Mrs Carl Leyel was the badge captain (see Figures 3.1 and 3.2). As Katherine E. Kelly has noted, the flower-carrying women in

3.1 The musicians' section of the AFL marchers in the 1911 Coronation Procession

3.2 Decima Moore in the Coronation Procession, 1911
© Museum of London

their matching scarves may have looked attractive, but the militaristic allusions of the procession were deliberate.⁷ A long list of rules entitled 'Hints for the Procession' was given to participating members – of which the following seem the most potentially challenging for actresses with a public profile:

DON'T forget that you are out to be seen, not to see.
DON'T try to see the procession
DON'T think of yourself, but of the League.
DO keep line, especially when turning corners. Remember that the outside left marcher is responsible for keeping pace.

DO see that the left shoulder is in line with the right shoulder of the neighbour on the left.
DO march eyes front, like a soldier in the ranks.
DO remember that you are just a unit in a great whole.
DO realize that upon each individual rests the responsibility of securing the complete perfection of the whole spectacle.[8]

These instructions enforced a formality that did not permit overt interaction with the spectators or other participants – and may perhaps have been difficult to follow for performers who were used to celebrating their individuality when appearing as their professional selves in public. While not 'in character' during processions and demonstrations in a traditionally theatrical sense, the actresses were costumed and performing as part of the sisterhood of suffragists. Without words, either her own or others given to her, each League member became a powerful visual symbol for both her profession and her sex, a single performative body contributing directly by her presence to the larger performative body of the AFL and the still larger one of the procession. The instructions invited actresses to imagine the impact and scale of the spectacle of so many women marchers from their position within the procession and to focus on and project their own feelings of sisterhood and solidarity. The shared experience of participation was physically sensed through rhythm and movement, rather than verbally articulated, creating a bond between the marching women that was keenly felt. Lena Ashwell remembered taking part in the Coronation Procession and the positive and negative reactions of the watching crowds (see Figure 3.3), while Beatrice Forbes-Robertson recalled that she was moved to tears when witnessing a suffrage parade in America and, having participated in many herself, found the spectacle unexpectedly resonant with meaning.[9]

There was pressure to be part of actively representing the sisterhood of suffragists. Christabel Pankhurst wrote an article entitled 'The Sisterhood of Women' in the 20 May 1910 edition of *Votes for Women*, urging readers to participate in the procession for the sake of not only the suffrage cause but also all womankind. It was presumably not directed towards working women but to the leisured middle classes:

> Any suffragist who, on that day, elects to stand out of the ranks will be diminishing the strength and volume of the demand which will go out from this great concourse of women to the Government. And how much

3.3 Lena Ashwell and Gertrude Elliott in the Coronation Procession, 1911

poorer she herself will be because of the knowledge that while she sits at home, the flag is flying, the drums are beating, and her sister women in their thousands are marching through London to demand political freedom![10]

A similar emotive exhortation by Christabel Pankhurst is mentioned in the suffrage play *How the Vote Was Won*. Lily, a 'maid of all work', explains to her employer why she is going on strike:

> LILY: Miss Christabel – she told us. She says to us: 'Now look 'ere, all of yer – you who've got no men to go to on Thursday – you've got to go to the

Union', she says; 'and the one who 'angs back' – and she looked at me, she did – 'may be the person 'oo the 'ole strain of the movement is restin' on, the traitor 'oo's sailin' under the 'ostile flag', she says; and I says, 'That won't be me – not much!'"[11]

While there is no specific piece that describes or recreates a suffrage procession, a representation of a large gathering of women appears at the end of Laurence Housman's play *Alice in Ganderland*, first performed at an AFL grand matinee at the Lyceum Theatre on 27 October 1911.[12] Accompanied by 'a procession of very ragged sandwich-men, carrying "Anti" posters', women process on stage in 'the colours of the different Unions' and mix with the characters, who leave the stage en masse in a triumphant suffrage march.

> *The* March Hare *strikes up the Marseillaise on his concertina. The* Dormouse *sings 'Rule, Britannia' to it, and the* Hatter *another tune of his own. Alice's voice, backed up by a chorus of Men and Women behind the scenes, emerges from the rest. She sings the first verse of the Women's March.*[13]

This sudden mustering of a suffragist crowd at the end of *Alice in Ganderland* seems rather incongruous aesthetically. The Lyceum matinee also featured a *Pageant of the Leagues* and so it is possible that the end of *Alice in Ganderland* may have been specifically written to incorporate the mass of performers and the colours of various suffrage societies that would be backstage at the theatre for the performance on 27 October.[14] The sight of processing women en masse and the organised, militaristic formation and execution of large events such as the Coronation Procession provided images of sisterhood and female solidarity to those watching as well as those taking part. Barbara Green, in her focus on the spectacle of suffrage and of performative feminist activism, has noted that the movement 'allowed women to put themselves on display for other women', and her ideas have been influential in subsequent analysis of the theatricality and performativity of both militant and constitutional societies by historians building on Tickner's *The Spectacle of Women*.[15] The AFL was able to draw attention to its political message by taking part in these events, and, although its silent presence meant that this portrayal of sisterhood had one united face and voice, with no chance to address the complexities of the arguments for the cause or to publicly acknowledge differing views within the League, it directly challenged populist stereotypes of ugly, hysterical, disorganised militant suffrage campaigners. However, many members also participated as individuals in representing the suffrage societies on the streets of towns and cities and were able to directly engage with the general public and the press.

Selling suffrage

> Why will well-bred girls, as well as older women, sell Suffrage papers in the streets, go about as sandwich-men, and suffer the scant civility of the police and the horseplay of rowdies?[16]

In contrast to the uniformity demanded of AFL members during large organised processions and demonstrations, actresses appeared before the public as individuals to advertise their allegiance to the cause on the streets of towns and cities across the country, and particularly in London. This public presence created a new dynamic between performers and their audiences as well as challenging preconceptions about the visibility of women and suffragists on the streets. The common experience of female visibility on the street and in public was explored in many suffrage plays, which were predominantly performed to an audience of women who understood how the politicised and gendered bodies of women, and the suffragist sisterhood were portrayed in the popular press. *At the Gates*, written by AFL member Alice Chapin, is a short play that portrays a number of encounters between a suffragette and members of the general public, including a seamstress, a drunken man and a member of Parliament. Performed for the WFL at Caxton Hall on 1 March 1910, it varies stylistically from reportage to melodrama to polemic. Susan Carlson has praised the range of characters and the complexity of the political arguments presented, and Susan Croft has applauded Chapin's attempt to 'find a theatrical language to describe an experience of multiple brief encounters'.[17] Presented for a suffragist audience by suffragist performers, it can be considered as a heightened reflection of the variety of encounters and responses that both the audience and performers might have experienced themselves when on the streets. This performative presentation therefore validates and explores the experience of suffragist women in public, incorporating a range of characters and situations that are both common and unusual. And, indeed, the disparate elements and characters are held together by the constant presence of the character of the Suffragette who is presented as plucky, passionate, determined and able to defend and assert herself intellectually when challenged by men unsympathetic to her cause. The audience experiences each situation with her as their champion, and she triumphs morally if not politically throughout the piece.

The sight of women selling suffrage literature and newspapers in public was part of the street theatre of representation for the campaign. Suffrage shops became a frequent sight in London and major cities across the country from 1908 to 1913.[18] The most prominent in the West End was the Women's Press shop at 156 Charing Cross Road, which sold literature, gifts, postcards and merchandise of all kinds, all branded with the WSPU colours of purple, white and green.[19] The shop environment, the range of items for sale and the humour of many of the displays – 'try some "militant jam with stones" or the "stoneless variety (stones extracted for other purposes)" – was a vital resource for the newspaper-sellers. It was also the place where paper-sellers would come to collect their stock to sell, thereby regularly immersing them in the propaganda of the movement and the camaraderie of their fellow suffragists and sellers, and making them simultaneously 'both consumers and vendors of suffrage'.[20] They could emerge refreshed and reinvigorated in the knowledge that they were part of a bigger, proselytising movement that was demanding, and getting, the public's attention. Kitty Marion recalled in her autobiography:

> One of the first things I learned was to sell 'Votes for Women' on the street … All new recruits who were anxious to 'do something' were told the best thing they could do was to take a bundle of papers and show the 'faith that was in them' by standing on the streets with them. Even if they didn't sell any, as long as they held up 'Votes for Women' to the public and advertised the cause.[21]

Votes for Women, which had previously been a monthly publication, was published weekly from 30 April 1908.[22] Vera Holme, a future AFL member, was in charge of a special committee set up in July 1908 to promote the sale of the paper and was instrumental in introducing the idea of WSPU members directly selling the paper on the street, where previously it had only been available at newsagents, suffragist meetings and from the WSPU offices.[23] Members of the WSPU sold the paper along the route of suffragist marches and at meetings, and even to queues of theatre audiences in the West End,[24] and by February 1909 there were 'several scores of women' street sellers in London, as well as sellers in Glasgow, Manchester, Leeds and Bristol' (see Figure 3.4).[25] Edith Craig sold newspapers on Chandos Street near Charing Cross outside the Eustace Miles, a popular vegetarian restaurant that had opened in 1906 and that counted Bernard Shaw and Charlotte Shaw among its shareholders. The Eustace Miles held the inaugural meeting of the MPU in January 1910 and was the site of regular suffrage

3.4 Joan Dugdale and her sister Daisy selling *Votes for Women* at the entrance to the Oval Cricket Ground, 1908

meetings and receptions, including two performances by the AFL in 1911.²⁶ Selling papers in the heart of her professional working environs, sited as she was close to St Martin's Lane and the theatres along the Strand, it seems likely that Craig's peers and colleagues, both pro- and anti-suffrage would have been aware of her presence and perhaps passed her on the street. It is interesting to speculate as to how anti-suffragist members of the profession might have negotiated a possible interaction with the paper-selling Craig as well as how she experienced reactions to her presence from contemporaries and colleagues. As the daughter of the actress Ellen Terry, her visibility as part of the suffrage sisterhood within the theatrical profession was guaranteed. Just how many of the general public passing through her Chandos Street pitch would have recognised her personally is impossible to estimate, but Craig's decision to place herself in the heart of the West End is indicative of her confidence in her political views as well as her desire to be seen to be expressing them in public. She noted, 'I generally sell the paper outside the Eustace Miles Restaurant, and I offer it verbally to every soul that passes ... Most of them reply, others come up, and we collect a little crowd until I'm told to let the people into the restaurant and move on. Then I begin all over again.'27

As with their appearances in suffrage marches and demonstrations, a different way of behaving before the public than actresses had trained for had to be negotiated. Kitty Marion was used to appearing on stages across the country and having the eyes of strangers on her, but paper-selling was a challenge, and a 'great lesson in ... self discipline. The first time I took my place on the "Island" in Piccadilly Circus, near the flower sellers, I felt as if every eye that looked at me was a dagger piercing me through, and I wished the ground would open and swallow me.'28 Public political actions and gestures such as paper-selling are acts which historian Martha Vicinus has described as 'liberating' for middle- and upper-class women: 'Freedom of movement came to symbolize the wider freedoms that women were seeking through the vote.'29 Women of different classes mixed regularly through newspaper-selling for the cause, partly because the hours were so flexible. In 1911, *Votes for Women* reported that a Balham member of the WSPU, a mother and full-time maid-of-all-work 'finds time to do a little selling on Fridays and Saturdays and has met with the greatest success'.30 Miss Gladys Evans, a worker at Selfridges and drum major in the WSPU's Drum and Fife Band, sold *Votes for Women* every Saturday afternoon outside Charing Cross, 'an act of considerable self-sacrifice on her part, seeing that that was her one half holiday which she had in each week'.31 There were regular columns in *Votes for Women* that reflected the experience of suffrage newspaper-sellers on the streets, and anecdotes and poems about the experience of selling were published frequently. Overwhelmingly positive or amusing, these give tips for sellers to help increase sales and build up a regular clientele and pass on messages of encouragement from their fellow WSPU members from across the UK. There were also pieces presented as verbatim extracts from conversations between sellers and the public, such as the following anonymous exchange entitled *A True Story*:

SUFFRAGETTE: May I sell you a copy of our paper?
SUPERIOR PERSON: Oh, no, thank you! I don't believe in it.
SUFFRAGETTE: *(surprised)* Oh, don't you?
SUPERIOR PERSON: *(emphatically)* No. I think a woman's place is in the kitchen.
SUFFRAGETTE: *(sweetly)* Well, you are not in the kitchen, are you?
SUPERIOR PERSON: *(very indignantly)* No, I should think *not* indeed!32

A short piece about paper-selling entitled *Su' L' Pave* was published in *Votes for Women* on 9 January 1914. The writer, Gladys Mendl, was a novelist, journalist and playwright who also wrote under the name 'Henrietta Leslie'.[33] With the subtitle 'Being half an hour in the life of a paper-seller', the paper-seller in *Su' L' Pave* has encounters with forty-three members of the general public, each responding differently to the sight of her. Susan Carlson has described the piece as 'one of many dramatic reflections on the ways in which the suffrage campaign was redefining public space as well as women's use of it', and for the most part the suffragist or anti-suffragist sympathies of the characters are quickly revealed, with the exception of some ambiguous and tantalising snippets of partially overheard lines from the various passers-by.[34] Kindness is shown by 'A Different Sort of Paper Seller' who is described as rather dilapidated and encourages the suffragette to 'Take cover, dearie. Come and 'ave a drink.'[35] The endorsements of the suffragette and her cause come from potentially unlikely sources – she is championed by an old gentleman and a Chelsea Pensioner, the latter appearing seemingly in support of the WSPU's militant strategy with his line, 'Soldiers get the Victoria Cross when they die in action. What did Miss Davison get?' The female characters buy the most copies of her paper – a 'plain woman' with kind eyes takes six to send away, saying, 'You are plucky creatures, you women', and an American 'damsel', who is bursting with enthusiasm, 'My, but you're great!' purchases ten copies. The suffragette does not respond to the words of the characters addressing her until the end of the piece when she stands up to a 'flashy man':

> FLASHY MAN: *(speaking with overbearing familiarity in order to impress his two companions)* What! Suffragettes still going strong? I've been abroad, but I thought Scotland Yard would have got rid of you before I came home. It won't be long now, though, I reckon. Yes, I'll have a paper. I always buy copies of last editions.
> SUFFRAGETTE: Well, you won't get this one under a guinea! It's the last copy of my week's stock.
> *(Flashy Man saves his face with gold)*
> SUFFRAGETTE: Thank you very much. Good afternoon!
> *(Exit in triumph, with the guinea and her empty bag).*

There appear to be a number of jokes for the readers of *Votes for Women* in the piece – the following exchange seeming rather fantastical:

> A PRIM PERSON: *(addressing a constable who happens to be passing)*: Why ever can't you stop those dreadful women selling their awful paper?
> CONSTABLE: We so often buy it ourselves, Madam.

And there are farcical elements too:

NON-VOTER: Well, you can have my vote.

Apart from the exchange with the flashy man, the silence of the newspaper-seller may be an invitation to the reader to picture themselves as the character of the suffragette and imagine or perhaps rehearse their own responses to the various people she encounters. Readers who also sold the paper would have found solidarity in the experiences portrayed and dramatised in *Su' L' Pave*, recognising themselves and others as part of a larger body of women who had knowledge of the realities of being visible as in public as suffrage activists. In her autobiography, the author described her own experiences as a seller of *The Suffragette* on the streets of Knightsbridge and at Piccadilly Circus: 'Two old men, one a professional paper-seller and one a military looking gent, had spat at me, and one lady with a dog had poked me with her umbrella, remarking that I ought to be boiled. For the rest, the public had been more than friendly.'[36]

A sketch entitled *The Mad Hatter's Tea Party Up to Date* by Helen MacLachlan, assistant secretary of the Edinburgh WFL, was published in *The Vote* in April 1912. MacLachlan parodies the songs in Lewis Carroll's popular book *Alice's Adventures in Wonderland* by giving them a suffragist theme. For example, 'You are old Father William' becomes 'You are old, Mother Despard', which features a verse about paper-selling.[37]

> 'Though I'm old,' Mother Despard replied once again,
> 'Suffragetting has kept me quite supple –
> Now I'm selling THE VOTE at a penny a time:
> Allow me to sell you a couple!'[38]

The Mad Hatter's Tea Party Up to Date reads like a revue sketch, with word play, comic songs and references to contemporary politics all spoken by familiar comic stereotypes in the guise of a classic of contemporary literature, using allusions to well-known songs, poems and patter and reminiscent of the call-and-response aspects of some popular theatre forms. A newspaper-seller also appears in Beatrice Harraden's 1909 play *Lady Geraldine's Speech*. Certainly the least bohemian of the guests at Dr Alice's suffrage gathering, Nellie Grant is a typist and shorthand writer and enters looking 'extremely fatigued' after selling *Votes for Women* all day.[39] She has had a successful day, selling all but one copy of the paper – an important plot point as she is therefore able to give it to the newly converted Lady Geraldine at the end of the play. This copy unites all the characters in the play in their suffrage allegiance, and Nellie gives it to Lady Geraldine as 'a present from us all!'[40] The symbolism of the last paper is referred to in an article by Evelyn Sharp in *Votes for Women*. 'I am always a little superstitious about the last paper', she writes, worrying that it will be bought by an undeserving member of the public who is unlikely to appreciate the message within. She mentions a number of types familiar from *Su' L' Pave*, not wanting to sell it to:

> a grudging purchaser, who grumbled while he bought, or to a laughing young woman ... urged forward by other laughing young women to 'buy the Suffragette's paper for a lark', or to a kind but condescending woman who thought I looked tired and that it must be very unpleasant for me to stand there ... all of whom had been my customers already.[41]

Sharp reports with theatrical flair that her last copy was given by her to an apparently deserving home: 'Then a poor bent old woman, in rusty black, hobbled by and smiled at me. No, she could not afford to buy it, but she thought it was good of us to try to get votes to help poor women. So I placed my last paper under her threadbare shawl, to bring hope to her and luck to the Suffragettes.'[42] The emphasis here is not on financial support for the WSPU but on the empathy of suffragists, the sisterhood of women, the spiritual enrichment of the deserving poor, and the socialist as well as the suffragist agenda. Sharp portrays suffragists as morally rich, despite what others may wrongly think, assume or say about them. This motif is repeated in *The Salvation of Her Sex*, a dialogue by Mabel Lawrence published in *Votes for Women* on 13 June 1913, in which a husband returns home to his wife and children after six weeks away from home. He is furious, having encountered a paper-seller on his journey:

> HUSBAND: Those Suffragettes again! They're actually daring to sell their paper outside the Tube, near my own house! The police ought not to allow it! *(Waits for the sympathy that does not come)* I got even with one of them, though; made her look silly!
> WIFE: What did you do?
> HUSBAND: She dared to offer *me* a paper! I snatched it from her and tore it up before her eyes. 'That's what I think of your paper,' I told her.

It becomes apparent during the rest of the dialogue that one of the children has been very ill, and nursed back to health by a Nurse Hayes. The wife reveals that she has asked Nurse Hayes to tea to meet her newly returned spouse.

Visibility

HUSBAND: I shall be proud to meet her. Women like that are the salvation of their sex! They make one believe in women in spite of those –
(*Ring at the bell*)
WIFE: There she is! (*The maid opens the door and shows in a prettily-dressed girl.*)
HUSBAND: (*recognizing the paper-seller*) My God![43]

In *The Salvation of Her Sex*, it is important that the suffrage paper-seller is revealed to be a 'prettily-dressed girl', as it not only challenges negative stereotypes of suffragist women but also heightens the moral injustice of her previous treatment at the hands of the husband and celebrates her spiritual goodness that has nursed a sick child back to health. The husband is even more of a monster therefore not to have recognised not only her good looks but her superior attributes – blinded as he is as an anti-suffragist. Playwright and actress Elizabeth Robins saw the female newspaper-seller and sandwich-woman as not only 'bearing witness to her faith and earning a few shillings for a particular society' but also as contributing to the perception of and prejudices against the visible female body and audible female voice in public space.[44] By being visible in public as part of a politically active sisterhood, the paper-sellers and sandwich-women forced the creation of new spaces for women's voices and presence in existing public areas. Rather than hiding, this suffragist sisterhood deliberately sought spontaneous, commercialised and politicised interactions in order to provoke discussion and argument and take their campaigning to every level of society, despite the potential risk of militant overtones.[45]

The Era and the AFL

In the editorial of the 16 January 1909 edition of the theatrical weekly newspaper *The Era*, written a few weeks after the AFL's inaugural meeting, the paper expressed surprise that 'some of our cleverest actresses are in favour of voting powers being granted to women'. The piece is defensive, ill-informed and surprisingly hostile, attributing the support for the vote from the members of the League as motivated by 'sympathy for their less fortunate sisters' but doubting whether 'the rank and file of the sex are sufficiently advanced and improved to do any good with the vote'.[46] The anonymous editorial writer champions the skill and independence of working women, offering a surprisingly diverse set of examples – 'female huntresses, hockey players, swimmers, acrobats, Dahomey Amazons, char-women, wrestlers, and political lecturers' – as proof that women are not the weaker sex but rejects the idea that women within the profession experience inequality within their professional or personal lives. A week later, *The Era* published a response from an anonymous member of the AFL who wrote in to say that that actresses did indeed need the vote 'because they are women, and women need it as a moral recognition of their responsibility and stake in the affairs of their country, and as a public acknowledgement of their capability of judging and speaking for themselves on matters that concern them'.[47] *The Era* was an influential journal within the theatrical profession. Performers used its pages to advertise their work and their availability, and it covered the professional industry across the UK, including backstage, venues and licensing, theatrical patents, reviews, gossip and news about music hall, variety and theatre. The paper been in existence since 1838 and had its offices in the heart of the West End. Other trade journals for theatre professionals included *The Stage*, founded in 1880, and *The Performer*, founded in 1906, but *The Era* was the largest and most dominant in the late Victorian and Edwardian periods.

Seeking continually to signal its disapproval of the AFL without directly being disrespectful to its influential members, the language used in *The Era* throughout the period 1909–14 regarding anything to do with the campaign for women's suffrage is negative, dismissive and often flippant. For example, an AFL event will be a 'monster' meeting, a review of a comic operetta entitled *Suffragettes in Power* begins with 'An appalling prospect is held out in the production above named', and disturbances caused by suffragists in the Bradford Empire protesting forcible feeding are mocked: 'This Suffragist "gag" has been worked before. Isn't it getting rather stale?'[48] The tone even becomes slightly threatening as the paper posits that having a vote might negatively affect future employment opportunities for actresses because: 'as most of the votresses would "register" somewhere in London, the approach of a general election would make travelling managers uneasy'.[49] There is of course no mention made of how touring male voters in the profession, where eligible, manage to cope with this burden of responsibility. This overtly negative and persistent comment on one issue is unusual even in the context of the theatrical gossip and variety gossip pages of the paper, and, as the comments are not attributable to a specific writer, they therefore represent the views of *The Era*. When reporting speeches made by prominent suffragist actors, however, the tone taken by the paper was more respectful. Johnston Forbes-Robertson's appearances at WSPU meetings in

Newcastle and Edinburgh in April 1909, and his involvement with the MLWS was acknowledged without praise or comment in the paper: 'Mr. Robertson's views with regard to the movement are well known, and his voice has often been raised in its behalf.'[50]

In August 1909, *The Era* produced a second editorial on the subject of 'actresses and politics', in which it conceded that the support for the vote was growing within the profession from not just 'eccentrics and advanced artists' but also 'many important actors' and declaring that the 'actress is, indeed, an ideal candidate for the vote' based on her equality within her profession.[51] Yet this apparent conversion to the cause is undermined as the editorial expresses bafflement as to what actresses would do with a vote and no confidence in their capability to make an informed decision on any topic other than their own individual careers. Confident in 'the humanizing effect of her calling', the paper cannot imagine 'an actress smacking the face of an Inspector of Police or wrestling with a wardress at Holloway', presumably unaware that some suffragist actresses had already been arrested for violent and non-violent direct action.[52] The following week, the paper again printed a letter from an AFL member in response to the its editorial. Actress and playwright Madeleine Lucette Ryley wrote to refute many of the points made, mentioning the subject of St John's play *The First Actress* in her reply: 'of all the women workers in the world the actress should be the greatest helper in this vital cause ... we know something of the stubborn prejudice which the female pioneer of the stage had originally to overcome.'[53] Underneath her letter, the editor of the paper commented, 'We shall be glad to hear from other actresses who are Suffragists.' This reveals, possibly, a more practical purpose to the antagonistic tone of previous *Era* editorials on the topic. As the most prominent and widely read of the theatrical newspapers and the one with the widest scope, *The Era* needed to keep up with current political issues and remain a source and forum for news and debate within the theatrical profession. Inviting, provoking and stimulating reactions from its readers kept them purchasing and reading the paper – and on the issue of women's suffrage the editorial team knew there was a diversity of opinion, strength of feeling and interest among its readership, as well as a growing national awareness of the movement. The editors of *The Era* were clearly not particularly interested in or disposed to favour the campaign for the vote per se – their lack of consideration for the constitutional arguments and inability to refrain from publishing constant small criticisms of the campaign where possible are too frequent to ignore. But their engagement with the debate, however unhelpful for the AFL and

WWSL in its negativity, at least shows an awareness of the importance of the movement within the theatrical professions and wider society. By 1913, *The Era* was again tackling the issue of 'votes for actresses' in its editorial column, expressing surprise at the ability of the AFL to organise 'weekly meetings [that] are conducted with a business-like order and sobriety which has usually been considered the especial property of the male'.[54] Central to *The Era*'s confusion as to why actresses were interested in the vote remained that the paper considered them to be on an equal footing with actors:

> The actress has already won for herself an enviable position of independence ... First of all she is self-supporting. She meets man on equal ground, rivals him, and often defeats him. An actress on tour is wearied by the same railway journeys, annoyed by the same difficulties about 'diggings', exhausted by the same rehearsals, aggravated, at times, by the same stage-managerial temper as the actor is. She takes an equal interest in the question of payment for rehearsals, and she suffers even more from an unhealthy dressing-room.[55]

The editorial then quoted an anonymous 'actress-suffragist' to confirm that actresses only wanted the vote in order to help their less fortunate sisters, just as they had claimed in 1909:

> 'Do you think,' she said, 'that we actresses are so selfish as, just because *we* have got what we want, to overlook the fact that thousands of our fellow-women are in a much less happy condition? No, we are loyal to our sex, and not to our interests. It is a question with us of sentiment, not of mean and narrow self-interest.'[56]

Views similar to the above had been expressed in public before, and by prominent AFL members and supporters. Gertrude Elliott said in an interview that 'ours is the only profession in the world where women and men have equal opportunities and equal pay'; Israel Zangwill cited the fact that women were paid the same as men in the profession as 'revenge from their ancient exclusion from the boards'; and Janette Steer had written an article in *The Vote* stating that actresses had equal pay and conditions with their male colleagues and that they were campaigning for the vote for their 'less fortunate' sisters.[57] Statements like Steer's were used by actresses to deflect accusations of privilege and to present themselves as altruistic as well as to quietly assert their professional accomplishments. They could also be used by others, however, to implicitly condone and disregard the inequalities, institutionalised sexism and legal discrimination affecting actresses and women. As an anonymous letter from 'ONE OF THE FIRST A.F.L. MEMBERS' in the following issue of *The Era* points out, the experiences of actresses were not consistent across the profession:

> Are not male 'supers' paid more than female for doing the same work, male choristers more than female, male understudies more than female ... ? Are salaries paid according to the length and importance of 'parts', or do not Mr. and Miss 'Star' command enormous salaries ... whereas Mr. and Miss 'Rankandfile' have to be content with anything they can get (the women usually less than the men for doing the same amount of work) for playing those same 'star parts' in which some often outshine the 'Stars'?
>
> Are all actresses 'self-supporting' ... Have not the majority an ungodly struggle to keep body and soul together on 'lowest terms'?
>
> The actress-suffragist who said '*We* have got what we want' seems rather confused as to what we have got and 'what we want'. We *want* the *vote*, which we have not got any more than other women, and which, God knows, we need as much for our own sakes as others![58]

The letter-writer is most likely to be music-hall artiste Kitty Marion, as the address given was that of a theatrical digs in Kennington where she was living at the time of her arrest for the militant act of setting fire to Hurst Park racecourse just two months later on 8 June 1913. Marion was often vocal about her concerns as a woman in the theatrical profession and when in court for window-smashing in December 1912, announced that her raids had not only been undertaken in support of the cause but also 'to attract attention to the conditions on the stage, under which it was "almost impossible" for a woman to earn an honest living'.[59] Her perspective is valuable in this regard and her frustration clear. It is interesting that she does not sign her name to the letter in *The Era*, as she had been not been afraid to identify herself when writing upon the same subject to both the *Sunday Chronicle* and the Variety Artists Federation's paper, *The Performer*.[60]

> Extreme measures usually are the outcome of extreme views, views created by extreme circumstances and extreme sufferings caused by extreme unfairness and injustice, the moderate protests against which are so unnoticed by those who have the power to rectify wrong, but prefer to do wrong instead of right.[61]

However, in court, in December 1912, Marion had told the magistrate that her openly expressed views on the topic had cost her many career opportunities; this is perhaps the reason why she did not want to be seen as the author of the letter to *The Era*, although she did respond as an AFL member.[62] *The Era* editorial expressed little sympathy with the militant cause and issued a challenge to its suffragist readers:

> A great argument in favour of giving the vote to any class is the demand for it by the class; and we hope next week to be able to give our readers facts and figures on the question: Do actresses as a body desire the franchise? Every actress in London and the provinces will receive to-day a pre-paid postcard asking her to state if she wants, or does not want, 'the vote'. The replies which we receive will supply us with the necessary statistics.[63]

Wanting to keep the issue current, but clearly anticipating a large response if such a survey was undertaken properly, all the professional actresses in England were given just one opportunity in less than a week to make their views known. With no account made for actresses away on European and North American tours, on holiday or presumably unreachable due to nightly touring, the undertaking of a spontaneous survey in this manner exposes again the flippancy with which the issue of women's suffrage was held by the editorial writers. That there is no similar poll of actors is disappointing – it is tempting to assume that *The Era* would not so confidently have asked for, assumed or reported the views of male readers so off-handedly or indeed considered them to be a homogenous mass as a professional group. A week later, the paper triumphantly reported: 'The result is that 244 actresses are in favour of women having the vote, and 346 are against their having it, while 845 are indifferent.'[64] There was no explanation given for the 'indifferent' category, which therefore can be presumed to have accounted for actresses who had neglected to reply, or whose replies had arrived too late for inclusion.

The 1911 census gives the number of actresses in Britain as 9,171 with 6,726 listed as working in theatres and 2,445 in music halls.[65] Accordingly, the membership of the AFL, at 550 in that year, seems only to represent 6 per cent of the profession. However, as census figures are not wholly trustworthy – there is, for example, no way of proving if all the women who were listed as actresses ever performed on the professional stage at all or were still working – *The Era*'s hastily arranged poll which considered 1,435 women to be actively worth contacting (some 15 per cent of the total number of actresses listed in the 1911 census) is, ironically, possibly more representative. *The Era*'s editorial did not state that the poll postcards were only to be sent to employed actresses, nor did it make apparently any differentiation between actresses who worked predominantly in the music halls and those who did not. In response to the poll, Winifred Mayo sent a list of 122 AFL members to *The Era*, which printed the names in full and without comment.

It is impossible to give a true figure of the number of supporters the League had. The annual report for June 1913 gives a figure of 760 members but does not list them, and there were many more actresses who are recorded as having supported suffrage that do not feature on the one early membership list of the organisation from c. 1910.[66] By summer 1914, the League had swelled to 901 actress members, a separate group of patrons of both sexes, and an affiliated men's group. While no list of the latter is known to exist, subscriptions for the men's group in the League's annual report of June 1914 are listed as £3 11s. which, if the joining fee was the same as for women, would mean that there were potentially seventy-one male members.[67] Michael Sanderson, in his analysis of the theatrical trade-union movement before the First World War, reports that the membership of the Actors' Union, which was founded in 1907, a year before the AFL, remained at around 840 from 1910 to 1914, despite absorbing the Actor's Association, which had had a membership of 797 in 1909.[68] The AFL seems therefore to have had a comparable number of active and activist members as the Actor's Union and was similar in having regional branches across the UK. Thus, the number of AFL members in 1913 suggests that the campaign for Votes for Women was more widely supported in the theatre than has been previously considered.

That the League had taken on the responsibility of sending out the postcards to its members on behalf of *The Era* is revealed in one letter printed a week after the poll, dated 10 March 1913, and sent by an actress called Rose Beryl, who was appearing in Horace Stanley's 1899 melodrama, *10.30 Down Express*, at the King's Theatre, Worksop.

> I have filled in the voting card sent me by the Actresses' Franchise League and returned it to 'The Era' office. But the next time that you wish to sound the opinions of the ladies in the theatrical profession on any important matter, would it not perhaps be as well to make the stipulations that any person recording a vote should –
>
> (a) Understand what they are voting for or against;
> (b) Give the matter, say, five minutes' consideration.[69]

Just one week later, *The Era*'s seeming distaste for the issue had returned. Towards the end of an interview with Adeline Bourne to promote

Forbes-Robertson's 'Farewell Season' at Drury Lane, she mentions her involvement in the New Players' Society, and continued:

> AB: 'I am also, may I add, a member of the Women's –'
> *Era*: 'Pray, do forgive my interrupting you, but all Political references in our columns are strictly taboo; and, besides, you know, we wish, if you please, our extensive area of office windows to remain intact.'[70]

It seems an extraordinary decision to include the interviewer's interruption in print rather than merely omitting his final question and her reply. Although it perhaps gave the editorial a theatrical feel, it also highlighted a negative and all too stereotypical view about militancy that had nothing to do with the rest of the piece. The paper did not interview any of the leading members of the AFL about their views on women's suffrage, relying instead on anonymous reviews, reports of meetings and items in their theatrical-gossip column for coverage of this important issue. Any positive accounts of the League's work appeared in published letters to the paper. This refusal of the paper to take the initiative and invite influential members of the profession to offer their views on and reasons for supporting the cause can only be read as deliberate editorial policy and a thinly disguised disapproval of the whole question of Votes for Women and, more specifically, votes for actresses. The editorials sometimes made a minimal acknowledgement of the presence of debate around the issue of women's suffrage but always stopped short of definitively allying with either side, instead attempting an uncomfortable and uneasy ambiguity. This may have been intended to avoid controversy among the paper's wide readership within the profession, but, by not engaging with the wider concerns around the agitation for the vote, *The Era* belittled and dismissed the arguments for and around equality. For interested actors and actresses not based in London or unable to attend AFL meetings, there was barely any useful information given to balance this bias, and no reports were made about the constitutional campaigning undertaken by the League. The other principal theatrical paper, *The Stage*, did not feature editorials and articles expressing opinion on either the AFL or the suffrage movement but before 1914 regularly ran an advertisement for the League. Actresses had therefore to rely on the papers of the suffrage societies to air their views and struggled to find a fair voice or hearing in the press that dominated, documented and shaped their professional lives. There has been no academic scholarship to date about *The Era* in this period and its influence upon the theatrical campaign for the vote, and this material offers new perspectives yet again on the complexities of the League's relationship to and status within professional networks of practice.

For members of the League, public visibility was an important part of their contribution to the suffrage movement. Through marches, processions and interactions with the public on the streets, actresses kept themselves fully immersed in the complexities of the campaign. They also saw at first hand how the movement was represented and misrepresented in the popular press and on the stage. Maud Arncliffe Sennett recognised what she regarded as the courage required from her colleagues to undertake public support for the cause in a letter to the *Manchester Guardian* in 1913, where she wrote that 'some of our most distinguished actresses pocketed their scruples and prejudiced their popularity by appearing in public upon a political platform'.[71] Their professional scruples regarding popularity among not only the public but also with those with influence in the theatre industry were not to be taken lightly, and the personal camaraderie and professional network of the suffragist sisterhood acted as both refuge and protection within the industry. Networked within the suffrage societies and the theatre profession, the League was in a unique position, able to adapt to the changing political landscape and to make sure up-to-date debates about suffrage were represented on stage. The next chapter explores the AFL's interaction with militancy, an issue that divided many suffragist women and suffrage societies. The chapter looks at actresses who were involved in militant actions, plays in which representations of militant women appeared and the debates within the League regarding militant tactics.

Notes

1 Eva Moore, interviewed in *The Vote*, 3 December 1910, p. 64.
2 B. Green, *Spectacular Confessions: Autobiography, Performance Activism and the Sites of Suffrage* (New York: St Martin's Press, 1997), p. 68.
3 L. Tickner, *The Spectacle of Women: Imagery of the Suffrage Campaign, 1907–14* (London: Chatto & Windus, 1987), p. 122.
4 *The Observer*, 18 June 1911, p. 33.
5 The Dorothy Perkins rose was developed in 1901 by the American company Jackson & Perkins. The rose won top honours at the Royal National Rose Society in 1908. Instructions for AFL members for Great Procession of Women, Arncliffe Sennett Collection, British Library.
6 Instructions for AFL members.

7. K. E. Kelly, 'Seeing through spectacles: the woman suffrage movement and London newspapers, 1906–13', *European Journal of Women's Studies*, 11:3 (2004), 327–53, at p. 344.
8. Kelly, 'Seeing through spectacles'.
9. L. Ashwell, *Myself a Player* (London: Michael Joseph, 1936), p. 169; B. Forbes-Robertson Hale, *What Women Want: An Interpretation of the Feminist Movement* (New York: Frederick A. Stokes, 1914), p. 183.
10. *Votes for Women*, 20 May 1910, p. 550.
11. C. Hamilton and C. St John, *How the Vote Was Won*, in N. Paxton, *The Methuen Drama Book of Suffrage Plays* (London: Bloomsbury, 2013), p. 9.
12. For more about Alice in Ganderland see N. Paxton, 'Will you, won't you, will you, won't you join the Suffrage Dance' in C. Riley and L. Rose (eds) *Women's Suffrage in Word, Image, Music and Drama* (London: Routledge, 2020)
13. L. Housman, *Alice in Ganderland* (London: The Woman's Press, 1911), p. 24.
14. E. Crawford (ed.), *Campaigning for the Vote: Kate Parry Frye's Suffrage Diary* (London: Francis Boutle, 2013), p. 556.
15. Green, *Spectacular Confessions*, p. 78.
16. E. Robins, 'Why?' in *Way Stations* (London: Hodder & Stoughton, 1913).
17. S. Carlson, 'Comic militancy: the politics of suffrage drama', in M. B. Gale and V. Gardner (eds), *Women, Theatre and Performance: New Histories, New Historiographies* (Manchester: Manchester University Press, 2000), pp. 198–215, at p. 212; S. Croft, *Votes for Women and Other Plays* (Twickenham: Aurora Metro, 2009), p. 122.
18. For more on this, see J. Mercer, 'Shopping for suffrage: the campaign shops of the Women's Social and Political Union', *Women's History Review*, 18:2 (2009), 293–309.
19. 156 Charing Cross Road was occupied by the Woman's Press from May 1910 to October 1912.
20. K. Lysack, *Come Buy, Come Buy: Shopping and the Culture of Consumption in Victorian Women's Writing* (Athens, OH: Ohio University Press, 2008), p. 164.
21. Kitty Marion, unpublished autobiography, New York Public Library, p. 6.
22. *Votes for Women Supplement*, 23 April 1908, p. 1.
23. *Votes for Women*, 30 July 1908, p. 338.
24. *Votes for Women*, 3 December 1908, p. 162.
25. *Votes for Women*, 4 February 1909, p. 312.
26. AFL, *Half Yearly Report*, 1911.
27. *Votes for Women*, 15 April 1910, p. 455.
28. Kitty Marion, unpublished autobiography, New York Public Library, p. 6.
29. M. Vicinus, *Independent Women: Work and Community for Single Women, 1850–1920* (London: Virago Press, 1985), p. 256.
30. *Votes for Women*, 11 August 1911, p. 736.
31. *Votes for Women*, 23 August 1912.

32 *Votes for Women*, 10 September 1909, p. 1152.
33 E. Crawford, *The Women's Suffrage Movement: A Reference Guide, 1866-1928* (London and New York: Routledge, 2001), p. 620.
34 S. Carlson, 'Suffrage theatre: community activism and political commitment', in Mary Luckhurst (ed.), *A Companion to Modern British and Irish Drama* (Oxford: Blackwell, 2006), pp. 99-109, at p. 102.
35 *Votes for Women*, 9 January 1914, p. 224.
36 H. Leslie, *More Ha'pence than Kicks: Being Some Things Remembered* (London: Macdonald, 1943), p. 99.
37 Charlotte Despard was the leader of the WFL.
38 *The Vote*, 20 April 1912, p. 12.
39 B. Harraden, *Lady Geraldine's Speech*, in N. Paxton (ed.), *The Methuen Drama Book of Suffrage Plays* (London: Bloomsbury, 2013), pp. 29-46, at p. 40.
40 Harraden, 'Lady Geraldine's Speech', p. 45.
41 *Votes for Women*, 18 June 1909, p. 807.
42 *Votes for Women*, 18 June 1909, p. 807.
43 *Votes for Women*, 13 June 1913, p. 538.
44 Robins, *Way Stations*.
45 For more on this, see S. Glenn, *Female Spectacle: The Theatrical Roots of Modern Feminism* (Cambridge, MA: Harvard University Press, 2000), p. 139.
46 *The Era*, 16 January 1909, p. 23.
47 *The Era*, 23 January 1909 p. 19.
48 *The Era*, 18 September 1909, p. 29; 15 February 1913, p. 24.
49 *The Era*, 16 January 1909, p. 23.
50 *The Era*, 10 April 1909, p. 10; 17 April 1909, p. 13; 18 September 1909, p. 14.
51 *The Era*, editorial, 21 August 1909.
52 *Actresses and Politics*, *The Era*, 21 August 1909.
53 *The Era*, 28 August 1909, p. 19.
54 *The Era*, 8 March 1913, p. 19.
55 *The Era*, 8 March 1913, p. 19.
56 *The Era*, 8 March 1913, p. 19.
57 'Miss Gertrude Elliott Says', *Nash's Magazine*, 3:2 (1913); *Votes for Women*, 5 December 1913, p. 142; 'The suffrage movement: the salvation of the race', in *The Vote*, 1 June 1912, p. 109.
58 *The Era*, 15 March 1913, p. 19.
59 *Daily Mail*, 19 December 1912, p. 3.
60 *Sunday Chronicle*, 3 and 10 October 1909, Kitty Marion Papers, New York Public Library.
61 *The Performer*, 13 January 1910, Kitty Marion Papers, New York Public Library.
62 *Daily Mail*, 19 December 1912, p. 3.
63 *The Era* editorial, 8 March 1913.
64 *The Era* editorial, 15 March 1913.
65 Sanderson, *From Irving to Olivier*, p. 26.

66 AFL, *Secretary's Report, June 1912–June 1913*, p. 5.
67 AFL, *Annual Report, June 1913–June 1914*, p. 5.
68 Sanderson, *From Irving to Olivier*, pp. 104–8.
69 *The Era*, 15 March 1913, p. 19.
70 *The Era*, 22 March 1913, p. 15.
71 Copy of original letter sent to *Manchester Guardian*, May 1913, Arncliffe Sennett Papers, vol. XXII, British Library.

4
Militancy

> From woman, marvel of the age
> Surprises still we get,
> And soon each actress on the stage
> Will be a Suffragette.
>
> And by their new found ardour stirred,
> The footlights' charming queens,
> Will make their gentle voices heard
> In 'Acts' as well as scenes![1]

The AFL has not been thought of as having had a significant role in the militant agitation for the vote, perhaps because the organisation remained neutral towards militancy as a matter of policy. The fourth item of the League's constitution stated that it was 'strictly neutral in regard to Suffrage Tactics' and therefore was not and subsequently has not been allied exclusively to any particular militant or non-militant society.[2] This neutrality was a decision that was practical professionally as well as politically, given the precariousness of the employment situation for members, the punitive legal response to militant actions and the hostility of much of the press coverage towards suffrage activism. Members of the League remained free to show their public support as individuals for militant actions, but when taking part they did not do so on behalf of the AFL, who in turn did not make special efforts to recognise or celebrate the militant actions of their members. As suffragist actresses gained familiarity with the day-to-day aspects of the campaign for the vote and the detailed political rhetoric surrounding it, it became increasingly problematic for them to publicly condemn all militant strategies outright, and few did. By 1908, 'many of the leading actresses of the day had already been converted to the cause by the Women's Social and Political Union', and, indeed, the founder members of the AFL included performers such as Sime Seruya and Winifred Mayo who had already been or would go on to be imprisoned for their militant actions in support for the suffrage campaign, and although openly supportive of militancy they perhaps 'prudently chose to play down their personal connections with the militants' in order to attract a wider range of influential performers to the League.³

With influential allies in the theatre industry and the suffrage societies, actresses and playwrights who chose to support the principal of militancy did so within a rhetorical and intellectual context that invited debate and challenged stereotypes, and the compromises members had to be prepared to make both within and outside of the League tested friendships as well as consciences. Education through propaganda plays, meetings and lectures was as much a tenet of the League as neutrality, and all of the League's productions, public events and activism could in some ways be categorised as militant, non-violent direct action.⁴ The belief of the organisation in the power of theatre as performative propaganda was directly linked to its desire to provoke profound political transformations in audiences as well as to entertain them. President of the AFL Gertrude Elliott believed strongly in the power of the theatre to transform an audience's understanding of the world: 'I have known whole lives to be changed ... That's why I think that the stage has a mission – to give the world a gilded pill, so to speak. You can teach anything on the stage, just because people don't realize they are learning.'⁵ The plays published by the League vary hugely in style, but none overtly condemn militancy, or conversely explicitly promote it.⁶ Instead, militancy and militants are part of the broader representation of the suffrage campaign, with militant and non-militant characters given a voice with which to present their constitutional argument for the vote. The AFL preserved good working relationships with all the suffrage societies, overcoming what June Purvis has called the 'formal dividing barriers' between the three largest organisations, the militant WSPU and WFL and the non-militant NUWSS,⁷ although other scholars have attempted to challenge the idea that such formal boundaries existed, particularly at local branch level.⁸

Money raised at events, performances and meetings was vital to the continuing work of the League, and, as tensions about militant prisoners and forcible feeding in prisons arose, inviting militant speakers to their platforms and 'at homes' perhaps helped to attract audiences keen to experience a frisson of unpredictability as well as providing much needed opportunities for militants to speak in public about their constitutional campaigning. Mary Jean Corbett has suggested that during this period 'both onstage and off, in the theatrical roles and their self representations, actresses learned to play the part of middle class women'.⁹ AFL 'at homes', often held in grand hotels such as the Dorchester or restaurants such as the Criterion in Piccadilly Circus, carefully cultivated an atmosphere of middle-class gentility within which discussions and debates could be held, bringing news and ideas from the heart of both the constitutional and militant campaigns into the world of middle- and upper-class leisure time and social networking. Aware of their appeal to both pro- and anti-suffrage theatre-goers, the League's elegant 'at homes' attracted audiences and participants able to offer significant financial support and social influence:

> we find they attract the most obstinate of Antis and, more important still, members of that class most difficult of all to get at 'the women who take no interest at all' in Votes for Women! and have never been to a Meeting before. Our Patrons Book bears witness to the fact that this is no longer true when they leave![10]

Maintaining the delicate balance the actresses needed to have between public profile and employment was difficult for some League members as the militant campaign became more divisive. Having looked at the ideas of sisterhood and visibility in the previous chapters, here I aim to explore the League's connections with militancy – both as an idea and as a form of action – taking into account how scholars have defined militant actions and considering the tactical neutrality of the League in the context of its activism and performance.

Narratives of militancy and the AFL: 'When you see the Light, follow it'[11]

Never again for her, or for her friends, any cobweb left of that old illusion as to the chivalry of the average official. 'This and this they did to me rather than admit my purpose honest.'[12]

Narratives of militancy and militant women have dominated public awareness and academic analyses of the British campaign for Votes for Women. Militant accounts were prioritised in histories of the campaign written during the 1960s and 1970s in the UK, with feminist scholars focusing their attention on the militant campaign as a precursor to the radical second-wave feminist movement. The first militant action is widely cited by historians to be the heckling of Sir Edward Grey MP by the WSPU's Annie Kenney and Christabel Pankhurst on 13 October 1905 in the Free Trade Hall in Manchester, and their arrest and imprisonment garnered widespread press coverage and began a national campaign of non-violent action and public protest.[13] However, the first arrests for violent action were not until 29 June 1909, when, unauthorised by their union, thirteen members of the WSPU smashed the windows of government offices in a symbolic action.[14] Hunger-striking by a suffragette prisoner as protest against her internment in the second division took place for the first time a week later – also apparently without sanction from the leadership of the WSPU.[15] That the leaders of the militant movement were involved in the first arrests and were themselves repeatedly imprisoned and on hunger strike helped to create a sense of camaraderie among campaigners as well as attracting publicity – a physical as well as political body of women who were prepared to surrender their health and reputations for the cause. As Laura Nym Mayhall notes, the WSPU have a 'stranglehold ... on the historical imagination' of the Votes for Women movement, and appear in a great deal of contemporary scholarship to represent the movement to the near exclusion of other large societies like the WFL and NUWSS.[16] Brian Harrison, who interviewed 205 former suffragettes and suffragists between 1974 and 1981, has expressed frustration that the work of militant societies has not been considered alongside 'the perspective offered by the National Union of Women's Suffrage Society (i.e. non-violent) literature'.[17] This may be because militant accounts were disseminated through organisations such as the Suffragette Fellowship, which maintained networks of former campaigners and collected archives, testimonies and ephemera. Formed in 1926 and initially named the 'Suffragette Club', the fellowship was made up of members of militant societies and those who had been in prison for their campaigning. Many actresses who were members of both the AFL and the WSPU, including Una Dugdale, Kitty Marion and Naomi Jacob, maintained links with the fellowship well into the 1950s, with Winifred Mayo becoming president of the fellowship in 1958. The fellowship opened a suffragette museum in London in 1947, and its collection became absorbed into the Museum of London's holdings in the 1950s.[18]

In fact, of the hundreds of thousands of active members of suffrage societies between 1905 and 1914, just over 1,000 women, mostly from the WSPU and WFL, were imprisoned for suffrage activities.[19] Concentrating on 'the bodies of women in pain' has meant that popular histories and scholarship have perpetuated the idea that 'to be authentic, suffrage militancy followed one trajectory: from militant action, defined narrowly as violence against property, through arrest, to incarceration and, eventually, the hunger strike and forcible feeding'.[20] This has created and justified misleading specialist and non-specialist accounts of the militants and the suffrage campaign and a narrow focus that has obliquely informed much of the recent academic analyses of the AFL. Actress Kitty Marion's accounts of her numerous arrests and forcible feeding in prison, among her other writings in her unpublished autobiography, complete versions of which are held in the Museum of London and the New York Public Library, has meant that she has been the actress most written about by suffrage scholars, but solely within this narrow focus.[21]

Mayhall, among other scholars, has argued for a more considered analysis of militancy in the cultural context of the late Victorian and Edwardian eras and a recognition of the relevance of all forms of protest by suffragettes and suffragists, suggesting that militancy should be defined as 'a set of political interactions, as a range of suffragist practices'.[22] The consensus among scholars seems to be an acknowledgement of the individual agency of each woman, both militant and non-militant, to demonstrate her support for the cause, and the WSPU and WFL continued to concurrently campaign through constitutional methods that proved largely unsuccessful. Thus, for June Purvis, there were two phases of militancy: the first involving 'various forms of peaceful actions' and the second attacks against property. Purvis also acknowledges that 'many of these guerilla militants acted on their own initiative' and that 'the aim throughout was always to damage property, not life'.[23] Neither of the phases of militancy that Purvis describes were alien to members of the League. They took part in peaceful actions to advertise events and raise awareness including demonstrations, newspaper-selling, sandwich-board parades and public outdoor meetings. As will be explored later in this chapter, members were arrested and imprisoned for participating in or even being close to peaceful demonstrations involving crowds of suffragist women that the police considered to be volatile. Purvis's second phase – that of attacks against property – also saw League members participating, and some were imprisoned for window-smashing and arson. In this chapter, my intention is not to perpetuate the idea of a strict division between the militant and non-militant societies but rather to highlight and examine the role of the League and its membership in both elements of the campaign. Here, first looking at constitutional methods, I collate some of the stories of League members who were arrested with those of women whose protests directly affected their subsequent contributions to the campaign.

Constitutional campaigning

The Executive of the AFL have done their best during the year to protest against the coercive legislation which has been the Government's only response to the women's demand for citizenship.[24]

The constitutional work done by actresses in the League in collaboration with all suffrage societies created narratives that blurred boundaries between militant and non-militant individuals through shared experiences of protest and debate. Prevented and restricted from accessing traditional political spaces, suffragists took their words to the streets, theatres and workplaces and provided their own forums for debate in meetings and newspapers. However, the reporting of the sensational aspects of the militant campaign in preference to the constitutional arguments in popular, non-suffragist newspapers gave a distorted and negative impression of the women involved.[25] This media scaremongering created an anti-suffragist anxiety that could be used to manipulate readers and suppress information about the movement itself. Choosing to be visible as suffragists made members of the AFL vulnerable to physical and verbal attacks from the public and to arrest and harassment by the police, and the AFL's constitutional work introduced members at first hand to the attempts from the police, government and press to suppress and intimidate suffrage activism and to discredit the movement. The police brutality that met a suffragist deputation to Parliament on 18 November 1910, a day that became known in the suffrage movement as Black Friday, was notorious in the campaign.[26] AFL member Kitty Marion was arrested, and other members, including Joan and Una Dugdale, Winifred Mayo and Maud Arncliffe Sennett were recorded as among those injured.[27] Una Dugdale remembered that her sister had been hit in the throat and head by two policemen, while Winifred Mayo recalled being seized 'by the throat' as did Ellison Gibb, who stated that a police constable caught her by the throat and bent back her head 'until it felt as though the neck were breaking'.[28] Previously a constitutional suffragist, actress Kate Parry Frye joined the WSPU after witnessing Black Friday:

> It was the most horrible experience ... the loud laughter & hideous remarks of the men – so-called gentlemen ... was truly awful ... Several spoke to me – many indignant: 'What good do you suppose this will do?' 'What else would you suggest?' said I. Then he began the usual – that the militant methods had disgusted all nicely feeling people etc. I turned his

attention to my two badges – constitutional societies, as I told him – and asked, 'What help have you ever given us?' He walked away.[29]

On public demonstrations and at open-air meetings crowds could be volatile, unsympathetic and even violent towards suffragist speakers, as Maud Arncliffe Sennett found when the League took part in a procession in Victoria Park, London, in May 1913. Marching alongside organisations including the Bow and Bromley Independent Labour Party trade unions and three men's suffrage societies, Arncliffe Sennett was shocked at the reaction of some of the crowd: 'Our banners were torn from the cart and our poles were smashed. Stones were hurled at us, together with the most filthy and foul-mouthed abuse. Our cart was dragged about to the utmost danger of its occupants and the crowd itself.'[30] On 8 July 1913, the League took part in protests against the treatment of suffragette prisoners and appeared at meetings and conferences, with one delegate experiencing 'rough treatment' for which 'the complaint of the League on this score to the Chief of police met with no success'.[31] For the most part, however, the organisation participated in successful open-air meetings on behalf of both militant and constitutional societies across the country with actresses speaking on platforms at each event. By summer 1913, the League had developed the experience and confidence to hold its own meetings every Sunday in Hyde Park, seemingly without significant disruption from either the police or a hostile public.[32]

After having publicly protested and been present in marches, deputations and exhibitions with other suffrage societies since its foundation, the League sent a memorial to the speaker of the House of Commons in December 1912, asking to be received at the Bar of the House to speak directly to Parliament about Votes for Women. Describing the process of appearing at the Bar as 'a dignified and picturesque procedure, with a touch of the histrionic', and suggesting wryly that that was perhaps why it appealed to the actresses, the *Evening Standard* openly encouraged and supported the AFL's memorial: 'The ladies, we are sure, will plead their case with dignity and moderation. They will enable Members of Parliament to receive an earnest and reasoned statement of the case for Votes for Women, free from the atmosphere of turmoil and excitement in which it is generally presented.'[33] The *Westminster Gazette* also supported the League's request on constitutional grounds, but it was rebuffed repeatedly by representatives of the speaker and prime minister, prompting Winifred

Mayo to seek advice from the Conservative MP and suffragist Lord Robert Cecil on how to proceed.[34] Cecil had publicly condemned acts of militancy but acknowledged the frustration of suffragists with the slow progress of the constitutional campaign, saying in the House of Commons that he thought they had 'no chance of receiving that justice which has been frequently promised them' from Parliament.[35] His advice to Mayo was that she organise a petition signed by representatives of all the suffrage societies, which he could then present to Parliament.[36] At the time, Mayo was in rehearsal for a Pioneer Players production of Cicely Hamilton's play *A Matter of Money*, and the Play Actors production of Bjornson's *The Gauntlet*, and sought the support of fellow militant sympathiser and AFL Committee member Maud Arncliffe Sennett: 'We certainly ought to lobby other MPs, but I can't do it for the moment. I am tied in knots, with rehearsals, and with finding bail for prisoners, and Police Court matters'.[37] Cecil did present a petition in favour of women's suffrage on 22 April 1913.[38] Representing twenty-seven suffrage societies in England, Ireland and Wales, it was submitted with another, presented by Keir Hardie, from the National Women's Labour League and allied societies on behalf of 34,500 working women. Together, the petitions represented 100,000 women, but neither they nor the requests made for time allotted in Parliament to discuss them had had any success by June 1913.[39]

Blurring the lines

> There had been quiet Suffrage work going on for forty years, but most of us had never heard of it ... and then this disturbing element came in, and those of us who had hitherto taken no part in Suffrage movements began to group ourselves into new societies, which represented our views and our powers of expressing them.[40]

Issues around both the nature and function of militancy are as challenging to academic commentators now as they were for the actresses in the League. Adeline Bourne recalled that, until she got to know them, she was 'was frightened of ... the militants at first', and while actresses may have identified with and admired the determination and passion of the militants, the consequences of openly stating this admiration could negatively impact on their public profile.[41] At an AFL 'at home' in June 1914, Eva Moore spoke in support of Mary Blomfield, who had caused a scandal by getting on her knees in front of the king and queen at Buckingham Palace to protest about forcible feeding of suffragette prisoners.⁴² In her autobiography, Moore recalled her feelings about the incident: 'It may have been, probably was, the wrong time to do it; it was probably the wrong way to attempt to do it; but I did feel, and still feel, that the girl must have called up every ounce of courage she possessed to say what she did.'⁴³ Moore concluded her speech at the 'at home' with 'We must all take our hats off to such terrific courage', a comment that was subsequently reported widely, prompting Moore to write to *The Times* in her own defence in order to clarify her position.⁴⁴ 'I admire Miss Blomfield for her courage; she was a subject appealing to her King to redress what she considers a great wrong ... Surely hers was quite a different action from those who burn and destroy, with whose methods I have no sympathy.'⁴⁵ Moore wrote in her autobiography of her shock and distress at the 'abusive, indecent' letters she received from male strangers during this period of publicity, asserting that if she had not already been a suffragist, those letters would have made her one.⁴⁶ Holledge has suggested that 'psychologically the actresses were inevitably attracted to the more theatrical methods' of the WSPU and the WFL, and one such was perhaps WFL and AFL member, Australian actress Muriel Matters, who took part in a protest in the Ladies Gallery of the House of Commons on 28 October 1908 for which she was imprisoned for a month.⁴⁷ Confident that gaining the vote would raise the status of women in Britain as she considered it to have done in Australia, where women had been enfranchised in some states since 1894, Matters spoke frequently on the industrial and economic position of women, as well as for the vote.⁴⁸ Matters was one of two women who chained themselves to the grille of the Ladies Gallery before taking part in an organised disruption of the Commons session by shouting, throwing leaflets and displaying suffrage banners. By interrupting parliamentary proceedings in this dramatic way, Matters and the other women present at the grille protest created a non-violent action that was full of symbolism. Drawing attention to the means by which women were kept apart from parliamentarians and the parliamentary process, 'the protest forced M.P.s to choose between listening to the women's claims for political representation and removing a symbol of their exclusion from that representation'.⁴⁹ The police were unable to release Matters from the grille while she was still in the Ladies Gallery and had to remove the part of the grille she was chained to in order to do so (see Figure 4.1). The WFL newspaper wrote that her action had not only made her nationally famous

4.1 Australian actress Muriel Matters being removed from the Ladies Gallery of the House of Commons

but that it also 'proved to us we had found a recruit of rare courage and initiative, one who could be trusted never to falter, never to turn back'.[50] Matters became an official WFL organiser and continued to participate in marches and non-violent actions, including hiring a hot-air balloon with 'Votes for Women' written on it in an attempt to drop propaganda leaflets over the Houses of Parliament on 17 February 1909.[51]

The grille protest was referenced in Cicely Hamilton and Christopher St John's 1909 suffrage play *Pot and Kettle*, with the character of Nell announcing that she met fellow suffragette Lady Susan Pengarvon when they 'were chucked out of the Ladies' Gallery the night the grille was shifted'.[52] The camaraderie between Lady Susan and Nell comes from their shared experience of observing – if not directly participating in – a militant action. *Pot and Kettle* provides a dramatised account of the heckling of an anti-suffrage speaker, another non-violent action. Lady Susan continually interrupts the speakers on the platform of an anti-suffrage meeting she and other suffragettes have attended specifically in order to create a disturbance. Concealed within her clothing she has a flag with 'Votes for Women' emblazoned on it and by continually interrupting, shouting and standing on her seat demonstrates that she is not inhibited by ideas of how women should behave in public nor by the disapproval of the anti-suffragists at the meeting. Nell's cousin Marjorie reveals that she has been arrested for inadvertently becoming overexcited during the protest and punching Lady Susan, but Nell is able to persuade her friend and campaigning colleague to drop the charges: 'You're used to appearing in police courts but she isn't; kindly take that into account.'[53] Intriguingly, a note in the programme for the first performance of *Pot and Kettle* at the Scala Theatre on 12 November 1909 stated that the idea for the play was 'suggested to the Authors by an incident which occurred at a Meeting held by the Anti-Suffrage League at Queen's Hall, London, in March, 1909'.[54] Whether Hamilton and St John were present at the incident referred to or just heard about it is not clear; however, the possibility that two prominent suffragists were attending an anti-suffrage meeting to observe and gain material for their own work is an interesting one, particularly as both would perhaps have been recognised by suffragists and anti-suffragists in the audience.

Members of the League appeared in court to defend themselves, and to testify in defence of their colleagues. Examples include Edith Craig, who was a witness at Sime Seruya's trial at Bow Street in 1911, and Eva Moore, who in 1912 appeared at the Old Bailey as a defence witness for Emmeline Pankhurst.[55] Stating that she had not attended meetings in which violent direct action was incited, Moore offered her own definition of militancy: 'Militancy, I suppose, means being very determined to work in every possible way for something that one thinks right.'[56] Unfortunately, for some members of the AFL participation in peaceful protests placed them under suspicion from the law.

Actresses under arrest: the radicalisation of peaceful demonstrators

> While public political space was not formally segregated along gender lines, men and women did not possess that space equally.[57]

The threat of arrest by police was constantly present for women in or near suffrage demonstrations and deputations after 1906. Two actresses, Annie Fraser and Maggie Moffat, became the first Scottish women to be arrested for suffrage activism when in February 1907 mounted police broke up a group of women marching to the House of Commons with a resolution for the prime minister.[58] Maggie Moffat was the Glasgow WSPU delegate for the Women's Parliament in Caxton Hall, and she, Fraser and fifty-three other women who had processed peacefully from Caxton Hall to Parliament were imprisoned in the second division in Holloway.[59] Her husband, playwright Graham Moffat, was a member of the MLWS, and he described himself and his wife as 'only mildly militant – a little fly bill-posting, and a little heckling of parliamentary candidates'.[60] Graham Moffat remained proud of Maggie's direct action and included a photograph of her prison medal in his privately published autobiography. He also wrote a suffrage duologue, *The Maid and the Magistrate*, first presented for the WFL in 1909 and later performed numerous times by the AFL, in which a suffragist has been arrested for 'chaining herself to the Prime Minister's door knocker'.[61] After detailing the constitutional reasons for her action, she declares herself unafraid of being imprisoned: 'Why the whole family will be proud of me when I win my Holloway medal. Even dad has joined the Men's League.'[62] Disapproving of 'extremely militant methods', Maggie Moffat later left the WSPU for the WFL, becoming treasure of the WFL Scottish Council.[63]

A year after Maggie Moffat's arrest, Winifred Mayo was arrested for the first time in February 1908 after attending the Women's Parliament at Caxton Hall and attempting to present the WSPU's resolution to a member of the government at the House of Commons. Her account of her arrest, trial and imprisonment was published in the *Idler* magazine a month later.[64] In it, Mayo stressed the different social backgrounds of the suffragists and the comradeship between them while they were detained, including another actress who had come from Birmingham to take part in the event. Taking care not to apportion blame to individuals, even those in authority, her writing is carefully presented as a measured account of her experiences, with herself and her fellow militants as victims of a system of government oppression. Mayo also introduces her readers to a different side of the suffragist sisterhood by detailing the work of the members of the WSPU who helped to care for arrested women, as she later would go on to do herself. She reports assistance for the detainees from the most well-known of the militant leaders: Emmeline Pethick-Lawrence sends in tea for the women, and her husband Frederick brings them the evening papers, writing paper and stamps. Later, the WSPU delivers baskets of food, and an anonymous suffragette spends hours outside the cells in the police station, writing down the women's messages for their families and friends. As a constructed autobiographical narrative of her experience, it is fascinating. She details her time in the demonstration, during and after arrest, being taken through London in a Black Maria and her subsequent trial and first days in prison with deliberate humour, taking care to keep the tone of the piece light and present herself as a likeable and reliable narrator. This lightness of touch allows Mayo to critique the treatment of suffragist women in the justice system while simultaneously challenging populist stereotypes and introducing suffragettes as gentle, misunderstood and passionately engaged in constitutional campaigning – a clever piece of writing that entertains as well as informs. One of the other women arrested at the same time as Winifred Mayo worked for League member and actress manager Gertrude Kingston:

> My reader of plays, height 4ft 6ins., accompanied by her mother, an elderly lady who could certainly not do much harm ... was seized by the throat by a tall policeman and used as a buffer against the other women behind her ... As she showed me the bruise of the finger-marks on her neck there was no doubt of the assault ... I rang up the Home Secretary ... I told him I wanted my reader back as he was upsetting the business of the Little Theatre.[65]

Kingston does not record if her appeal to the home secretary was successful and, although shocked at the violence her employee experienced, frames this memory in her writing in an offhand and yet dramatic context. She not only informs her readers that she had the telephone number of a cabinet minister but that she feels free to use it to campaign for woman's suffrage, berate the minister about the behaviour of the police and protest at the potential impact to her business. Whether the phone call took place or not, this light but pointed touch in her memoir shows her as aware of the need to balance public and private relationships from within the context of her wider political affiliations in order to sustain her career and commercial interests, even over two decades after the event. An article published in the *Daily News* the day after Mayo's arrest corroborates many of the details in her article for *The Idler* and reveals that Mayo was among fifty women from all over the UK who were arrested 'women in all stations of life – millhands, shopgirls, artists, actresses, and nurses.'[66]

AFL executive committee member Sime Seruya had first been arrested at the same time as Moffat in 1907 and served fourteen days in prison for her part in the deputation.[67] Her appearance in court on the day of her trial made an impression on one reporter who seemed keen to present her as having an amused disregard for authority:

> Miss Seruya was a graceful young lady with a laughing confidence … and chuckled silently at the tall, grim policeman in the box about to give evidence against her. 'She not only said she would not go away,' said Police-Constable 264A, 'but she also struck me with her clenched fist.' 'What!' exclaimed Miss Seruya, vivaciously; 'I struck you with this muff, which had a book inside it.' 'It seemed like a clenched fist,' remarked the magistrate pleasantly. 'Well I merely struck back,' declared Miss Seruya. 'Twenty shillings, or fourteen days,' said Mr. Curtis Bennett. 'Oh, the fourteen days' of course,' the defendant remarked sweetly, as she stepped into the care of the gaoler.[68]

The seeming levity in Seruya's reported responses implied a confidence that she herself later claimed she did not have. In February 1909, she was again arrested, this time with Christopher St John while they were walking in Whitehall near a suffrage deputation, and charged with obstructing the police.[69] At her trial, Seruya protested that she was merely 'looking on' but was convicted nevertheless, denied the option of a fine and imprisoned for six weeks.[70] St John pleaded her case more successfully, citing her role as a professional spectator:

> I realized in a flash that although my arrest was illegal and unjust any resistance would be to my disadvantage … My solicitor put me in the witness box and gave me an opportunity of saying on oath that I was not in Whitehall as a Suffragette, but as a journalist and a dramatist … I was discharged.[71]

St John's assertion that she was present as an observer in the crowd rather than 'as a Suffragette' was upheld in court, but it's clear that her appearance and behaviour at the time had not sufficiently differentiated her from the mass of protesting women to prevent her being mistaken for one of them. Her self-defined status as a 'journalist and a dramatist' was either not outwardly visible to the policeman who arrested her or not respected, an example of the one of the 'problems of spectatorship' that Barbara Green refers to in her analysis of the representations of militant women in and by the WSPU.[72] A committee member of both the Catholic Women's Suffrage Society and the WWSL, St John was arrested later in 1909 for setting fire to a pillar box and her experiences of militancy informed her writing directly.[73]

On 18 June 1909, *Votes for Women* published a duologue by Christopher St John entitled *A Defence of the Fighting Spirit*.[74] A short and passionate piece, it begins with a direct reference to militancy:

> DIANA: So we alienate 'people' by our violence. What people?
> GERTRUDE: Oh, I don't know! People I suppose who would otherwise sympathise with the cause.[75]

The militant suffragette character, Diana, immediately defends the use of non-violent militant tactics:

> DIANA: We don't care a rap for those people who preach moderation. We know that the moderate are not usually the most sincere, for the same caution which makes them moderate makes them careful of what might give offence.

St John seems keen to inform readers of *Votes for Women* of the constitutional basis of the upcoming deputation:

> GERTRUDE: It's all so foolish. If you know beforehand that the Prime Minister won't receive you, why do you go?
> DIANA: For one thing we cannot acknowledge the Prime Minister's right to deny to unrepresented women what he would not dare to deny to unrepresented men.

St John, who had said in February 1909 that she was 'not a Suffragette in the accepted term of the word' defended her use of it in the duologue.[76] 'We didn't invent the word, but ungrammatical, half-contemptuous as it is, there is not one of us who would exchange it now for a more refined and literary title.'[77] The piece appeared in *Votes for Women* one week before a high-profile WSPU deputation to the prime minster at the House of Commons. Hundreds of women gathered in Westminster, and a photograph of AFL member Vera Holme on horseback 'bearing the Despatch to the House' was published in the *Daily Mirror* and subsequently in *Votes for Women*.[78] When the prime minister refused to see

Mrs Pankhurst, she refused to leave, and the police attempted to drive the women away. Among those arrested were AFL members Kitty Marion, Winifred Mayo and Christopher St John. Writing in *Votes for Women* just over a week after her arrest, St John made plain her motivation for taking part: 'My reasons for joining the deputation to the Prime Minister can be summed up in a single sentence. I was ashamed to stay away.'[79] St John saw her participation in the June 1909 demonstration as a turning point in not only her personal political views but in her artistic career, having felt ashamed of herself at the 1909 Women's Exhibition the month before: 'At every corner I saw brave women who had served long sentences ... they could look at me cheerfully, straightly. But I, meandering in and out of my artistic subtleties, how could I look at them?'[80] Resolving to take a more active part in the campaign for the vote in future through her writing and her practical support, St John thoughtfully unpacked the issues and ideas around WSPU militancy in *A Defence of the Fighting Spirit* but would continue to use her personal experiences of non-violent direct action to inspire perhaps more subtle but no less fervent pieces of propaganda for the militant campaign.

Sime Seruya was taken into custody for a third time on 27 October 1911 after being arrested on the steps of the Lyceum Theatre just before the AFL's grand matinee. Charged again with obstruction, her trial at Bow Street Magistrates' Court a week later saw Edith Craig and Winifred Mayo among the eyewitnesses who testified in her defence, and when Sir Albert de Rutzen, the chief magistrate of the Metropolitan Police told her at her trial that the situation 'was nothing to laugh at', she attributed her apparent amusement to nervousness.[81] In the AFL secretary's report for 1911–12, the Lyceum matinee is referred to as 'a very delightful afternoon' and no mention is made of Seruya's arrest.[82] Perhaps by drawing attention to any evidence of militant actions by members of the organisation, the committee of the League was concerned that they might alienate other members and supporters, whose views and allegiances – professionally and personally – could not be assumed to be favourable to militancy. The incident on the steps of the Lyceum and the events of the trial could, if the League had desired, have been made much of in the press but would certainly have overshadowed the work and generosity of the members who had taken part in the matinee performance and the amount of money raised. Fundraising was, as ever, a priority. Seruya managed the International Suffrage shop and told the *Standard* that she very much wanted to 'be on the best of terms with the officers of the E Division, in whose district the International Suffrage shop in Adam

Street is situated'.[83] Reliant on the police for protection and yet wary of their arbitrary definition of 'obstruction', suffragists who supported non-violent actions placed themselves continuously and sometimes unknowingly on the boundaries between legality and illegality.

Violent direct action

For much of 1910 and 1911, the WSPU suspended militancy as an act of good faith in the prime minister. Suffragists were delighted when the Conciliation Bill passed a second reading on 12 July 1910 with a majority of 110, and the optimism of the suffrage societies culminated in a mass meeting and demonstration in London on the 23 July, organised jointly by the WSPU and WFL, in which the AFL took part.[84] That same day, the prime minster halted the progress of the bill, and it made no further progression in the House of Commons during the rest of 1910. Despite the police brutality on Black Friday in November 1910 and assurances from the government but no actual progression of the bill, the WSPU truce remained. Maud Arncliffe Sennett, representing the AFL, took part in a deputation to Downing Street on 17 March 1911 and made a speech to the prime minister in which she claimed the right to vote for actresses as 'wage earners and human beings'.[85] Non-violent demonstrations and deputations continued throughout 1911, but suffrage campaigners were horrified when, on 7 November, the prime minister announced a Manhood Suffrage Bill. The AFL, represented by Maud Arncliffe Sennett, Lena Ashwell, Eva Moore and Winifred Mayo took part in a deputation of the major suffrage societies to the prime minister to discuss the situation, but their appeal was unsuccessful. The AFL, having had such close dealings with all suffrage societies, was understandably sympathetic to the frustration felt by both militant and constitutional campaigners (see Figure 4.2).

Lillah McCarthy was quoted in *Votes for Women* as saying 'the offer of a Manhood Suffrage Bill scarcely seems to come from minds friendly to the cause of Women's Suffrage', and, indeed, the optimism of the past year, the patient constitutional campaigns, the hope in the Conciliation Bill and even the suspension of militancy by the WSPU seemed to have been for nothing.[86] The militant campaign resumed on 21 November 1911, when Emmeline Pethick-Lawrence led a deputation from Caxton Hall to the House of Commons armed with bags of stones to break government office windows. Groups of women gathered in different areas to break windows, among them many members of the AFL. It is indicative of the strength of feeling among the League members that so many took part.

4.2 Cartoon from *Votes for Women*, with the caption 'THE W.S.P.U.: "One or two more shots and we'll have it down."'

Maud Arncliffe Sennett received letters from the WSPU on 16 and 18 of November planning the action.[87] She was informed that she was to meet at the WSPU's Charing Cross Road shop on the night of 21 November and advised not to wear anything that might identify her as a suffragist. She also received instructions in case of arrest:

> In the event of arrest, you will be taken to Cannon Row or another police station and charged, when it is advisable <u>to make no statement,</u> as anything said to the Police may be used in evidence against you next day. After an interval, you will be bailed out until the following morning, when you will be ordered to appear at Bow Street, or any other police-court named on your charge-sheet. Bring with you to the police court the next morning a HANDBAG containing night things and a change of clothing, brush and comb etc., also <u>do not forget to come provided with food sufficient to keep you going for the day</u>, as the proceedings may be lengthy.[88]

Arncliffe Sennett was arrested, along with over 200 others, including fellow League members Kitty Marion, Vera Holme, Janette Steer, Winifred Mayo and Ellison Gibb on 22 November 1911.[89] Marion was tried on 23 November and given twenty-one days; Holme was tried on 28

November and given five days; Steer and Gibb were tried on 27 November and given five and fourteen days respectively; and Mayo was tried on 29 November and given twenty-one days.[90] At her trial, Arncliffe Sennett was charged with disorderly and threatening behaviour and was fined 40 shillings or seven days' imprisonment. *Votes for Women* reported the speech she made, which stated clearly her motive for becoming involved in the protest: 'I broke the windows of the *Daily Mail* as a protest against the corruption of the Press for withholding, with malice aforethought, the truth about the Suffrage Movement from the great British public.'[91] Arncliffe Sennett's fine was paid, against her wishes, by the proprietor of the *Daily Mail*, Lord Northcliffe, who disapproved of militancy, to deprive her of the publicity of imprisonment for the cause.[92] Kitty Marion was accused of throwing two stones at the windows of the Home Office and proudly quoted the following press report of her trial in her unpublished autobiography: 'In reply to a remark by the defendant, the magistrate said "Possibly you women will get votes if you behave properly." Miss Marion at once retorted, "Men don't always behave properly and they have the vote."'[93] Janette Steer was charged with 'trying to break through the police line near St. Margaret's Church'. In her trial, Steer said that she was not there as an offender, 'but on the defensive against a Government that has shamefully insulted the women of England'.[94] Ellison Gibb, honorary secretary of the Glasgow branch of the AFL, was charged with breaking the windows of the local government board offices.[95] Gibb was imprisoned numerous times for militant actions between 1910 and 1912, went on hunger strike and was forcibly fed.[96] Ada Cecile Wright wrote to Arncliffe Sennett in July 1912 about her time in Aylesbury prison, describing Gibb as a '"Tubeite" and a great brick'.[97] Vera Holme was charged with breaking through a police cordon and trying to take hold of the mounted men's horses to pull them round. Holme said that, 'as the Government would not accept them as citizens no one could blame them for acting as outlaws'.[98] Mayo was charged with breaking two windows at the Guards' Club, causing £4 (about £367 in 2015 values) of damage.

> I took out a stone and hurled it and to my great joy and satisfaction it broke the window ... A number of the servants came out and I addressed them, telling them what the point of the attack was. 'Well!' said the porter, 'Why the Guards? They don't know nothing about woman's suffrage.' I said, 'That's exactly my point! Now they will.' Meantime the policeman arrived and grasped me firmly by the arm. 'Did you do that?' he said. 'Yes' I said ... I was sent to prison.[99]

The incident was mentioned in brief in *The Stage* newspaper, with Marion and Mayo named as being involved in 'stone-throwing and promiscuous window-breaking'.[100] At the next AFL 'at home' held for members only on the afternoon of 24 November 1911, Arncliffe Sennett, Mayo and Muriel Matters gave speeches 'on the Deputation to the Prime Minister and the Militant Agitation'.[101] The imprisoned League members did not hunger-strike in prison because, although they were not treated officially as political prisoners, they were granted some privileges including being able to wear their own clothes and being allowed to exercise together.[102] As with previous arrests of members, no mention was made of militant activities in the AFL's 1911–12 annual report. The committee of the League may not have wished the names of militant members to be highlighted in the formal reporting of the business of the League, but the regular 'at homes' and meetings often featured militant speakers and debates about militancy. On 1 December 1911, at a packed public AFL meeting at the Criterion, WSPU leader Christabel Pankhurst was one of the speakers.[103] According to a report of the meeting, Janette Steer, as chair,

> appealed to her audience to follow in the footsteps of the women who had protested against the Government's action. Miss Christabel Pankhurst dealt with the political situation in a rousing speech, which, in spite of a few male interruptions, won the prolonged applause of her hearers. She explained the reason for the recurrence of militant tactics, and demanded that the Government should stand or fall by the incasure of Woman's Suffrage.[104]

Pankhurst published an article entitled 'Broken Windows' on the same day, defending the militant attack on government property and referencing one of the most popular suffrage plays:

> In that delightful and instructive play, 'How the Vote Was Won' ... the tactics resorted to by women ... win the sympathy and enthusiasm of all ... and many have wished, no doubt, that this same policy could be adopted in real life. What is the essential difference between such a policy and that actually adopted on Tuesday night by the window-breakers? It is actually cheaper to pay for mending a shop window than to maintain, for a considerable period, several female relatives.[105]

Equating a play that focuses entirely on collective non-violent action by women with the deliberate violent campaign of the WSPU may not have been tactful, but it was certainly provocative for the audience, many of whom would contribute to the entertainments for the WSPU's Christmas Fair and Fete, three days after the meeting, on 4 December 1911. The

League continued to maintain close public links with both militant and constitutional societies throughout 1912 and 1913. In February 1912, the League performed two plays at a WFL 'Hard Up Social' in the Gardenia restaurant.[106] In May, it took part in a deputation to Ramsay MacDonald MP alongside the New Constitutional Society for Women's Suffrage, and the 'Actresses' League' platform at a WSPU demonstration in Hyde Park on 14 July was one of twenty platforms at the event, which also featured a massed band of 150 performers conducted by Ethel Smyth. Speakers on the League's platform included Decima and Eva Moore, Adeline Bourne and Miss Sidney Keith.[107] Nine members of the League, including Gertrude Elliott, Adeline Bourne, Lena Ashwell, Decima and Eva Moore, and Margaret Morris wrote 'New Year's Good Wishes' for publication in the WSPU's newspaper *The Suffragette* in January 1913.[108] The League needed to maintain the neutral reputation that made its fundraising work so successful, but members noticed how useful the passionate defence of militancy was when it came to raising financial support. In an interview in *Votes for Women*, Lena Ashwell noted:

> Militancy? No, I'm not a militant myself. I haven't the temperament for it. But when I am asked, as I was the other day, whether I think militancy has put back the cause, I can only say that all the eloquence of many speakers and all the enthusiasm of a crowded audience at our big Actresses' meeting, the other day, produced about £400, whereas, at the Albert Hall, the militants raised about £15,000 in something like a quarter of an hour.[109]

The meeting Ashwell referred to, held in May 1913, is one of the few events held by the League for which there is a range of press coverage, giving scholars access to accounts of the strength of feeling from members around militancy at that time.

The 1913 Drury Lane meeting

Hoping to reach a larger audience than could attend their 'at homes', the AFL held a mass meeting on 2 May 1913 in the Theatre Royal, Drury Lane, a venue that could hold 3,000 people.[110] Tickets were priced between 6d and 3s (approximately £2 to £13 in 2015 values), and the reported ticket sales of £89 (nearly £7,900 in 2015 values) evidence a large audience. The meeting, which the League subsequently 'acclaimed a brilliant success from the propaganda point of view', was open to all and the press reported that the theatre was 'full to overflowing', with the dress circle of the auditorium was decorated with banners representing both militant and constitutional suffrage societies.[110] Thirty-five members of the AFL acted as programme-sellers inside the auditorium, with additional members and male supporters working as literature-sellers and stewards. Fifty-nine women sat on the stage representing the AFL, NUWSS, WFL and WSPU, including Charlotte Despard and Millicent Garrett Fawcett – leaders of the WFL and NUWSS respectively – and of the ten speakers, eight were directly affiliated with the AFL. Reports of their speeches provide an indication of how outspoken they were prepared to be in their public support for the cause, particularly in front of the press. Most negotiated a fine line: keen to express their solidarity with imprisoned suffragettes as fellow campaigners while not necessarily endorsing their militant actions. To this end, the speeches were focused on issues affecting the wider constitutional campaign and not on the government's treatment of imprisoned women. The 'Cat and Mouse' Act – the Prisoners (Temporary Discharge for Ill Health) Act 1913 – had been passed exactly one week before the Drury Lane meeting, and allowed hunger-striking suffragette prisoners to be released when they became dangerously ill, only to be rearrested once recovered, to continue their sentence.[112] For the AFL to be holding a tactically neutral meeting at this time could be seen to be rejecting the debate around the passing of the act and the immediate threat to the lives of militant prisoners, but it was an unfortunate coincidence of timing. Perhaps hoping for open criticism of the government, the meeting was well attended by the national press who were quick to pick up on the volatility of the vocal pro-militant audience, with *The Stage* describing the atmosphere as 'charged with the electricity of militancy'.[113]

Lady Willoughby de Broke opened the meeting, and novelist Marie Corelli told the packed auditorium that she wanted the vote 'in order to raise the economic and social position' of sweated workers.[114] Corelli was followed by Gertrude Elliott, who mentioned the success of the vote for women in the state of Colorado in her native USA and focused her speech on 'reforms for working women [and] protection for little children' and the difference she hoped that the female franchise would make to future legislation in these areas.[115] Arncliffe Sennett spoke condemning the government and the prime minister directly and 'confessed that she was militant in spirit – (loud cheers) – and although she dare not that afternoon talk of militancy, she would never repudiate it'.[116] Carrie Chapman Catt, the president of the International Women's Suffrage Alliance, spoke diplomatically about both the militant and constitutional sides of the campaign and about the position of the women's movement throughout the world. The next speaker, Miss Compton (the stage name of Katharine Mackenzie Compton), mentioned the support of many of her male colleagues for the cause and said that she wanted the vote as an income-tax payer 'because she had a share in the British Empire, Limited. Whether it was a gamble or an investment she did not know, but she was not satisfied with the Board of Directors, and her hands were tied'.[117]

Irene Vanbrugh spoke next to say that she was 'wholly out of sympathy with militant methods', and blamed the militants rather than the government for the 'present deplorable state of disorder'.[118] Press reports of her speech revelled in the hostile and vocal reaction Vanbrugh apparently received from the audience. The *Morning Post*, *Daily Chronicle* and *Era* mentioned cries of 'It is the Government's fault'; the *Westminster Gazette* quoted the audience calling 'No, no'; and the *Telegraph* and *Manchester Guardian* reported that members of the crowd shouted 'Three cheers for Mrs. Pankhurst', to which Vanbrugh retorted that 'members of the Actresses' Franchise League have the right of individuals individually to express their opinion. I am sorry I have had to say what I have, but it is what I feel'.[119] Unable to continue speaking because of the noise, Vanbrugh sat down. Eva Moore then 'spoke passionately of crimes against childhood' and the short sentences served by men who were convicted of criminal offences against young girls.[120] ' "What," said the speaker, amid applause, "should I do if my little girl was so treated? No law would hold me! Men who had been guilty of such atrocities should not be given short sentences, but treated as mad dogs and destroyed." '[121] Moore was followed by Russian actress Lydia Yavorska (the stage name of Princess Bariatinski), who expressed her surprise that a country such as England, 'which had always been in the forefront of the struggle for freedom', should deny women votes. Lena Ashwell spoke 'with feeling and sincerity on behalf of sweated women workers', and, perhaps in an attempt to mollify the supporters of militants in the audience, encouraged them not to lose focus on the campaign for the vote or be distracted by 'any criticism of anybody'.[122] Miss Lind af Hageby, a Swedish anti-vivisection campaigner, was the final speaker. She appears to have attempted to mollify the situation:

> it was evident that the meeting held divergent views as to methods of fighting for the vote, but every one, she thought, glorified in the devotion shown by women to the cause, and believed that it was going to bear fruit. They must all be militant in one form or another, even if not in the revolutionary way.[123]

Most speakers, with the overt exception of Irene Vanburgh, obliquely referred to the issues affecting militant women and acknowledged the audience's concerns about the Cat and Mouse Act without directly stating their views. The silent show of support from the other women on stage perhaps reinforced this cautious attitude, although it must have been tempting for the militants among them to respond candidly to Vanbrugh's words. With a considerable press presence and a large audience, the meeting was a financial success for the League. After expenses, the AFL made £442 2s (over £39,000 in 2015 values) from the meeting, much of that from a public collection in which prominent members of the League offered contributions of increasing size in a theatrical display of largesse that delighted the crowd.[124] The positive press coverage of the event was, however, short-lived.

Aftermath of the Drury Lane meeting

> I accepted an invitation to occupy a seat on the platform at the Actresses' Franchise League meeting on Friday on the distinct promise from the organizing secretary that militant speeches would not be made. The great majority of the long list of speakers honourably observed this undertaking; but a few did not, in consequence of which I and some others left the platform and the theatre before the end of the meeting. I make no charge against the organizing secretary, in whose good faith I have absolute confidence.[125]

Three days after the meeting, the *Manchester Guardian* published a letter from the president of the NUWSS, Millicent Garrett Fawcett, stating her unhappiness at the militant sympathies of the Drury Lane meeting. Arncliffe Sennett, frustrated with the sudden and unwelcome negative publicity for the League, was quick to respond, writing letters to the *Manchester Guardian, Daily Herald, Standard* and *Telegraph* to defend herself and the League.

> May I ask you to give the same publicity to my letter as has been given to that of Mrs. Fawcett, because I happen to be the only speaker at the meeting who has ever been known in connection with militancy? It was not suggested that I should suppress my natural self or sail under false colours 'as an honourable undertaking'. I was asked not to speak of militancy, and did not. I said: 'I cannot compromise the constitutional women who have come upon our platform to support us in our demands for a Government measure. I am not here, therefore, to defend the militants, though with Heaven's help I never will repudiate them.'[126]

Privately, Arncliffe Sennett was puzzled by Fawcett's letter and questioned the veracity of her statement: 'How can Mrs. Fawcett say ... that I drove her off when she remained on the platform a full hour after I had spoken?'[127] For her, the interest of the press in reporting negative propaganda surrounding the militant campaign deliberately obscured the efforts of the constitutional suffragists, and she wrote as much to the *Manchester Guardian*: 'Is it justice only to publish that which may injure a great movement and withhold that which might help the people to understand it?'[128] Emphasising the support for the movement from within the theatrical community, Arncliffe Sennett listed the famous actors and actresses present at the meeting in her letter to the press, enclosing a plan of the platform and asking for the full list of names to be published. Winifred Mayo, described privately by Arncliffe Sennett as 'a famous militant ... Mrs. Fawcett knows she has smashed windows and things', sought to reassure her that she had the full support of the committee of the AFL, but seems to have been less irritated by Fawcett's letter to the press: 'Did you see Mrs. Fawcett's letter in the Observer? She is so ratty. I have to go and see her this afternoon and dread it. It is the one blot on an otherwise complete success.'[129]

The upset at the meeting was felt inside the membership of the AFL, with both Irene and Violet Vanbrugh resigning their roles as vice presidents and leaving the League altogether. Arncliffe Sennett was scathing in her private view of Irene Vanbrugh at the time, saying that Vanbrugh had 'never put out a finger for the cause or given money. Those who make sacrifices and do all the hard work should not be sacrificed to those whose only contribution to the Cause is criticism.'[130] Her view seems to have been shared by Mayo, who wrote to her on 21 May 1913:

> The Vanbrughs are not Suffragists and I have always greatly disliked having them as Vice Presidents. I don't think you are responsible for their leaving, actually. Irene was tactless at the Meeting, and got herself into trouble, and her motive throughout is a personal one. She has probably talked to her sister, and it is 'a good riddance'.[131]

Irene Vanbrugh's resignation from the AFL was reported in the *London Budget*, which billed itself as 'The Best FAMILY PAPER for the BEST FAMILIES of Great Britain'. The article described Vanbrugh as still 'an ardent and sincere suffragist [who] feels the treatment she has received very keenly, but prefers not to make any statement at the moment.'[132] A few pages later in the same paper, there was an article by the American poet Ella Wheeler Wilcox denouncing militant methods as 'only suitable for people suffering from brain storms and hysteria'.[133] Vanbrugh seems to have made no public statement about her resignation, only writing about it in her autobiography long after the event: 'By speaking at this meeting I could make it clear that I certainly was an adherent to the cause but against the militant methods, and that if I found the constitution of the AFL was in sympathy with rioting, then naturally I should resign my membership.'[134] Vanbrugh, whose husband Dion Boucicault was an anti-suffragist, did not resume her public involvement with the League until the 1930s, after his death, although she did support its philanthropic projects during the First World War. A month after the Drury Lane meeting, actresses representing the AFL attended the funeral of Emily Wilding Davison, the WSPU militant suffragette who had been fatally injured in an accident at the Derby. Masterminded by the WSPU, the procession was open to both militant and constitutional societies. Winifred Mayo wrote to Maud Arncliffe Sennett on 8 June 1913 that '<u>Certainly</u> the A.F.L. must be represented ... We ought to have a <u>big</u> contingent.'[135] Between thirty and forty AFL members and many members of the WWSL took part in the funeral procession that marched through central London to St George's Church, Bloomsbury, and presented a wreath of trumpet lilies with a tempered message of support: 'From some members of the Actresses' Franchise League, in memory of Emily Wilding Davison.'[136]

The large crowds and the formality of Emily Wilding Davison's funeral procession seem to have inspired Christopher St John to again tackle issues around militants and militancy in her 1914 play *Her Will*. Produced by Edith Craig at the women's section of the Children's Welfare Exhibition at Olympia, *Her Will* alludes to two of the most famous militant members of the WSPU: Emily Wilding Davison and Constance Lytton. Both had captured the imagination of suffragists and suffragettes with their physical and psychological sufferings at the hands of the authorities. Lytton's health had been permanently damaged by her treatment in prison, and her book about her experiences as a militant prisoner, *Prison and Prisoners*, included evocative, graphic and disturbing descriptions of forcible feeding and hunger-striking suffragettes. In November 1910, she had spoken at an AFL 'at home' and had appeared in the cast of *Pageant of Great Women* for the League's fundraising matinee at the Aldwych Theatre.[137] *Her Will* is set after the funeral of a wealthy suffragette, Helen Wilton. Her relations, unsympathetic to the cause and eager to discover their legacies, gather to hear her will being read. A member of the fictional 'Forward Suffrage Union', Wilton has died from medical complications brought on by forcible feeding in Holloway prison. St John fabricates a debate in the House of Commons and a fictional suffrage newspaper regarding her death ('Mr. Drinkwater drew the Home Secretary's attention to the statement in "The Torch" and other suffragist journals that the illness from which Miss Helen Wilton died was directly due to her treatment in Holloway prison last year when she was forcibly fed no fewer than fifteen times'), and has one of her characters read a newspaper report about the funeral procession.[138]

> Twelve young girls dressed in white and wearing the colours of the Forward Suffrage Union were the pall-bearers, and white was almost universally worn by the hundreds of women who followed the hearse to Kensal Green. All carried bunches of gay spring flowers, and another brilliant note of colour was supplied by the band of the Union in their scarlet and purple uniforms with gold sashes on which the word 'Equalitas' was conspicuous. The demeanour of the crowds lining the route was on the whole profoundly respectful, death for the time making the public forget their resentment at recent Suffragist outrages ... [139]

The parallels between the fictional funeral of Helen Wilton and the actual funeral of Emily Wilding Davison are obvious. St John also writes in *Her Will* that at the time of her death Helen Wilton had been writing a book called 'Prisoners and Prisons' – a reversal of the title of Lytton's book which had been published just a few weeks before the first production of *Her Will*. The choice of this piece – full of overt allusions to two of the WSPU's most famous militants – for presentation at an event organised by the NUWSS, seems, in some ways, surprising. Christopher St John and Edith Craig had been on stage at the Drury Lane meeting and witnessed both the fervent feeling in the auditorium and the later accusations made by Fawcett. Perhaps the presentation of *Her Will* was not only an attempt to respond quickly to an event that had given the movement tremendous publicity and momentum but also to draw direct links between the constitutional and militant methods of campaigning and the lack of clear distinction between them.

The Drury Lane meeting shows how divisive the issue of militancy was for League members and supporters and how difficult it was for them to negotiate the complexities of it in public, but it also indicates that the League as an organisation took its neutral position seriously. The success of the meeting was not spoiled by the Vanbrughs' resignation, and the League continued to organise large-scale events where ideas could be expressed and shared. The programme for a grand meeting, held by the AFL at the Shaftesbury Theatre on 18 November 1913, shows thirty-three members of the League sat on stage behind Lena Ashwell, who was chairing the event, and seven male speakers including Roy Horniman and Israel Zangwill.

Representations of militancy and militants on stage

> Militancy and propaganda were campaign strategies that interacted, the former creating organizational resources and an audience for the latter's positive 'spin' on militancy and the militants. This constant interaction indicates that propaganda's place was as a direct counterpart to militancy, not merely a minor strand of a campaign that offered more dramatic elements.[140]
>
> Each individual woman ... became a centre of enlightenment for all whom she might thereafter reach.[141]

Becoming what Elizabeth Robins called 'a centre of enlightenment' for their colleagues, friends and families, many women who experienced arrest or ill-treatment at the hands of the police or public had not previously been in trouble with the law. Winifred Mayo mocked her own naivety on her first arrest in 1908: 'I was still under the impression that you must do something illegal to get arrested.'[142] Actresses who chose to join militant societies might discover, as Kabi Hartman describes in her analysis of conversion narratives, that 'their subsequent shared experience of protesting, being arrested, and going to prison produced in turn a spiritual narrative common to all classes.'[143] This narrative of feminist activism and the camaraderie it engendered among suffragists was disseminated most quickly in the suffragist press, at public meetings and through suffrage plays and novels. Representations of militant women and militant acts appeared frequently in suffrage plays and on stages across the country. The publicity achieved by militant actions as well as the negative propaganda towards suffragists and suffragettes had created repetitive visual tropes that the public had been taught to recognise and that suffragist writers sought to challenge. Despite the actual and visible presence of suffragists in and around theatres, and the numerous attempts the suffrage societies made through exhibitions, demonstrations and marches to show militant women as politically engaged campaigners, the negative stereotypes dominated, meaning that while some plays can be considered to have constructively contributed to the debate, others relied on

MILITANCY

mockery of a fictional and yet populist target to undermine the campaign. The damaging propaganda that the government and newspapers spread about the Votes for Women campaign was pervasive, and performers and writers could most easily and quickly adopt and reference it through broad, comic characters and misogynistic representations of women and suffragists, often performed by men.

There are numerous examples of men dressing as militant suffragettes on stage in revues and music halls. *The Era* reported that an impromptu impersonation of a suffragette speaker drew the interest of a volatile public crowd in Liverpool when, in January 1909, the comic Arthur Rigby, dressed as a pantomime dame, decided to make a spontaneous pastiche of a suffrage speaker from a motor bus while travelling back to the Court Theatre after a charity performance at the Hippodrome. The crowd following the bus began to heckle him and attempted to physically prevent him from leaving the vehicle at his destination.[144] One popular revue show, H. P. Pelissier's *Follies*, regularly included caricatured versions of suffragettes in order to make fun of the movement and the individuals involved. In 1910, Pelissier inserted a verse that made fun of forcible feeding into one of his comic songs, perhaps inspired by the pantomime *Aladdin* at the Theatre Royal Drury Lane in 1909 which had included it as a topical reference: 'when Abanazar hears a hubbub without he says, "They are only feeding a suffragette"'.[145] Suffrage campaigners were horrified by this, and at one performance of Pelissier's *Follies*, 'a man in the audience stood up and protested, pointing out that Mr. Pelissier would not sing it if he understood what forcible feeding really meant'.[146] It seems not to have deterred Pelissier, as in 1911, costume designs were drawn up for a 'Suffragette Maud Allan' skit, which portrayed a militant suffragette in a 'knocked about' and 'torn' skirt with a 'very mannish cut', with a newspaper satchel, metal chains and a bodice with two 'prison plates with 2nd division on them'. There are notes on the costume design that the performer should wear 'very severe make up' (see Figure 4.3). This representation of Maud Allan as a suffragette would have been read in many ways by the *Follies* audiences. Allan was known to have Margot Asquith, the prime minister's wife and an anti-suffragist, as a patron.[147] With her most famous dance, the *Vision of Salome*, first performed at the Palace theatre in March 1908, she 'introduced a set of codes for female bodily expression', contributing not only to new forms of dance on the London stage but to new ways of presenting the female body.[148] Allan did not speak during her performances, and it is easy to see a silencing of the constitutional arguments for women's suffrage within the parody,

4.3 Costume design for Lewis Sydney as a 'suffragette Maud Allan' for *Pelissier's Follies of 1911* at the Apollo Theatre

as well as a facile regurgitation of populist and anti-suffragist imagery in the use of her name and style in Pelissier's work, reducing the politicised woman into a figure of fun for the audience to laugh at, not with. Not surprisingly, Pelissier's company does not seem to have included any AFL members, although Fay Compton, Pelissier's wife, who made her stage debut aged sixteen in the 1911 *Follies*, was the younger sister of League member Viola Compton.[149]

Occasionally stereotypes of suffragettes appeared in suffrage plays to highlight the absurdity of such representations, using them to the advantage of the movement by contrasting them with the actual presence of popular suffragist actresses on stage. By 'playing up' to comic stereotypes of militant women they could appropriate them by contrast, much as Cicely Hamilton's suffragette in 'quaint dress, and self-imposed heavy chain' had done in her *Anti-Suffrage Waxworks*. The art of eloquent persuasion by suffragist and suffragette speakers is a feature of many of the most popular suffrage plays, but the comic militant character is often initially recognisable by her dress rather than by her language. A significant number of plays, a number of which have not previously been analysed by academics, feature both non-violent and violent militant characters, although none commit militant acts on stage. Instead, the arguments used are constitutional, and militancy is either implied or referenced. The following examples offer a brief glimpse into the varied portrayals of suffrage militants and militancy, both positive and negative, that were written to entertain the general public.

Novelist and playwright Netta Syrett used negative stereotypes of militant suffragettes to comic effect in her one-act play *Might Is Right*, performed as a curtain-raiser at the Haymarket Theatre in November 1909.[150] Set at an unspecified future date, the play sees a group of suffragist women plotting to kidnap the prime minister. Enlisting a variety actress to entice him to a private house, they then dress him in a lace-trimmed dressing gown and refuse to release him until he agrees to give the vote to women. There were AFL members among the original cast, including Gillian Scaife, Sydney Fairbrother, Doris Lytton and Ada Palmer, who played the militant suffragette character, Miss Finch, described in the original stage directions as 'lanky and untidy in appearance. She is dressed in floppy clothes of purple, green and white, and wears the Votes for Women badge in the orthodox fashion across her chest.'[151] The *Daily Telegraph* thought she was a 'dreadful person' but at the same time 'the most amusing character in the piece'.[152] The *Globe* declared Miss Finch 'the only real Suffragette of the lot', and *At The Play* considered that 'a suffragist of the raucous order is well caricatured'.[153] In the piece, Miss Finch wants the prime minister, Beauchamp, to suffer in captivity as the suffragettes have done: 'He'll be treated as a second class prisoner, I hope! Prison rules, prison fare, one clean pocket handkerchief a week –'. She is not amused when told he will be treated well and allowed a valet:

> MISS FINCH: *(rising and speaking with sarcasm)* May I enquire whether there is any proposal to influence the <u>mind</u> of Mr. Beauchamp? From all I can gather, he is to live here in luxury, with a man to wait on him, and all the rest of us slaving for his comfort. I strongly advocate prison life, prison fare and prison rules, but failing such wholesome discipline, surely some

appeal should be made to his intelligence? I suggest first that all books with the exception of suffragette literature should be removed. Secondly, that at stated intervals our members one at a time should interview him on the subject of the vote; thirdly –

Miss Finch is interrupted but goes on to make continual attempts to lecture the prime minister on the constitutional arguments for female enfranchisement and places WSPU flags and placards in his room. In a final comic touch, she carves the words 'Votes for Women' in the butter on the breakfast table. Her efforts to educate him about the constitutional campaign are attempts to convert him through reason rather than incarceration, but he does not want to listen to her:

> MISS FINCH: You have probably never studied our question, never attempted, except in the most superficial manner, to acquaint yourself with our arguments? I have been at some pains to marshal those arguments and to embody them under various headings, in a pamphlet which I have called How Long? This I propose to read to you. In a couple of hours I undertake to convince any sane man that –
> BEAUCHAMP: *(alarmed)* My dear Miss Finch, please spare me. I know all your arguments inside out.
> MISS FINCH: You only know a wretched travesty of them.

At the end of the play, the prime minister agrees to introduce a government bill for women's suffrage but uses his assent to bargain with one of his kidnappers, with whom he has fallen in love. The victory is won through the militant but non-violent actions of the suffragist women, and the play presents the women as triumphing within a domestic setting, using feminine wiles to trick men but constantly being close to succumbing to the lure of romance. The prime minister's life is not truly in danger, and he never seems to be genuinely fearful of his female kidnappers. Although he is forced to wear a feminine garment while the women are in charge, he is not emasculated, having everything he needs 'barring his liberty, and his coat and trousers'.[154] Not surprisingly, the play was a success, widely and favourably reviewed. The humour of the piece and the portrayal of suffragists seemed to evoke laughter rather than hostility, with the AFL members in the cast happy to show their support for the cause by participating in a fun piece with a large female cast that managed to get many of the constitutional arguments for women's suffrage across to the audience through its lightness of touch.

An entirely different depiction of a militant leader on stage is present in *The Reforming of Augustus* by Irene Rutherford McLeod, first produced

MILITANCY 139

by the AFL at the Rehearsal Theatre on 15 January 1910 and published by the Woman's Press later that year. Set in a dining room, the play opens with an argument between a brother and sister about equality of opportunity, reminiscent of that between the siblings in Inez Bensusan's 1909 suffrage play *The Apple*. Halfway through the piece it changes stylistically, when a fairy deputation arrives to report to the queen of justice. Named 'By-Election', 'Protest Maker', 'Hunger Striker', 'Courage' and 'Stone-Thrower', they are preceded by Jingles, the spirit of youth, described in a review by *Votes for Women* as 'Puck under another name'.[155] Jingles boasts about 'Portia'.

> JINGLES: Portia is a Suffragette. Portia and I live together in the same house – at least, our shadows do ... and a head, covered with brown hair, that is soft as the softest silk, and is always tumbling about in little wavy strands. She has blue eyes – bluer than yours, bluer than mine. Our eyes beside hers are like grey pools that lie in the shadow, for they cannot flash as her flash, nor laugh as hers laugh ...
> MARY: Why, that's Cr –
> JINGLES: Now, didn't I tell you not to interrupt? If you know who it is, so do we all, don't we? *(To audience)* Anyway it's the most delicious house to occupy. Portia and I snuggle up together in the coziest corner of that house, the corner of the Heart, and when she is tired or sad she calls 'Spirit of Youth, Spirit of Youth, where are you?' and I answer, 'Here am I, here am I.' Then she has no more fear. *(Laughing)* When she is cross-examining Cabinet Ministers she calls, 'Portia, Portia, I want you; and Spirit of Youth, you, too.'[156]

McLeod is referring to Christabel Pankhurst's legal training through the allusion of Portia from Shakespeare's *The Merchant of Venice*, confident that the audience will not only recognise the idealised description of Pankhurst but will also agree with the idealised image of her. A noble, glorious militant suffragette is represented by the fairy hunger-striker: 'I left a dark punishment cell, and the last thing I saw was a white face peering out of the darkness, and a flame of golden hair. That was all. The girl was ill, but still determined.'[157] Clearly written for a militant audience, the play proved very popular with groups of younger militant WSPU groups, including the Drummers Union and the Young Purple, White and Green Club, who organised a performance of the piece at the Boudoir Theatre, Kensington, in May 1910.[158]

There are few surviving examples of suffrage plays directly set in prison or featuring police brutality, and the experiences of militant suffragettes were disseminated more easily among the suffragist and general public through speeches, articles, novels and poems. One of the reasons for this may be the censorship of plays containing politically sensitive material pertaining to militancy by the Lord Chamberlain's office. A four-act play written by Marie Robson in 1914 entitled *The Suffragette; or, A Woman's Vote*, about a Lancashire woman who leaves her husband and child to join the militants in London, originally contained scenes which the censor refused to license. A scene in which the heroine was imprisoned, went on hunger strike and was forcibly fed was considered inappropriate: 'The stage direction is that "this business must be done as delicately as possible, mostly hidden from the audience," but even so the passage is clearly inadmissible.'[159] The Lord Chamberlain's office also censored the scenes set in a police station with a rather optimistic remark that they 'are, as a whole, a libel (I hope) on police methods'.[160] This 'I hope' is interesting – implying a lack of knowledge and understanding of the treatment of suffragettes by the police, despite the frequent and explicit public-awareness campaign run by the militant suffrage societies. Perhaps that is too generous an interpretation, however, as the Lord Chamberlain's office, responsible to the government, could not sanction negative portrayals of police brutality on stage, thereby creating further propaganda for the suffrage movement. This example of censorship might offer a fresh perspective on the number and popularity of the comedic and figurative pieces that featured in the AFL's repertoire. More politically explicit or daring plays could be presented privately at play societies, but the suffrage plays that remain the most widely known treat the issues facing militant women in prison through allusions and topical references with a necessary subtlety that would have suggested much more, and much more implicitly, to contemporary audiences well versed in the complexities of the imagery and debate around the campaign. The presence of openly suffragist actresses in plays that gently challenged stereotypes, such as *Might Is Right*, was less 'safe' than it perhaps first appears. Appearing in the piece created a layering of representations of suffragist women, and suffragist actresses, for the audience that allowed for subtleties of interpretation of both the play and the cause it was promoting.

Militancy and the AFL

> No, I am certainly not an advocate of militancy, but I do see that it is horribly difficult to view things fairly when we are right in the middle of them.[161]

> Women are changed. They are more changed than their critics
> know ... Is it rational to expect these experiences to leave a woman
> unchanged?[162]

Viv Gardner is right in her assertion that 'it is difficult to assess the real extent of support for the militants at any one time' in the League.[163] It is certainly difficult to map the changing opinions of the membership as, apart from the summaries of activities given in the League's annual reports, some press interviews and autobiographical accounts written years later, we have only snapshots of moments such as the Drury Lane meeting through which to judge the mood of the League as a whole. However, the public actions, plays, performances, appearance and writings of very active League members affirm the level of support given by hundreds of individual members to militant societies. In the 1910 Grand Procession, for example, rather than joining the contingent from the AFL, Sime Seruya marched with the WFL prisoners, as did Muriel Matters, who carried a grille-protest banner.[164] The participation of individual members of the League in public militant actions ensured that the neutral stance of the organisation needed to be continually maintained, emphasised and renegotiated in order to keep good relations with activists on both sides of the debate. The League did not compromise its position in order to gain more financial support or to ally itself with particular individuals, but it didn't shy away from engaging with the issue. In 1913, the committee publicly condemned 'the abominable and cruel' forcible feeding of suffrage prisoners, calling on the Home Office to end the 'vindictive persecution of women'.[165] Although the raw data of who wrote and was in performances of suffrage plays, who supported or spoke at suffrage exhibitions and who actively contributed their time and public profile to the movement may seem bland in comparison to diary entries, articles or memoirs, it is perhaps a more accurate indication of the strength of support for militancy within the League. Where personal accounts do survive, they are coloured by their intended or perceived audiences, and, similarly, when non-violent and violent 'acts' were performed by actresses, the audiences for such acts were and remain varied and subjective.

However, there is no one definition of militancy – it is a flexible term, the meaning of which is tied into a very specific moment in time. This is especially so in regards to the suffrage campaign or the work of the AFL within it – with the responsibility for defining what actions, words and alliances were or were not militant as open to interpretation by those spectating at first, second and third hand, as well as those participating. Far from reducing either the audience or themselves only to suffragists and suffragettes, the ambiguity and fluidity of the changing strategies in the campaign for the vote could be seen onstage and off in their feminist theatrical activism. Previous scholarship on the AFL has not considered in detail the range and variety of its membership, events or the plays it generated in relation to the League's militant connections. This has meant that many of the League's plays have not been examined within the context of their creation and subsequent success. Describing militancy as 'feminist praxis', Laura Nym Mayhall suggests a consideration of a less antagonistic relationship between militant and non-militant campaigning than has been hitherto explored.[166] The idea of this feminist praxis makes sense in relation to the development of the AFL's work in the theatre, on the streets, in the press and in meetings. Members could react to, anticipate and promote the changing position of women in society and engage in feminist activism through creative, practical means. It may be that the best way to assess the militancy of the AFL as an organisation is through its praxis – by focusing their work on education through the use of propaganda plays they invested their resources in non-violent public political activism and debate. Active campaigning by the League in all areas had produced an efficient and confident organisation that considered itself capable of successfully implementing change within the theatre industry as well as in wider society. This confidence would lead to the Woman's Theatre project, intended to change the way women could participate in the professional theatre industry forever, and would also go on to underpin the work of the organisation during the First World War, both of which are explored in the next chapter.

Notes

1. F.J.C., '"Acts" and actresses', *Sunday Times*, 20 December 1908, p. 8.
2. AFL, *Annual Report 1913–1914*, p. 2.
3. J. Holledge, *Innocent Flowers: Women in the Edwardian Theatre* (London: Virago Press, 1981), p. 51; C. Hirshfield, 'The Actresses' Franchise League and the campaign for women's suffrage, 1908–1914', *Theatre Research International*, 10:2 (1985), 129–53, p. 130.
4. A.J.R. (ed.), *The Suffrage Annual and Women's Who's Who 1913* (London: Stanley Paul, 1913), p. 11.
5. 'Miss Gertrude Elliott says', *Nash's Magazine*, May 1913.

6 They are *A Woman's Influence, Miss Appleyard's Awakening, The Apple, The Anti-Suffragist; or, the Other Side, The Maid and the Magistrate, The Mother's Meeting, Mary Edwards, An Englishwoman's Home, A Junction, A Chat with Mrs Chicky*, and *An Allegory*.
7 J. Purvis, 'The prison experiences of the suffragettes in Edwardian Britain', *Women's History Review*, 4:1 (1995), 103-33, p. 103.
8 See S. S. Holton, 'Women and the vote', in J. Purvis (ed.), *Women's History: Britain 1850-1945* (London and New York: Routledge, 1998), pp. 277-306; and A. V. John, 'The privilege of power: suffrage women and the issue of men's support', in Amanda Vickery (ed.), *Women, Privilege and Power: British Politics, 1750 to the Present* (Stanford, CA: Stanford University Press, 2001), pp. 227-52.
9 M. J. Corbett, *Representing Femininity: Middle Class Subjectivity in Victorian and Edwardian Women's Autobiographies* (Oxford: Oxford University Press, 1992), p. 117.
10 AFL, *Secretary's Report, June 1910-1911*.
11 Muriel Matters, interviewed in *The Vote*, 19 February 1910, p. 196.
12 Elizabeth Robins, 'Woman's war', *McClure's Magazine*, March 1913.
13 J. Purvis, 'The suffragette and women's history', *Women's History Review*, 14:3-5 (2005), 357-64, at p. 357.
14 A. Rosen, *Rise Up, Women! The Militant Campaign of the Women's Social and Political Union 1903-1914* (Aldershot: Gregg Revivals, 1993), p. 120.
15 Marion Wallace Dunlop was sentenced on 2 July 1909 to one month in prison for 'defacing the wall of St Stephen's Hall'. Her request to be treated as a political prisoner was denied. Three days later, she began a hunger strike and was released after ninety-one hours. Rosen, *Rise Up*, p. 123.
16 L. N. Mayhall, 'Creating the "suffragette spirit": British feminism and the historical imagination', *Women's History Review*, 4:3 (1995), 319-44, at p. 320; see, for example, D. Atkinson, *Purple, White and Green: Suffragettes in London* (London: Museum of London, 1992); and D. Atkinson, *The Suffragettes in Pictures* (London: The History Press, 2010); A. Raeburn, *Militant Suffragettes* (London: Michael Joseph, 1973); Rosen, *Rise Up*.
17 B. Harrison, '*The Militant Suffragettes* by Antonia Raeburn', *Oral History*, 2:1 (1974), 73-6, at p. 76. The recordings of Harrison's interviews – *Oral Evidence on the Suffragette* and *Suffragist Movements: The Brian Harrison Interviews* – are held at the Women's Library, 8/SUF/B.
18 E. Crawford, *The Women's Suffrage Movement: A Reference Guide, 1866-1928* (London and New York: Routledge, 2001), pp. 663-4.
19 Purvis, 'The prison experiences of the suffragettes', p. 103.
20 L. N. Mayhall, 'Defining militancy: radical protest, the constitutional idiom, and women's suffrage in Britain, 1908-1909', *Journal of British Studies*, 39:3 (2000), 340-71, at p. 342; L. N. Mayhall, 'Domesticating Emmeline: representing the suffragette, 1930-1993', *NWSA Journal*, 11:2 (1999), 1-24, at p. 3.

21 Including Viv Gardner, Julie Holledge, June Purvis, Fern Riddell and Christine Woodworth.
22 Mayhall, *Defining Militancy*, p. 371.
23 J. Purvis, 'A lost dimension? The political education of women in the suffragette movement in Edwardian Britain', *Gender and Education*, 6:3 (1994), 319–27, at p. 323; J. Purvis, 'Deeds, not words: the daily lives of militant suffragettes in Edwardian Britain', *Women's Studies International Forum*, 18:2 (1995), 91–101, at p. 92.
24 AFL, *Annual Report, June 1913–June 1914*.
25 See M. DiCenzo, 'Unity and dissent: official organs of the suffrage campaign', in L. Delap, M. DiCenzo and L. Ryan, *Feminist Media History: Suffrage, Periodicals and the Public Sphere* (Basingstoke: Palgrave Macmillan, 2011), pp. 76–119.
26 C. Morrell, *'Black Friday' and Violence against Women in the Suffragette Movement* (London: WRRC Publications Collective, 1981).
27 Kitty Marion, unpublished autobiography, New York Public Library, p. 204; list of women and men injured, Papers of Emily Wilding Davison, Women's Library at LSE, 7EWD/D/1.
28 *Treatment of the Women's Deputations by the Police*, Women's Press, 1911, pp. 57, 44, 48, Papers of Emily Wilding Davison, Women's Library, LSE, 7EWD/D/1/2.
29 E. Crawford, *Campaigning for the Vote: Kate Parry Frye's Suffrage Diary* (London: Francis Boutle, 2013), p. 33. See also http://womanandhersphere.com/2013/05/20/campaigning-for-the-vote-kate-frye-and-black-friday-november-1910/ (accessed 20 October 2017).
30 Letter from Arncliffe Sennett to the editor of the *Christian Commonwealth*, 26 May 1913, Arncliffe Sennett Collection, British Library.
31 AFL, *Annual Report June 1913–June 1914*.
32 AFL, *Annual Report June 1913–June 1914*.
33 *Evening Standard*, 20 December 1913.
34 'London letter', *Westminster Gazette*, 13 January 1913; letters from Edward Cadogan to Gertrude Forbes-Robertson, 9 January 1913, Arncliffe Sennett Collection, British Library.
35 *Hansard*, 27 January 1913, vol. IV, cols. 1019–91.
36 Letter from Lord Robert Cecil to Winifred Mayo, 30 January 1913, Arncliffe Sennett Collection, British Library.
37 *The Era*, 25 January 1913, p. 14; *The Era*, 22 February 1913, p. 15; letter from Winifred Mayo to Maud Arncliffe Sennett, 2 February 1913, Arncliffe Sennett Collection, British Library.
38 *Hansard*, 22 April 1913, vol. LII, cols. 213–14.
39 *Daily Telegraph*, 22 April 1913; AFL, *Secretary's Report, June 1912–June 1913*.
40 Eva Moore, interviewed in *The Vote*, 3 December 1910, p. 64.
41 Adeline Bourne, interviewed for *Home This Afternoon*, BBC, 13 May 1964, British Library.

42 *New York Times*, 6 June 1914, p. 1.
43 E. Moore, *Exits and Entrances* (London: Chapman & Hall, 1923), p. 96.
44 *Votes for Women*, 12 June 1914, p. 560.
45 *The Times*, 11 June 1914.
46 Moore, *Exits and Entrances*, p. 96.
47 Holledge, *Innocent Flowers*, p. 53.
48 All the states of Australia had extended the franchise to women by 1905.
49 Mayhall, *Defining Militancy*, p. 359.
50 *The Vote*, 19 February 1910, p. 196.
51 Crawford, *The Woman's Suffrage Movement*. p. 392.
52 C. Hamilton and C. St John, *Pot and Kettle*, in N. Paxton, *The Methuen Drama Book of Suffrage Plays* (London: Bloomsbury, 2013), pp. 47–66, at p. 64.
53 Hamilton and St John, *Pot and Kettle*, p. 63.
54 Programme for the Scala Theatre, 12 November 1909, p. 3.
55 *Votes for Women*, 10 November 1911, p. 85.
56 *Proceedings of the Central Criminal Court*, 14 May 1912.
57 J. Lawrence, 'Contesting the male polity: the suffragettes and the politics of disruption in Edwardian Britain', in A. Vickery (ed.), *Women, Privilege and Power: British Politics, 1750 to the Present* (Stanford, CA: Stanford University Press, 2001), pp. 201–26, at p. 204.
58 L. Leneman, *'A Guid Cause': The Women's Suffrage Movement in Scotland* (Aberdeen: Aberdeen University Press, 1991), p. 46.
59 *Votes for Women*, 26 February 1909, p. 373; National Archives of Scotland, JC 26/1551.
60 G. Moffat, *Join Me in Remembering: The Life and Reminiscences of the Author of 'Bunty Pulls the Strings'* (Camps Bay: W. L. Moffat, 1955), p. 53.
61 AFL, *Half Yearly Report*, 1911.
62 G. Moffat, *The Maid and the Magistrate*, in C. C. Nelson (ed.), *Literature of the Women's Suffrage Campaign in England* (Peterborough: Broadview Press, 2004), pp. 256–64, at p. 262.
63 Moffat, *Join Me*, p. 52; Leneman, *'A Guid Cause'*, p. 266.
64 Winifred Mayo, 'Prison experiences of a suffragette', *The Idler*, April 1908, pp. 85–99, at p. 85.
65 G. Kingston, *Curtsey While You're Thinking* (London: Williams & Norgate, 1937), p. 190.
66 *Daily News*, 12 February 1908.
67 *Votes for Women*, 26 February 1909, p. 373.
68 *Marlborough Express*, 12 April 1907, p. 3.
69 *Votes for Women*, 2 July 1909, p. 879.
70 *Votes for Women*, 10 November 1911, p. 85.
71 *The Weekly Despatch*, 21 February 1909.
72 B. Green, 'From visible flâneuse to spectacular suffragette? The prison, the street and the sites of suffrage', *Discourse*, 17:2 (1994–5), 67–97, at p. 71.

73 K. Cockin, 'St John, Christopher Marie', *Oxford Dictionary of National Biography* (Oxford: Oxford University Press, 2004). Available at www.oxforddnb.com/index/57/101057057/ (accessed 12 July 2017).
74 *Votes for Women*, 18 June 1909, pp. 808–9.
75 *Votes for Women*, 18 June 1909, pp. 808–9.
76 *The Weekly Despatch*, 21 February 1909.
77 *Votes for Women*, 18 June 1909, p. 809.
78 *Votes for Women*, 2 July 1909, p. 874.
79 *Votes for Women*, 9 July 1909, p. 903.
80 *Votes for Women*, 9 July 1909, p. 903.
81 *Votes for Women*, 10 November 1911, p. 85.
82 AFL, *Secretary's Report June 1911–June 1912*.
83 *Votes for Women*, 10 November 1911, p. 85.
84 Crawford, *The Woman's Suffrage Movement*, p. 744.
85 Arncliffe Sennett Collection, vol. XV, British Library.
86 Lillah McCarthy, in *Votes for Women*, 8 December 1911, p. 161.
87 A committee member of the AFL, Arncliffe Sennett had performed under the name Miss Mary Kingsley, retiring from the stage when she married. As Mary Kingsley she performed in the West End (Creusa in *The Bride of Love* by Robert Buchanan, Lyric Theatre, June–July 1890), as Joan of Arc in *Henry VI* for the 1889 Shakespeare Commemoration in Stratford-upon-Avon and on tour around the UK and Australia.
88 Arncliffe Sennett Collection, vol. XV, British Library.
89 *Daily Express*, 22 November 1911, pp. 72–3.
90 *Votes for Women*, 1 December 1911, p. 144.
91 *Votes for Women*, 24 November 1911, p. 126.
92 *New York Times*, 5 October 1913; Crawford, *The Women's Suffrage Movement*, p. 451.
93 *Daily Telegraph*, 24 November 1911, quoted in Kitty Marion, unpublished autobiography, New York Public Library, p. 212.
94 *Votes for Women*, 1 December 1911, p. 146.
95 *Votes for Women*, 1 December 1911, p. 144.
96 A.J.R., *The Suffrage Annual*, pp. 250–1.
97 Arncliffe Sennett Collection, vol. XVIII, British Library.
98 *Votes for Women*, 1 December 1911, p. 148.
99 BBC, 13 July 1958. Available at www.bbc.co.uk/archive/suffragettes/8301.shtml (accessed on 12 July 2017).
100 *The Stage*, 23 November 1911, p. 18.
101 *Votes for Women*, 24 November 1911, p. 130.
102 Kitty Marion, unpublished autobiography, New York Public Library, p. 212.
103 *Votes for Women*, 24 November 1911, p. 130.
104 *Votes for Women*, 8 December 1911, p. 166.
105 *Votes for Women*, 1 December 1911, p. 142.

MILITANCY 147

106 *The Vote*, 20 January 1912, p. 155.
107 *The Stage*, 16 May 1912, p. 6; *Official Programme of Great Suffragette Demonstration in Hyde Park, Sunday, July 14th 1912*, Papers of Emily Wilding Davison, Women's Library at LSE, 7EWD/C/2/5.
108 *The Suffragette*, 3 January 1913, p. 171. and 10 January 1913, p. 187.
109 *Votes for Women*, 4 July 1913, p. 582.
110 D. Howard, *London Theatres and Music Halls, 1850–1950* (London: Library Association, 1970), p. 66.
111 AFL, *Secretary's Report June 1912–June 1913*; *The Stage*, 8 May 1913, p. 24; *Manchester Guardian*, 3 May 1913.
112 Parliamentary Archives, HL/PO/PU/1/1913/3&4G5c4.
113 *The Stage*, 8 May 1913, p. 24.
114 *Morning Post*, 3 May 1913.
115 *Daily Telegraph*, 3 May 1913.
116 *Daily Telegraph*, 3 May 1913.
117 *The Era*, 10 May 1913, p. 11.
118 *The Standard*, 3 May 1913; *The Era*, 10 May 1913, p. 11.
119 *Daily Chronicle*, 3 May 1913.
120 *Manchester Guardian*, 3 May 1913.
121 *The Era*, 10 May 1913, p. 11.
122 *The Era*, 10 May 1913, p. 11.
123 *Manchester Guardian*, 3 May 1913.
124 AFL, *Accounts*, June 1912–May 1913; clipping from *The Era*, in Arncliffe Sennett Collection, vol. XXII, British Library.
125 *Manchester Guardian*, 5 May 1913, p. 5.
126 *Manchester Guardian*, 6 May 1913, p. 12.
127 Arncliffe Sennett Collection, vol. XXI, British Library.
128 Arncliffe Sennett Collection, vol. XXI, British Library.
129 Handwritten letter to Arncliffe Sennett from Winifred Mayo, 4 May 1913, Arncliffe Sennett Collection, vol. XXII, British Library.
130 Arncliffe Sennett Papers, British Library.
131 Letter to Arncliffe Sennett from Winifred Mayo, 21 May 1913, Arncliffe Sennett Collection, vol. XXII, British Library.
132 *London Budget*, 11 May 1913. Arncliffe Sennett Collection, British Library.
133 *London Budget*, 11 May 1913.
134 I. Vanbrugh, *To Tell My Story* (London: Hutchinson and Co., 1948), p. 83.
135 Letter from Winifred Mayo to Maud Arncliffe Sennett, 8 June 1913, Arncliffe Sennett Collection, British Library.
136 *The Era*, 21 June 1913, p. 12.
137 *Votes for Women*, 4 November 1910, p. 78; *The Times*, 7 November 1910, p. 16.
138 Christopher St John, *Her Will*, unpublished, LCP Collection, British Library, LCP 1914/14.

139 St John, *Her Will*.
140 J. Mercer, 'Media and militancy: propaganda in the Women's Social and Political Union's campaign', *Women's History Review*, 14:3–4 (2005), 471–86, at p. 483.
141 Elizabeth Robins, 'In conclusion', in *Way Stations* (London: Hodder & Stoughton, 1913), p. 353.
142 Mayo, *Prison Experiences*, pp. 85–99.
143 K. Hartman, 'What made me a suffragette: the new woman and the new (?) conversion narrative', *Women's History Review*, 12:1 (2003), 35–50, at p. 41.
144 *The Era*, 2 January 1909, p. 21.
145 *The Times*, 28 December 1909, p. 8.
146 *Votes for Women*, 7 January 1910, p. 238.
147 J. R. Walkowitz, 'The "vision of Salome": cosmopolitanism and erotic dancing in Central London, 1908–1918', *The American Historical Review*, 108:2 (2003), 337–76, at p. 342.
148 Walkowitz, 'The "vision of Salome"', p. 345.
149 J. C. Trewin, 'Compton, Fay', *Oxford Dictionary of National Biography* (Oxford: Oxford University Press, 2004). Available at www.oxforddnb.com/view/article/30957 (accessed 12 July 2017).
150 Netta Syrett, *Might Is Right*, unpublished, LCP Collection, British Library, LCP 1909/24.
151 Syrett, *Might Is Right*.
152 *Daily Telegraph*, 15 November 1909.
153 *The Globe*, 15 November 1909; *At The Play*, 27 November 1909, University of Bristol Theatre Collection.
154 *The Referee*, 14 November 1909, University of Bristol Theatre Collection.
155 *Votes for Women*, 25 March 1910, p. 406.
156 I. Rutherford McLeod, *The Reforming of Augustus* (London: The Woman's Press, 1910), pp. 17–18.
157 McLeod, *The Reforming of Augustus*, p. 22.
158 *Votes for Women*, 6 May 1910, p. 538.
159 LC Office, letter for *The Suffragette or A Woman's Vote*, LCP No. 2338, 1914, British Library.
160 Lord Chamberlain's Plays, British Library.
161 *Votes for Women*, 4 July 1913, p. 582.
162 Robins, *Way Stations*, pp. 350, 354.
163 V. Gardner, *Sketches from the Actresses' Franchise League* (Nottingham: University of Nottingham, 1985), p. 3.
164 *The Vote*, 25 June 1910, p. 100; for the full text of the AFL's resolution see *The Suffragette*, 14 November 1913, p. 105.
165 *Votes for Women*, 7 November 1913, p. 85.
166 Mayhall, *Defining Militancy*, p. 344.

5
Hope

Building the future: a woman's theatre

In summer 1913, with the AFL's membership nearing 800, Inez Bensusan and the League's play department began developing an ambitious project, the Woman's Theatre, intended to change the way women participated in the theatre business forever (see Figure 5.1).[1] The play department had ventured into production already with *The Better Half*, a satire by novelist and suffragist Alison Garland, in which women are enfranchised and men are lobbying for the vote, at the King's Hall, Covent Garden, in May 1913, and a one-off matinee of new plays at the Arts Centre in Langham Place in July 1913.[2] League members were already part of other small groups and societies that produced new work, but women with experience of managing large producing and receiving houses and venues were relatively unusual and at a disadvantage financially as compared to their male contemporaries.[3] Tracy C. Davis has written about the 'truly uneven' playing field for female theatrical managers of the Edwardian period and the difficulty they faced in raising capital and securing guarantors, both formally and informally.[4] Familial and marital connections were a way around the problem for some women, but even those with private capital were prevented by their gender from accessing the networks of business and finance necessary to participate in the commercial management system. As syndicates and larger companies became more prevalent, women were further excluded. Few were able to lease venues in addition to managing them and were therefore unable to establish a sustained period of management, which in turn compromised their gains by limiting long-term planning and the possible extension of successful seasons.[5] This undermined their authority as initiators and creators of work, meaning that women had fewer opportunities to build and sustain reputations as producers and managers. There were exceptions, including Emma Cons, Annie Horniman, Gertrude Kingston and Lena Ashwell, all of whom were suffragists, but they were comparatively rare.[6] Davis has lamented the collectivism of women in organising ventures around the suffrage agitation, wishing instead that they had made new 'kinds of

5.1 Woman's Theatre logo, 1913

leaps into the financial environment'.[7] However, designed as it was to directly address these fiscal inequalities as well as further feminist and suffragist agendas, it is arguable that the Woman's Theatre was indeed this kind of leap. Bensusan spoke confidently about supporting the professional skills of women on stage and off: 'I want it to be run entirely by women. The whole business management and control will be in the hands of women … there will be women business and stage-managers, producers, and so on.'[8] Opening up other avenues into and through the professional theatre world for women and taking 'the feminist struggle into the heart of the mainstream industry' created opportunities for change at every level.[9] The Woman's Theatre was keenly aware as an organisation of advancing both the commercial and artistic opportunities for women in theatre – more roles for and about women, more employment on and off stage for women, an emphasis on collaboration in the wider feminist community and a shared profit for the financial backers. No aspect was overlooked – Bensusan wanted to 'bring about a revolution in the way in which less important actresses are treated at some theatres' and cited examples of exhausted walking-on actresses who were expected to stand throughout rehearsals and the 'insolence and bad language from stage employees' that women were subject to.[10] This holistic view included fighting discrimination based on physical attractiveness rather than talent in the casting process. Bensusan considered that she had suffered personally from such treatment: 'A woman of talent ought not to be compelled to go through the ordeal of being regarded much as if she were some prize animal ... if our organization does nothing else but eliminate this low sex standard it will have done a fine thing.'[11] Bensusan's new project, intended to financially support all the suffrage societies and to 'spread accurate knowledge through the educational medium of the theatre' was both timely and exciting.[12] The aims of the Woman's Theatre were:

To present plays, written either by men or women, which show the woman's point of view.
To provide a new outlet for the activities of women members of the theatrical profession.
To run the theatre on a co-operative basis, guarantors sharing in the profits.
To help and forward the Women's Movement to enfranchisement, and to promote the unification of all suffrage and feminist societies.[13]

The general committee for the Woman's Theatre was made up of ninety women, and, whereas membership of the AFL was restricted to women who were or had been performers, there was no such qualification required of the Woman's Theatre committee members, who included leading representatives of both the militant and constitutional suffrage societies, including the WSPU's Georgina Brackenbury, Emmeline Pethick-Lawrence and Charlotte Despard from the WFL, and Millicent Fawcett, the leader of the NUWSS. This collaboration between the militant and non-militant leaders for a feminist theatrical venture shows how successful the AFL's strategic position of neutrality was and had been in ensuring the sustainability of the organisation. High-profile women with specialist areas of interest, experience of political campaigning at every level and influential contacts and supporters gave the Woman's Theatre project and its ideals a profile outside of the theatre profession as well as within it. Bensusan, inspired by the dissent demonstrated by suffragists, the vocal support the suffrage societies could call upon and the involvement of prominent individuals in the theatre profession was not alone. Actresses, playwrights and theatre professionals abroad with shared interests in the enfranchisement of women as well as many other social issues related to gender and economic inequality saw the potential of a female-led theatre to create positive change, not only for themselves but for their contemporaries.

A woman's theatre in Europe and America

There was an international movement towards a woman's or women's theatre that had been active throughout Bensusan's working lifetime within professional networks of feminist actresses. In 1896, plans were announced for a woman's theatre in Copenhagen. The first season was to include work by Danish playwright, poet and novelist Magdalene Thorensen, a friend and colleague of Henrik Ibsen, who had staged her plays, attended her literary salons and married her daughter.[14] Bjornstiern Bjornson, one of the playwrights chosen for Bensusan's inaugural Woman's Theatre season, had published a book of Thorensen's poetry in 1860.[15] Featuring an all-female orchestra, chorus and conductor, the project intended to solely produce plays written by female playwrights.[16] The year 1897–98 saw the first feminist theatre season in Paris, founded by Polish dramatist Marya Cheliga. Cheliga wanted her Théâtre Feministe to champion women playwrights, announcing that 'women are to have precedence over men in at least one theatre', and her first and only season had full houses and positive press coverage.[17] Glad that she had attempted the project, even though it had not proved financially sustainable, Cheliga considered the venture a success in retrospect.[18] The year 1902 saw a woman's theatre proposed in New York, which, with a female owner, business manager and press agent, intended to have men involved as 'necessary parts of the cast and audience' only.[19] Gertrude Andrews, a playwright and press agent, was to manage the new theatre with actress Etta Reed as owner.[20] The Criterion Theatre in Brooklyn was renamed Mrs Payton's Playhouse when Etta Reed opened it on 15 January 1903, with an all-female orchestra and female ushers.[21] Ten years later, *Jus Suffragii*, the journal of the International Woman Suffrage Alliance, reported in October 1913 that dramatist Frank Wedekind was on the committee of a society formed in Munich to produce plays by women playwrights that hoped to 'overcome the prejudice of managers to women playwrights, which has forced women to write under a male nom de plume'.[22]

Bensusan intended to start a women's theatrical agency in connection with the Woman's Theatre, inspired by the success of two transatlantic colleagues, Elisabeth Marbury and Jessie Bonstelle, who had tried to build on their success and experience in the theatre profession by creating opportunities for other women. Elisabeth Marbury, an influential, well-connected literary agent in New York, London and Paris, had represented Elizabeth Robins since 1898, and also counted among her clients prominent supporters of the League including J. M. Barrie, Jerome K. Jerome, Arthur Wing Pinero and George Bernard Shaw.[23] In 1912, she was reported to be part of a project for a new theatre to be built in New York that would produce plays for and by women. Called the Woman's Theatre, it was to be financed by Anne Morgan, daughter of financier J. P. Morgan, with Marbury as business manager and actress Minnie Madern Fiske as artistic director.[24] Marbury and Morgan had previously collaborated in 1903 to found New York's first women-only club, the Colony Club, which was reported to 'have a considerable interest in the undertaking' of the Woman's Theatre.[25] The year 1912 also saw Mary Moncure Parker, a writer and actress, make plans for a Woman's Theatre in Chicago that would be owned and operated solely by women. 'A woman will manage the new theatre … there will be a woman ticket seller, a woman stage manager, a woman press agent, women scene shifters, women ushers, and an orchestra composed of women.'[26] Actress-manager Jessie Bonstelle began working with American actress and suffragist Mary Shaw on establishing a women's national theatre in 1913 – a venture that eventually did not come to fruition due to lack of investment.[27] Mary Shaw, who had played the lead in Elizabeth Robins' play *Votes for Women* on Broadway in 1909 and who had written suffrage plays of her own, was passionate about the positive influence theatre could have on the treatment of women in society.[28] At a mass meeting of the Woman's National Theatre League in May 1913, she spoke about the subsuming of actresses and female characters to a 'man cut pattern': 'A woman's theatre, then – since there is slim chance for women to work out any but men's ideals of womanhood in the existing theatre – a woman's theatre because women must themselves make the proving, must show the men.'[29] Mary Shaw's frustration shows how similarly actresses in the commercial theatre in the UK and the USA felt about their limited professional career opportunities.

Creating space for a woman's theatre

Late-nineteenth- and early twentieth-century European and American initiatives to develop a woman's theatre had in common the desire for a new physical as well as theatrical space. Wanting to attract and maintain a female audience, each project considered as a matter of priority the creation of opportunities in their ventures for networking, learning and socialising as well as theatre-going. Gertrude Andrews was keen that her theatre should appeal to all women, with an in-house nursery to encourage mothers to attend: 'we have a well-equipped nursery ... so that mothers can bring their babies to the matinee and be free to enjoy it ... it enables them, too, to come with their husbands, when otherwise they would be compelled to stay at home'.[30] Mary Moncure Parker's project of 1912 was for a theatre that would cater to a female audience by having daily matinees and providing 'tea and social rooms', and Mary Shaw's Woman's National Theatre building, which she hoped would eventually be in 'all the cities of the United States', envisioned a venue with a training school, free performances for school children, and a roof garden in which to show moving pictures.[31] Similarly, the woman's theatre in Copenhagen was intended to be part of a larger, purpose-built building, containing 'lecture rooms, a restaurant, tea room, baths, gymnasium and reading-room'.[32] A purpose-built space did not appear as part of the Bensusan's initial plans for her woman's theatre. The AFL used its offices as flexible working space in which members could plan projects, rehearse, network and teach, and rooms were regularly let for rehearsals as a way of supporting the organisation.[33] However, with suffrage shops, women's clubs and the public support for the cause from many prominent businesses and theatre managers, perhaps the communal space of the League's woman's theatre had the potential, in an abstract sense, to share intellectual and social as well as physical space, including the whole of the West End as well as other theatres, towns and cities across the country.[34]

It is clear that with their constant interest in outreach and support of the work of all suffrage societies, the AFL's Woman's Theatre project intended to have a national stage. Jacky Bratton's work on mapping the West End performance history of the late Victorian period sees theatrical clubs and the traditional male spaces for professional networking as 'the matrix of working practice' and shows that women's exclusion from these spaces meant it was more difficult for them to be part of the creation of wealth or have frequent and relatively informal access to powerful individuals in their industry.[35] However, Bratton notes that 'in the theatre, capital was cultural and corporeal and women were partly its possessors for that reason.[36] The League had created capital that had undeniable currency in both suffragist and theatrical worlds. The Woman's Theatre project, with its intention of creating a professionally transformative space for women, found precedence within the European and American theatrical and feminist communities. There was also the advantage that, unlike the efforts of Marbury, Andrews, Moncure Parker, Bonstelle, Shaw, Cheliga and Thorensen, the Woman's Theatre was supported artistically and financially by a large and established organisation with proven successes in producing propaganda theatre and events.

First season of the Woman's Theatre: December 1913

The Woman's Theatre intended to harness the potential of the League's existing audience to establish a competitive and profitable theatre business. Bensusan was proud of the financial arrangements, which she considered 'the most original part of the new scheme', and directly targeted the suffrage societies for their support.[37] Guarantors were allotted five seats worth 25s 6d in total (relative to £113 in 2015) for every £1 (relative to £88 in 2015) given. Bensusan suggested that suffrage societies who became guarantors could sell their allocation of seats at 'ordinary theatre prices', potentially doubling their profits by gaining 5s 6d (approximately 27 per cent) in the pound as well as their weekly receipts. The scheme also allowed for individual guarantors to nominate a suffrage society to which their profits would be automatically paid. After covering the weekly running costs of £450 (relative to nearly £40,000 in 2015), a third of the total profits would go directly to the AFL, and the remaining two-thirds was to be divided among the guarantors.[38] Profit was important in creating an attractive and sustainable model, and, by producing the work of two well-respected European male playwrights in her first season, Bensusan actively deflected private fears and public accusations of prejudice against men and male writing while simultaneously showing the Woman's Theatre to be part of a modernist, European theatre movement that was embracing new forms, ideas and intellectual debates (see Figure 5.2). George Bernard Shaw had championed the English theatre's engagement with Brieux two years earlier, describing both Brieux and Ibsen as 'prophets as well as playwrights', challenging traditional, entrenched notions of what could be portrayed on stage.[39] Janette Steer produced Charlotte Shaw's translation of Eugene Brieux's *Woman on Her Own* (*La Femme seule*),

5.2 Leaflet advertising the first season of the Woman's Theatre, 1913

and Winifred Mayo, who had been part of the cast in February 1913 when it was presented by the Play Actors at the Court Theatre, produced Robert Farquharson Sharp's translation of Bjornstiern Bjornson's *A Gauntlet*.[40] The themes in both plays included many issues that concerned League members – double standards, sexual harassment and unequal pay – and that they had frequently spoken about in public. Recent academic claims that 'in order to find sufficiently demanding roles, the company had to resort to male playwrights' show a lack of research into and understanding of the context of the project.[41] Other scholars have stated from a more knowledgeable position that the choice of two male playwrights showed the organisation to be 'intellectually serious and professionally capable' and meant that the financial success of the venture would not only be seen to be proof of women's business ability but also an example of competitive commercial success.[42] Cicely Hamilton sought to deflect the matter with humour in the Woman's Theatre Week souvenir programme: 'Possible the choice may have been accidental and possibly it may have been Hobson's; but, whatever it was, I consider it wise and fortunate.'[43] Hamilton focused her essay on the business aspects of the venture and the increased opportunities for women to become involved: 'Women stage-managers and women business-managers, we think, are still regarded with suspicion; we wish to show there is no cause for it.'[44] Keen to refute any notion of intellectual elitism, Hamilton dryly stated that as a commercial venture, the Woman's Theatre could not afford to only attract 'a thinking public', ending with a sardonic defence of the Woman's Theatre from the possible charge of being unadventurous in their exploration of new European theatre. The programme essays by Bernard Shaw and William Archer made no comment about the feminist statement inherent in the creation of the Woman's Theatre, but the essay by the president of the WWSL, Flora Annie Steele, praised the efficacy of suffragist actresses: 'good luck to you, sisters of a sister art! You should have a great future before you, since you can hammer hard facts into dull brains; you can open still duller eyes that will not trouble to read a page of print!'[45]

Reviews for Woman's Theatre Week were largely positive from both the suffragist and popular press. Suffragist actresses were not only involved on stage and backstage but, as with many fundraising events held by the League, engaged in direct contact with the public front of house, as souvenir- and literature-sellers.[46] This show of support helped to attract audiences and offer them the chance to debate issues around the venture with those directly involved. The League was pleased with the project, announcing proudly in its 1914 annual report that not only was it an artistic success but that the 'financial results exceeded all expectations'. Net profit was £442 (over £39,000 in 2015 values), and all the shareholders received a 57.5 per cent return on their investment. This commercial and artistic success of the first season of the Woman's Theatre was enormously encouraging to the

League, and Bensusan immediately made plans for a second season, hoping that 'in a few years' time the Woman's Theatre will become a permanent institution'.[47] In triumph, and brimming with hope for a successful future for the Woman's Theatre, the AFL postponed its annual birthday party until the New Year and prepared for its work in 1914.

The first half of 1914: looking towards a bright future

> The new year opens with very happy auguries for the future work of this League ... Our new 'Men's Group' is in process of being formed, and it is hoped that all our good friends, and many not yet known to us, will rally to our aid now there is an organisation that will provide a sphere for their activities.[48]

Just as the League announced the formation of a men's group, many of its members became part of a new suffrage society, the United Suffragists, formed on 6 January 1914.[49] The United Suffragists had offices close to the League's and welcomed female and male members of all other suffrage societies, both militant and non-militant, creating a new platform for the movement that was in theory undamaged by the issues of leadership, partiality or bias: issues that had dominated particularly the militant societies in the preceding years.[50] The first six months of 1914 were busy ones for the League, and the range of activities, events, appearances, performances and meetings programmed shows the organisation brimming with confidence in its capabilities. A glimpse of this confidence can be seen in the playful and unusual publicising of an encounter one of its members had when arranging the League's birthday party. This event was scheduled for 29 January as an AFL fundraiser at the Empress Rooms in Kensington. As at other similar events, League members intended to act as hostesses and, in this case, waitresses. However, the manager of the venue was uncooperative: 'For [according to the *Daily News*] when the manager of the hall heard that women were to carry tea trays he declared it to be impossible. "Only a man waiter," he vowed, "is capable of this feat."'[51] *Votes for Women* was surprised: 'Women? Going to the polling booth is an amateur feat in comparison!' and reproduced two sketches drawn by an anonymous member of the AFL after her interview with the manager, 'which are imaginary pictures of what that gentlemen evidently had in his mind when he thought of the expert waiter handing

5.3 'The Enfranchised Waiter'

over his perfectly balanced tea tray to the lady who is – off the stage – only a very charming amateur' (see Figures 5.3 and 5.4).[52]

Votes for Women did not report, however, that the manager had said that only male waiters could handle the round trays used at the Empress Rooms and that if the trays had been 'ordinary' ones, of course the actresses would have been welcome to use them.[53] The *Daily News and Leader* quoted an unnamed League member's defiant response:

> Of course we shall do our own waitressing, and I would like to invite your readers who are accustomed to this sort of thing with male waiters – to come and enjoy quick and efficient waiting – as it will be performed by the Actresses' Franchise League on the 29th inst. at the Empress Rooms.[54]

However, the manager did not relent. This defeat for the League was not acknowledged by *Votes for Women*, and the report of the event that appeared in the paper a week later was ambiguous: 'true Suffragists, the actresses were undismayed by the dismal tales of refractory trays and falling crockery, and their clever member … has now sketched what one is used to with a waiter in attendance, and what may be expected from the actresses' (see Figures 5.5 and 5.6).[55]

5.4 'The Voteless One'

The League's public and good-humoured mocking of this situation is admirable, and the light touch of the drawings both charming and pointed. Choosing to expose such petty discrimination and embarrass the perpetrator in the press was a bold move and showed that the League was not afraid to challenge and ridicule sexist and illogical ideas. It was also perhaps, in hindsight, an unwelcome glimpse of the wider institutional prejudice the actresses would face when they tried to assert themselves as working women in assisting the war effort just six months later.

February and March saw the League constantly active in performances, rehearsals, demonstrations and meetings. League members took part in a poster parade at the opening of Parliament and a deputation to protest against forcible feeding, sent delegates to conferences on election

5.5 'The Absent Waiter: Wake Me When He Comes'

work and women's work and wages and held a reception for the Northern Men's Federation for Women's Suffrage at Caxton Hall.[56] In April, the League was present at Women's Exhibition Gallery for the Children's Welfare Exhibition in Olympia, where it provided two weeks of performances and entertainments, and in June an *Entertainment and Pageant of Famous Men and Women B.C. 7000–A.D. 2914*, organised by the AFL and WWSL, was presented at the Hotel Cecil.[57] The pageant, arranged by Edith Craig and introduced by Cicely Hamilton, represented internationally famous women throughout history, and over seventy League members and supporters took part. The description of the 'Futurist' section of the June 1914 *Pageant* in the programme gives a tantalising glimpse of the characters presented, including a futurist fury and a mother of the futurists. The optimism of both the AFL and the WWSL is evident in this inclusion of future men and women – another example of

5.6 'The Present Actress'

the playful, ambitious camaraderie created by the political activism of the members of both leagues, and bolstered by the success of the Woman's Theatre project. July saw the AFL providing entertainment to delegates of the Woman Suffrage Alliance, British Dominions Overseas, and the beginning of what would be a three-month presence by the League in the social economy and education section of the Anglo-American Exhibition in White City.[58] Members, including Edith Craig, Decima Moore, Inez Bensusan and Madeleine Lucette Ryley, volunteered to manage the League's stall 'for propaganda work among visitors to the Exhibition' six days a week between 2 July and 19 September, a huge commitment of time and resources.[59] The League also resumed its Hyde Park meetings in July, with members chairing and speaking on Sunday afternoons throughout August and September. With the prospect of a second successful season of the Woman's Theatre, the AFL had every reason to feel confident that its work was moving forward and that 1914 might see hopes of a successful suffrage bill finally come to fruition.

The Women's Emergency Corps

> Aug 4 – All so strange, unreal – wild rumours of naval engagements, ships sunk – the streets as we walked home were full of excited people waving flags ... then the tension – the rumours – the hopes the fear ... and life went on ... the A.F.L. started organizing The Women's Emergency Corps, meetings every day – women came from all over the Country to register for Service, and here the work for Suffrage showed its value – women were organised trained, ready to face dangers.[60]

Two days after the outbreak of the First World War on 4 August 1914, the Women's Emergency Corps (WEC) was founded by Lena Ashwell, Decima Moore, Eva Moore and Eve Haverfield. The WEC was formed to be 'A nucleus of an organisation to co-operate with the authorities without loss of time or energy, without red tape ... to be elastic, unhampered by political or social prejudices, and prepared to undertake any work that should be useful, whatever that work might prove to be.'[61] Within just four days of its existence, *Votes for Women* reported that 2,000 women had volunteered 'to drive motor-cars, to ride or drive horses ... to take care of crèches, of kindergartens, to cook, to sew, speak several foreign languages, or serve in any other way they can suggest'.[62] Quickly outgrowing its first home, Gertrude Kingston's Little Theatre, the WEC headquarters moved to the Old Bedford College on Baker Street in September 1914.[63] By January 1915, the corps had fifteen branches across England and Wales, a branch in Edinburgh in collaboration with the Edinburgh United Suffragists, and eighteen departments including clerical work, housecraft, interpreting, land development, medical and nursing, national food fund, needlework, toy industry and the Women's Volunteer Corps.[64] The Corps organised the teaching of French and German in over forty military centres outside London, and published two booklets of French and German phrases, subtitled 'The Soldiers' "First Aid" to Foreign Languages', for English soldiers abroad.[65] The idea for the phrasebooks had come from H. M. Paull, playwright, novelist, journalist and honorary secretary of the Dramatists Club, whose gently comic suffrage monologue *An Anti-Suffragist; or, The Other Side* had been published by the AFL in 1910. With the Women's Imperial Health Association, the WEC published a wartime directory of societies engaged in war work and briefly opened a shop at 180 Oxford Street in which to sell the goods made in their workshops alongside 'Work done by Women of the Artistic Professions (Painting, Music and Stage)'.[66] The Corps' toy department in particular was a huge success, developing original designs and registering a trademark. The enterprise was widely reported in the press soon after it began:

> At Old Bedford College the Women's Emergency Corps have for the past fortnight opened workrooms for the employment of women in this industry. The results even in that short time have been remarkable, and the big shops like Harrod's, the Army and Navy Stores, Peter Robinson's and Selfridge's have given them large orders. One firm has ordered six gross of one toy alone.[67]

Keen to keep the Corps in the public eye, less than a month after the visit by *The Times* reporter, the WEC workrooms had produced the 'Guy-ser', a figure of the Kaiser to be stuffed with straw and burnt on Guy Fawkes night.[68] The 'Guy-sers' were on sale at WEC public meetings in aid of another AFL satellite project, the Three Arts Employment Fund, as well as at a special stall in Selfridges on Oxford Street from 4–5 November run by members of the WWSL, which was ensuring that articles and news items about the Corps remained in the press.[69] Lena Ashwell told the *Daily Chronicle* that she took 100 'Guy-sers' to Cardiff for a WEC meeting and 'could have sold three or four times that number'.[70] Other caricatures of prominent wartime figures were made from designs by artist W. A. Wildman, and the WEC toy-making department also began working with the curator of the Tower of London Armouries, Charles ffoulkes, to design a wooden model of Henry VII.[71] By February 1915, the number of women working in the toy-making department had grown considerably, with the WEC reporting that there were twenty branches across the UK employing 228 women workers and that the number of girls making toys at Bedford College had grown from twelve to 111 in less than six months.[72] In March 1915, the WEC exhibited its toys at the British Industries Fair, held at the Agricultural Hall in London. *Games and Toys*, the trade journal of the toy industry, described the diverse range of goods at the WEC stand:

> They are specialising in the manufacture of wooden toys, and are turning out in large quantities such lines as Noah's arks, model ambulances, Belgian dog carts, doll's bedsteads, etc. They are also making dolls … Alsatian Peasants, Boulogne Fishwives and toy soldier dolls in khaki uniforms. Other lines they are making in wooden toys are bathing machines, doll's houses, engines, elephants, ducks, Boy Scouts, etc.[73]

They were not alone in representing women's labour at the fair, as the newly formed East London Federation of Suffragettes Toy Factory also had a stand, selling dolls and wooden toys.[74] The WEC drew formal support from thirty different societies, and both national and international support for their work in the press and at public meetings also helped to keep the profile of the organisation high.[75] Relying entirely on donations and the sale of their products to keep going, the WEC was constantly fundraising and promoting its work. The Corps' half-year report, published at the end of January 1915, announced that the executive committee was 'fully aware of the great responsibility it incurs in employing so many women' and included details of a reserve fund amounting to over £900 (over £65,000 in 2015 values) which would be sufficient to pay salaries, wages and running expenses for one month if the WEC should have to close. So successful was its toy-making factory that Lena Ashwell approached Lloyd George to obtain protection from the government for the enterprise in order to secure the continuation of British toy manufacturing after the war was over, but he refused in the interests of free trade.[76] Ashwell was also heavily involved on the executive committee for the corps' land scheme, which aimed to train middle-class women 'in poultry-keeping and market gardening'.[77] The diversity of the provision made by the corps in all areas of industry and the organisation of funds and personnel was exceptional – as novelist and playwright Arnold Bennett noted in an article describing his visit to the WEC headquarters for the *Daily News and Leader* in December 1914.

> On the day of my inspection it had two thousand voluntary helpers, and was employing considerable over 1,000 girls and women on wages who might otherwise have been starving ... It is the medium between intelligent charity and distress, between organisation and the disorganised, between cheerful enterprise and desperate discouragement.[78]

Actresses were personally involved with the work of the WEC alongside their theatre work – Eva Moore recalled spending her days at the Little Theatre and her evenings performing at the Vaudeville Theatre in August 1914 and her sister Decima Moore, who had travelled extensively, ran the interpreting department, sending female interpreters to meet and help refugees from the war upon their arrival in London.[79] Freed from any negative association with the suffrage movement and in spite of the involvement of prominent militant suffragettes such as Emmeline Pethick-Lawrence on its committee, anti-suffragists were as welcome as suffragists to volunteer their services. Perhaps this prompted support from Violet Vanbrugh, who had resigned from the AFL after the Drury Lane meeting of May 1913, to write to *The Times* in January 1915 to appeal for funds for the WEC.[80] The Corps provided a safe space for such reconciliation – united as it was around the war effort and the employment of women, rather than political activism. WEC meetings were frequently held in theatres, utilising the League's contacts and influence. For example, there were simultaneous WEC meetings on 30 October 1914, with Lena Ashwell speaking in Cardiff's City Hall and Eva Moore in the Theatre Royal, Manchester, while on the 9 December 1914, Lady Tree and Emily Pertwee spoke for the WEC in Bournemouth's Theatre Royal while Lena Ashwell and Eva Moore were at the Tyne Theatre, Newcastle.[81] The speed and efficiency with which the WEC began and was run was, like the Woman's Theatre, due to the networks built up by the League.

'Feminist theatre in camouflage'[82]

> I did all I could to be of service in the only way I knew – the theatre way.[83]

There were a number of active charities run by and for the theatrical profession during this period – and a culture of charitable activities attached to venues, managements and individual performers. The AFL joined established theatrical charities such as the Theatrical Ladies Guild and the Actors' Benevolent Fund in financially supporting theatre performers and workers suffering hardship and loss of employment due to the war, administering the *Era* War Distress Fund and the Three Arts Employment Fund which gave work to unemployed theatre professionals.[84] Tours had been cancelled, and 'all the girls who were beginners in the professions – drama, music, painting – were all thrown out of work with no means of making a livelihood'.[85] Applications for help were received by Winifred Mayo at the League's offices on behalf of the *Era* War Distress Fund, and by July 1915, over £1,800 (over £130,000 in 2015 values) had been collected.[86] Mayo appealed to suffragists by reporting some of the requests for help that the League received to raise awareness of the issue in *Votes for Women* in November 1914:

> Miss D. C. – A girl of 22, deserted by her husband, in pitiful health ... Has been offered work in a laundry, for which she is totally unfitted ... she is being placed in comfort in the country till the pantomime season comes round, when it is hoped an engagement may be found for her.
>
> H. F. – A worker in the property department of a London theatre now closed; has a wife and four little boys under 10. He is in wretched health ...

> Our visitor found them with bare bedstead and no bedding left – all were in pawn.
>
> R. K. – has a husband who works as advance agent for touring companies; there are six little children. The husband has now enlisted … but back debts press heavily on them. We were able to take out of pawn all her blankets and the warm clothing of the children 'put away' in the warmer weather.[87]

The precarious financial situation faced by unemployed theatre workers meant that few performers could afford to donate their time for the suffrage cause as freely – if at all – as they had done before the commencement of war. The distress and financial hardship described in Mayo's report was taken into account when the AFL agreed to provide the entertainments at the United Suffragists Christmas Sale, held at the Eustace Miles restaurant on 4 December 1914. A special appeal was made in the pages of *Votes for Women* for donations for the performers:

> We appeal to our readers to remember the many services rendered to the cause by these most generous members of a generous profession, and now that the war has brought them within sight of destitution, to enable us to help a few of them in their hour of heed by sending us special donations with which to pay their fees at the Christmas Sale.[88]

The AFL continued to take part in suffrage meetings after the outbreak of war and maintained a presence at important exhibitions and demonstrations, including the United Suffragists Christmas Sale in 1914 and 1915 and the Women and Army Work Exhibition held in Caxton Hall in May 1915. Gertrude Elliott represented the Actresses' Franchise League in a 1917 women's suffrage deputation to Prime Minister Lloyd George, along with over 80 suffrage campaigners including Millicent Garrett Fawcett and Emmeline Pankhurst. League members were directly involved in the day-to-day life of British and Allied military personnel through a number of different projects, two of which were the YMCA (Young Men's Christian Association) Shakespeare Hut in Bloomsbury and the Endell Street military hospital in Covent Garden. The Shakespeare Hut, a large collection of mock-Tudor buildings, was erected in land on the corner of Keppel Street and Gower Street that had been bought by the Shakespeare Memorial National Theatre Committee in 1914. Intended to be the site of a monument to celebrate Shakespeare's tercentenary and eventually to be the location of a new national theatre, the land had been offered to the YMCA in 1916 by Israel Gollancz as a contribution to the war effort. The Hut, which included a dedicated theatre space, was built for the use of Australian and New Zealand Army Corps soldiers on leave in London.

Gertrude Elliott and Johnston Forbes-Robertson, whose Bedford Square residence was very close to the Hut, were both heavily involved in its drama and music committee and garnered support from suffragist and theatrical colleagues alike in programming and producing the entertainments at the Hut, which often were mixed bills of music, recitations and one-act plays by suffragist playwrights including J. M. Barrie, Evelyn Glover and Gertrude Jennings.[89] The military hospital on Endell Street was found in 1915 by Dr Flora Murray and Dr Louise Garrett Anderson, both former members of the WSPU, and was unique in being an official military hospital funded by the army and administered and staffed entirely by women. The hospital was proudly suffragist and militant and bore the WSPU motto 'Deeds Not Words'. With over 500 beds on site, the hospital was busy from the moment it opened and catered to patients' psychological as well as medical needs, boasting a library, gardeners, sports days and a huge variety of entertainments.[90] AFL and WWSL members were involved as volunteers, with Beatrice Harraden and Elizabeth Robins as librarian and assistant librarian, and Inez Bensusan, Bessie Hatton, Liza Lehmann and May Whitty on the entertainment committee.[91] Harraden, in an article for the *Windsor* magazine praising the work of female medics, ambulance workers and support staff in wartime, described the Endell Street hospital as a place where 'the men are looked after … with the greatest skill and devotion … everything is done by the whole staff to make them happy, and to maintain a homelike and cheery atmosphere, which greatly helps in their recuperation'.[92]

Members of the League were involved with public fundraising for a number of different military and civilian societies and charities throughout the war years, at home and abroad. One example, 'Lamp Day', was held on 12 May 1916 to commemorate Florence Nightingale's birthday and to raise funds for organisations including the WEC, the Women's Service Bureau and the British Women's Hospital. Six thousand women were reported as being in central London selling small cardboard lamps at 1d, 3d and 1s each. Nina Boucicault, Gertrude Kingston, Janette Steer and May Whitty were stationed outside the Star and Garter Fund offices in Bond Street while Lilian Braithwaite, Gladys Cooper and Marie Lohr were in Harrods.[93] Some League members found the experience difficult. Gertrude Kingston wrote an article in the *Daily Mail* entitled 'Never Again' about her experience, describing the positive and negative reactions of the public and asserting that taking part was worse than 'the horrors of a first performance of a new play to an actor', while May Whitty's daughter Margaret Webster disliked the public visibility of street fundraising but later conceded that 'it was good training in making contact with your audience'.[94] The League maintained a positive public presence, becoming involved with fundraising events throughout the war for societies including the Young Women's Christian Association and the Women's Army Auxiliary Corps. These organisations joined many others in the 'complex range of visible and invisible charity work undertaken by actresses during the First World War', and, as Catherine Hindson has explored, their success and versatility changed and challenged ideas about the function and value of performance and performers.[95] Without government support, the League's projects relied on sponsorship, gifts in kind, fundraising and appeals to those in positions of power and influence. Unhindered by pre-war debates around the effectiveness or appropriateness of suffragette militancy, the League's many wartime projects had titled ladies as founders, members and patrons – the beginning of formal connections with the upper classes that would be maintained and go on to characterise much of their later charitable work.

The Woman's Theatre during wartime

The war interrupted plans for the second season of the Woman's Theatre, which had been scheduled to run from 30 November to 5 December at the Coronet Theatre. Cicely Hamilton was commissioned to adapt Elizabeth Robins' novel about white slave-trafficking *Where Are You Going To?* into a play for the Woman's Theatre, but it was refused a licence by the Lord Chamberlain after some debate about the appropriateness of a scene set in a brothel. Letters from and to the censor's office regarding the play reveal that it was actually refused a licence because of the controversy surrounding George Bernard Shaw's play, *Mrs Warren's Profession*, which had been refused a licence in 1894 and would not be licenced until 1925. Squire Bancroft, when consulted about *Where Are You Going To?* wrote 'I fail to see how The Lord Chamberlain can grant his licence to the second act of this play and refuse it to "Mrs. Warren's Profession".'[96] Incensed by the prevarication – the piece had originally been recommended for licence – Bensusan wrote to the censor asking for the refund of the licence fee, but her request was refused.[97] Perhaps due to this setback as well as to availability of artists, just two months before the event the League announced that the programme would consist of short plays and 'other interesting events constituting what is described as a "high-class variety entertainment"' – an announcement that Katharine Kelly describes as a 'masterful understatement'.⁹⁸ Despite the change of plans, the League declared that:

> The programme will include 'stars' from the theatrical, musical, and music-hall professions on a scale that has never before been presented. These are giving their services, that the rank and file may be paid.⁹⁹

Unfortunately, the second season of the Woman's Theatre was cancelled a month before it was due to start. Citing 'the darkening of the streets and stricter regulations regarding traffic', the committee postponed the variety week until the New Year, assuring shareholders that their shares would be taken forward.¹⁰⁰ Although the Woman's Theatre season would be further delayed, the organisation did not disappear from the AFL's portfolio and, like the League, adapted and diversified according to the changing environment brought about by the war. The Woman's Theatre produced war relief matinees in June 1915 at the London Pavilion consisting of the 'high class variety entertainment' intended for the second season of Woman's Theatre Week.¹⁰¹ Wide support from the theatrical community made the 1915 Women's Theatre matinees reminiscent of the entertainments programmed and presented by the League for the 1909 Women's Exhibition, and there were sixty listed acts – sketches, short plays, dances, music, recitations and monologues all with 'a distinct whiff of feminism'.¹⁰² True to the aims of the Woman's Theatre, there was also a large female backstage team. The first performance featured appearances from May Whitty, Lilian Braithwaite and Louie Pounds alongside a scene from the London Pavilion's 'Moulin Rouge' revue, Madge Titheradge reciting Victor Hugo and dances from 'Little June, from the Empire'.¹⁰³ The second matinee, in aid of the WEC, included an appearance from Hilda Bewicke, one of Diaghilev's English dancers at the Ballets Russes who had performed at the 1909 Women's Exhibition, and acting and recitations from Eva Moore, Nigel Playfair, May Whitty and Godfrey Tearle.¹⁰⁴ Bensusan's description of the Woman's Theatre in the 1915 programme was slightly altered from the original in 1913, although the aims for the organisation remained consistent. A notable addition is the reference to the general advisory committee as 'representative of all shades of political, social and economic thought' and the introduction of the Woman's Theatre Camps Entertainment project to support the war effort, intending that it should 'fulfil the dual service of offering distraction for the troops in camp, and of providing an avenue of employment for artists'.[105] A souvenir programme was produced featuring essays in support of the work of the Woman's Theatre Camps Entertainments, and Elizabeth Robins' essay 'In The Front Row' celebrated the success of the Woman's Theatre in wartime and the transforming power of theatre among wounded troops.

> The closer we women come to the realities of war, the better we understand the function of the theatre in such times as these ... Not for this was the Woman's Theatre founded, but the Woman's Theatre has taken up with energy and marked success its rightful share in war service.[106]

The League's president, Gertrude Elliott, became president of the Women's Theatre Camps Entertainments which gave its first performance at

5.7 The Woman's Theatre Camps Entertainments logo

Aldershot on 6 November 1914.[107] The years 1915 and 1916 saw demand for the League's suffrage propaganda fall, but its war work flourished, with the Woman's Theatre Camps Entertainments giving 300 entertainments in 1915 and over 630 entertainments the following year in clubs, huts, hospitals and camps (see Figure 5.7).[108] Averaging six to eight concerts per week, the League employed 451 artists over this period.[109] Bensusan was excited by this new addition to the League's portfolio, seeing 'no reason why this Emergency work should not crystallize into a permanent activity' and regarding the continued success of the venture as further proof of the potential efficacy of her idea of a woman's theatre.[110] The all-female backstage teams pioneered by the AFL and the Woman's Theatre had encouraged women to be involved in the physical labour and creative industry of backstage work, and League members and supporters seem to have embraced this where possible. Lena Ashwell's decision to employ women as backstage staff at the Kingsway Theatre in 1915 was reported in the press as not only pragmatic, given the shortage of men available due to the war, but as a feminist action. *The Times* announced that, 'There will be a woman stage manager, a woman assistant stage manager, and a woman property "man". The limelights will be worked by women who have been coached by the electrician, and there will be women scene-shifters and an orchestra composed of women' describing it as 'an interesting development of the woman's theatre movement'.[111] Johnston Forbes-Robertson employed a female business manager, Dora Fellowes Robinson, and a female stage manager, Ethel Griffiths, for his production of *The Passing of the Third Floor Back* at the Playhouse in 1917, with the *Evening Standard* noting the latter as a 'novel and remarkable feature' of the run.[112]

The Woman's Theatre remained active, giving three matinees of new plays at the Margaret Morris Theatre in Chelsea from 28 February to 1 March 1916.[113] The owner of the theatre, dancer Margaret Morris, was an AFL member. True to their original aims, the organisation and production was done entirely by women.[114] Other activities included a fundraising matinee tea for the Woman's Theatre Camp Entertainments held in conjunction with the Women's Reserve Ambulance at the Piccadilly Hotel on 23 May 1916, attended by the League's most prominent members, including Gertrude Elliott, Lilian Braithwaite, Lillah McCarthy, May Whitty and Lady Wyndham.[115] The AFL organised an entertainment in Sunderland House under the banner of the Woman's Theatre on 27 June 1916 in aid of the Patriotic Thrift Campaign of the National Food Reform Association. The programme included *A War Committee* by Edward Knoblauch and *The Meeting* by Robert Ganthony with Lady

Tree, Lottie Venne, May Whitty and Ben Webster among the cast.[116] *A War Committee* had first been produced at the Haymarket Theatre on 2 July 1915 and mocked the formation of committees of women wanting to do war relief service and the hierarchies, self-interest and hypocrisy of do-gooders. The piece was dedicated by Knoblauch to 'Lady Muriel Paget, whose committees give this committee the lie'.[117] As in many of the most popular suffrage plays, the negative stereotypes of women in the piece were tackled directly by the involvement of a cast for the original production that included League members Jean Cadell, Lilian Braithwaite and Sydney Fairbrother, all of whom subsequently appeared in the piece for the Sunderland House Entertainment. Knoblauch donated *A War Committee* to the League's entertainment committee in May 1916.[118] The last known performance of the Woman's Theatre Camps Entertainments was on 31 July 1917 at the Gables Theatre in Surbiton. The performance was typically eclectic, featuring storytelling, short plays, songs and music recitals with a cast that included Inez Bensusan, May Whitty and Ben Webster. The programme for the performance proudly stated that over the first six months of 1917, 426 concerts had been given by the Woman's Theatre Camps Entertainments.[119]

The Woman's Theatre project was a bold, pragmatic and impressive undertaking, with a wide-ranging and ambitious strategy designed to maximise success and to make an enduring change in the way women could participate in professional theatre. Katharine Kelly's view that the project was 'both more focused and potentially more effective than the feminist movement had been to date at creating change in the theatre' is supported by not only the stated aims of the Woman's Theatre but also the opportunities the Woman's Theatre Camps Entertainments gave to performers to develop and showcase their own work, but does not consider the effect of the many small gains made by actors and actresses in their dedicated work for the suffrage cause before 1913.[120] Without these experiences, it is unlikely that such a scheme would have received the financial backing it needed. The Woman's Theatre had proved a financial success, but the Woman's Theatre Camps Entertainments were a 'considerable achievement both in administrative and artistic terms', backed as they were by fundraising events and the generosity of supporters.[121]

The British Women's Hospital

The British Women's Hospital Fund was formed in July 1915 and was based at the AFL's offices at 2 Robert Street.[122] Run by a subcommittee of the League that was only open to AFL members, the purpose of the fund was initially to raise the monies to found and maintain a British women's hospital unit that could provide care for wounded soldiers in the UK and in France.[123] The minute books of the committee show that support for the project gathered quickly and that the League's existing contacts and networks were used extensively to seek public and press backing for the idea. Securing Dr Flora Murray from the Endell Street hospital on the medical committee and an extensive list of titled women as patrons of the fund, the governing committee liaised with Edith Craig and the Pioneer Players, the WEC, publishers, politicians and theatre managers to arrange public meetings and fundraising opportunities. The subcommittee asked a number of leading performers including Cicely Courtneidge and Matheson Lang to mention the British Women's Hospital to the press during provincial tours, and the League held a poster parade in the West End on 25 September 1915.[124] The parade included the uniformed Girls' Band of the Church Nursing and Ambulance Brigade and was reported widely in the national press.[125] Postponing the project to set up a French hospital unit, the British Women's Hospital committee instead directed its resources to raising £50,000 to refurbish the Star and Garter Hotel in Richmond and turn it into a respite home for disabled soldiers and sailors that could then be given to the Red Cross (see Figure 5.8). Queen Mary became patroness of the new Star and Garter Building Fund, and the offices moved to a larger space in Bond Street.[126] Women's organisations from all around the world contributed to the Star and Garter Fund, and the lists of gifts given and wards, rooms and beds endowed shows how broad support for the project was – including girls' schools, suffrage organisations, clubs, groups of British women overseas, peers, military societies, and other wartime charities. In recognition that 'the British Women's Hospital Committee had its origin in the Actresses' Franchise League', a special room bearing the name of the League was built and equipped.[127] League members were unafraid to appeal directly for help to potential female supporters on feminist, suffragist, theatrical and patriotic grounds. Adeline Bourne wrote to Maud Arncliffe Sennett on 27 October 1915 to ask her to speak on behalf of the British Women's Hospital, candid about the outcome she wanted: 'It is really a recruiting meeting, the subject to stir them is Edith Cavell.' Cavell, a nurse stationed in Brussels, had been shot at dawn by the German army on 12 October for assisting the escape of allied soldiers. International protests had followed her arrest and execution, and her story and memory were potent with patriotic and moral

5.8 'Haven'

power. Bourne reported that the committee of the British Women's Hospital had decided that to 'associate and perpetuate' the name of Edith Cavell at the Star and Garter Home, and they should raise funds to name a wing of the building after her.[128] An appeal was duly made in the press, and Bourne publicly sought and gained the approval of Edith Cavell's sister for the campaign.[129] The British Women's Hospital Fund to restore and rebuild the Star and Garter Home was one of the League's most successful ventures, and by November 1916, £150,000 had been raised – three times the amount initially sought. A second home was acquired in Sandgate, Kent, for the injured men to be housed while the Richmond home was being refurbished, and, by 1919, nearly £224,000 had been raised for the homes through the British Women's Hospital committee, equivalent to £10 million in 2015 values. The committee also raised funds for the Scottish Women's Hospitals and the Lord Roberts Memorial Fund, and set up the Nation's Fund for Nurses. League members were at the heart of all these initiatives and helped to organise performances and events.

In June 1916, the British Women's Hospital organised a star-studded matinee performance at the London Coliseum. Produced by Lillah McCarthy, the matinee was well supported by the theatre industry, with over sixty performers, including Adeline Genée, Nigel Playfair and Gertrude Kingston, volunteering to sell programmes in the auditorium.[130] The programme featured musical performances, a full production of J. M. Barrie's *The Admirable Crichton*, and four topical comic sketches also by Barrie.[131] These sketches, collectively called *Irene Vanburgh's Pantomime*, included duologues for Johnston Forbes-Robertson and Gertrude Elliott, and Irene Vanbrugh and Lilian Braithwaite, and a monologue for Mrs Patrick Campbell.[132] A special souvenir edition of *The Admirable Crichton* was published by Hodder & Stoughton to be sold in aid of the fund. Other entertainments held for the British Women's Hospital include concerts, revues, swimming galas and fairs, and actress Lily Elsie donated her entire salary for appearing as the title role in *Mavourneen* at His Majesty's Theatre in 1915–16.[133] Johnston Forbes-Robertson came out of retirement to appear in a successful charity matinee performance of *The Passing of the Third Floor Back* in March 1917 at the Coliseum, and the play transferred to the Playhouse for a three-week run, with the proceeds going in full to the Scottish Women's Hospitals.[134] The cast, who all appeared voluntarily for eight shows a week, included Elliott and Whitty. This generosity was matched by Frank Curzon, who lent the Playhouse for free for the run and Jerome K. Jerome who waived his author's fee.[135] At the matinee performance on the 18 April 1917 many performers including Eva Moore and Adeline Genée worked as programme-sellers inside the auditorium alongside the daughter of the prime minister, Elizabeth Asquith, who was by then on the committee of the British Women's Hospital.[136] In total, the funds raised by the British Women's Hospital Committee in four and a half years were nearly £390,000, equivalent to over £16 million in 2015 values.

No women need apply

> If women counted in this country as they will count some day when the State recognises them, the work of the WEC would have been more widely acknowledged, and, we think, also more effective. As it stands, it is one more evidence of the absurdity of denying citizenship to women.[137]

What becomes evident in the few first-hand accounts of the League's wartime work from those involved is the difficulties women faced when wanting to assist the government war effort. Initially, the voluntary work by women was barely acknowledged, financially unsupported and undervalued by the very organisations the League was trying to help (see Figure 5.9).

Lena Ashwell remembered that 'Weekly lists were sent to the War Office, containing full particulars as to the numbers of women we could supply for transport, cooks, interpreters, and so forth; and each week a letter was received in acknowledgement, saying that women "were not needed".'[138] Decima Moore verified this in a letter to *The Times* in 1938: 'The Army Council had not at that time risen so far as to visualize the immense value of the use of such a body of women.'[139] The WEC saw this as 'ludicrous and shameful', noting that the home secretary had refused the services of women interpreters and the offer of:

> twenty-five women motor-cyclists, able to repair their own and other people's machines, has been similarly neglected. And how about the post-office work, the ticket-selling, the express-message carrying, and other useful and necessary employments that are now suspended or working short? Women could carry them on just as well as men, while men are in the field. But 'No women need apply' has been this narrow-minded Government's rule, whether for votes or anything else.[140]

Despite the willingness of taxicab owners in London to let women drive their cabs, Scotland Yard refused to license them, stating that women could not handle luggage and would be 'exposed to unpleasant experiences at night'. Unusually, the *Daily Mail* was on the side of the women in this matter:

5.9 'How Much More Effective My Work Would Be If My Hands Were Unfettered!'

> If Scotland Yard would sanction the experiment, a plentiful supply of women, trained drivers and well disciplined, could be obtained through such bodies of hard working, patriotic women as the Women's Emergency Corps ... These bodies have already offered to come to the aid of the cab companies and the public, but the police say 'No'.[141]

This exposure in the press did not create change. It would be sixty-one years until, in 1977, the first female taxi driver, Marie White, was licenced in London.[142] League members also became directly involved in war work outside of their theatre-related projects – for example, Cicely Hamilton spent most of the war working for the Scottish Women's Hospitals in France; Adeline Bourne served overseas as an officer in Queen Mary's Army Auxiliary Corps and worked as an acting paymaster in the War Office; Decima Moore helped run the Army and Navy Leave Club in Paris; while Olga Nethersole joined the Voluntary Aid Detachment and nursed at Hampstead military hospital, later founding the People's League of Health in 1917.[143] It is admirable that League members persisted in their efforts despite the dismissive attitude of the organisations they were trying to help. May Whitty described the Red Cross as 'very prejudiced against women's work', but the undeniable success and royal patronage of the British Women's Hospital committee in restoring the Star and Garter Home led to an invitation for her and Lady Cowdray, as chairman and treasurer of the fund, to join the previously all male Red Cross committee of the Star and Garter, and Whitty later became the first actress to receive a damehood when the Red Cross recommended her for a DBE (Dame Commander of the Order of the British Empire) in 1918.[144] Before 1914, only 58% of men had the vote. By 1916 it had become clear that the next general election could not use the pre-war electoral register, as many men on military service had been out of the country too long to meet the residency qualifications. There was also a strong feeling among politicians on all sides that previously unenfranchised men who had been conscripted into the forces or otherwise contributed to the war effort deserved the vote. A cross-party conference of thirty-two MPs and Peers was formed to discuss electoral reform. Women's suffrage campaigners saw their opportunity and lobbied politicians extensively. Concerned about enfranchising too many women by giving them the vote on the same terms as men, in January 1917 the conference recommended that an age limit of thirty or thirty-five be set and left the House of Commons to debate which. Two months later Gertrude Elliott, representing the Actresses' Franchise League, took part in a deputation to the prime minister. Led by Millicent Garrett Fawcett, the deputation included Emmeline Pankhurst, Charlotte Despard, Eleanor Rathbone and over eighty women representing thirty-three suffrage societies. Garrett Fawcett made it clear to the prime minister Lloyd George that the deputation was against the age bar and was asking for the equal franchise for all women, but that they were prepared to compromise in order that the principal of votes for women, even some women, would be established. Lloyd George said in response that he considered the proposed age bar for women 'illogical' and 'unjustifiable'. However he advised the deputation not to challenge the recommendations, warning that if calls were made for votes for women on the same terms as men there was likely to be opposition from anti-suffragist MPs.[145] The WEC was formally disbanded in November 1919, a year after the First World War ended, having been the foundation organisation for a number of other groups including the Women's Volunteer Reserve. With so many League members heavily involved in wartime work at home and abroad, celebrations of the limited franchise in the form of the Representation of the People Act in Feburary 1918 were muted, and many actresses over the age of thirty remained ineligible to vote because they did not meet the property and marital-status qualifications.[146] The fight for the equal franchise was still to be won, and the AFL was determined to continue campaigning.

Almost without exception, scholarship on the work of the AFL by suffrage and theatre historians has focused on the years before 1914.[147] This does both the suffrage and theatrical history a disservice and almost by default implies that suffragist networks in the theatrical profession ceased to be formally politically active and integrated after the start of the First World War. It is true that the outbreak of war and the division and refocusing of both militant and constitutional suffrage societies from August 1914 slowed down what had become an increasingly crammed schedule of performances, meetings and appearances by League members, but actresses continued to campaign for women's suffrage as well as social and economic issues that affected working women. Academic analyses of the wartime work of the League are rare perhaps due to the scarcity, and sometimes the obscurity, of archival material available. From the documents that have survived, it is clear that emboldened and empowered by their experiences before the outbreak of the First World War, the actresses and the League developed projects, founded organisations and extended networks in wartime to further their work and foster new collaborations with activists across social and political boundaries.

After the war: women, citizens and artists

Both the AFL and the Woman's Theatre were listed in the *Era* Annual of 1919, with the entry for the latter brimming with optimism for the future:

> This organisation owes its inception to the Actresses' Franchise League. Its aims are to present plays which truthfully set forth the woman's point

of view: to provide a new outlet for the energies of the women members of the theatrical professions; and to help forward the woman's movement to enfranchisement.[148]

On 20 June 1919, the League met at the St James's Theatre to discuss 'The Artist's Place in Reconstruction'. May Whitty chaired the meeting, saying that despite their wartime projects, the organisation 'had not lost sight of the fact that the League was a suffrage society first and foremost. They were very much alive and kicking, as of old, against injustice and inequality, and trying to better conditions.'[149] Maud Arncliffe Sennett reiterated Whitty's comments, saying that 'they had not got complete equality of the sexes either in Parliament or out of it, and until they did she could not believe there would be a really settled world'.[150] Sir Frank Benson also spoke, describing the League as 'being composed of women, citizens and artists' and emphasising its continued constitutional work for the suffrage cause, which he referred to as 'a great crusade'.[151] The 1920s saw the AFL continue the 'great crusade' for the vote as well as remaining active in social, political and theatrical initiatives. In 1921, a number of League members and supporters joined the Six Point Group, a non-party political organisation founded by Lady Rhondda to establish equality for women. The executive committee, social committee and vice presidents of the Six Point Group included Clemence Dane, Eva Moore, Elizabeth Robins, Nina Boucicault, Una Dugdale and Ethel Smyth, with Winifred Mayo as the organising secretary, and Cicely Hamilton, Christopher St. John and Elizabeth Robins were among the regular contributors to the weekly magazine *Time and Tide*, also founded by Lady Rhondda.[152] The Six Point Group was one of the forty-nine societies affiliated to the Consultative Committee of Women's Organisations, first formed in 1916 by the NUWSS and then reorganised by Lady Astor in 1921 to promote 'networking ... among women activists and politicians, seeking to draw women into the normal processes of political lobbying'.[153] The Six Point Group and the AFL continued to share membership and fundraising opportunities as well as build on the success of the League's networks. During the fifth annual meeting of the Consultative Committee of Women's Organisations, Winifred Mayo announced that the AFL would be giving half the funds raised by its 1926 December birthday party to the committee.[154] Held at the Hyde Park Hotel, the twenty-three hostesses at the event included Madge Kendal, Gertrude Elliott, May Whitty, Decima Moore, Inez Bensusan, Clara Butt and Gladys Cooper.[155]

The League continued to campaign alongside other suffrage societies, appearing at large events including the Women's Equal Political Rights procession on 3 July 1926.[156] The demands of the procession were for an immediate government measure giving votes to women at twenty-one on the same terms as men, and for peeresses to have in their own right a seat, voice, and vote in the House of Lords. The AFL, 'under the patronage of Miss Ellen Terry and Miss Lillah McCarthy' was one of forty societies that marched from Charing Cross to Hyde Park, and was represented by Maud Arncliffe Sennett, Inez Bensusan, Winifred Mayo, and Adeline Bourne, among others, all dressed in the League's colours of pink and green.[157] Actor, writer and playwright Arthur Applin marched with the League alongside WWSL member Margaret Nevinson, who had spoken on the WFL platform when the meeting began in Hyde Park to champion 'the cause of the professional woman under 30, who had not only qualified for a profession, but was frequently married as well, with husband, children, and home to manage'.[158] The *Manchester Guardian* recognised the League, 'remembering that since they marched in the last great procession they had set going the schemes of service that led to the wide development and organisation of women's war work'.[159] A year later, the League was signatory to a letter from Lady Rhondda – who had first petitioned in 1920 for the right to take her place as a hereditary peer in the House of Lords, based on the Sex Disqualification (Removal) Act 1919[160] – on behalf of the Equal Political Rights Campaign Committee to the government to demand that Votes for Women at the age of twenty-one be included in the king's speech at the opening of Parliament in 1927.[161] Again the suffrage societies joined to show support for the Equal Franchise Bill, and the WFL held a mass demonstration in Trafalgar Square in July 1927 calling on the government to pass an equal franchise measure 'so as to ensure the inclusion of the new women voters ... in time to vote at the next General Election'.[162] Adeline Bourne represented the AFL and spoke to remind her audience 'that, before the war, people were full of reasons against giving women the vote; after the war, no one could find any reasons against'.[163]

Alongside members of the WFL, the NUWSS and WSPU, May Whitty, Decima and Eva Moore and Edyth Olive represented the AFL at Emmeline Pankhurst's funeral, held in St John's Church, Westminster on 18 June 1928.[164] The Equal Franchise Bill was passed a month later,[165] and the AFL were part of the evening victory reception of the Equal Political Rights Campaign Committee on 24 October 1928 at Caxton Hall. Nearly twenty years after its original production, Winifred Mayo and Kitty Willoughby produced *How the Vote Was Won* at the victory reception, 'with some members of the original cast and in the fashion of 1908', the last known performance of a pre-war suffrage play by the League.[166] The first general election at which women could equally vote with men was held in May 1929. In September of that year, Sybil Thorndike was the guest of honour at a reception held by the Edinburgh National Society for Equal Citizenship. Speaking of the campaign for the vote, she urged younger women to use the opportunities won for them wisely and for the good of society.[167]

During the years between the outbreak of the First World War and the passing of the Equal Franchise Bill, the League supported female-led initiatives and put the ideas of its members into action on new and distinguished stages at home and abroad, claiming and producing new roles and spaces for women's work, voices and skills. The Woman's Theatre and the Woman's Theatre Camps Entertainments had created discussion and action around the role of women in professional theatre and kept a feminist and suffragist presence and visibility throughout wartime work, while the WEC and the British Women's Hospital Committee worked collaboratively and creatively inside and outside of the theatre industry, giving women the opportunity to develop and run large-scale projects. After 1928, the AFL continued to open up new opportunities for actresses and female theatre professionals to become involved in political and feminist activism by extending its work as an organisation across a diverse portfolio of social, political and philanthropic projects. The next chapter explores the work of the League in the 1920s and 1930s, during and after the Second World War, and the legacy of half a century of activism, political campaigning and collaboration.

Notes

1 AFL, *Annual Report June 1912–June 1913*, p. 5.
2 The plays were *The Iron Law* by Ruth Young, which tackled unequal wages; *Two of the Odd Boys* by Winifred St Clair, in which a young woman impersonates her brother; and *Ten Shillings* by Hilda C. Adshead in which the effects of the financial inequalities faced by a number of women are explored.
3 For example, Edith Craig's Pioneer Players; the New Players' Society of which Adeline Bourne was honorary secretary; the Jewish Drama League, the Play Actors, the Incorporated Play Society, and the Oncomers' Society.
4 T. C. Davis, 'Management and the structures of industrial capitalism', in M. R. Booth and J. H. Kaplan (eds.), *The Edwardian Theatre: Essays on Performance and the Stage* (Cambridge: Cambridge University Press, 2008), pp. 111–29, at p. 113.

5 Davis, 'Management and the structures of industrial capitalism', p. 115.
6 Davis, 'Management and the structures of industrial capitalism', p. 118.
7 Davis, 'Management and the structures of industrial capitalism', p. 126.
8 *Votes for Women*, 23 May 1913, p. 498.
9 J. Holledge, 'Innocent flowers no more: the changing status of women in theatre', in L. Goodman (ed.), *The Routledge Reader in Gender and Performance* (London and New York: Routledge, 1998), pp. 92–6, at p. 95.
10 *Boston Evening Transcript*, 3 December 1913, p. 27.
11 *Boston Evening Transcript*, 3 December 1913, p. 27.
12 *The Stage*, 21 August 1913, p. 18.
13 Women's Theatre Week programme, p. 7, Museum of London.
14 J. Templeton, *Ibsen's Women* (Cambridge: Cambridge University Press, 1997), p. 41.
15 The volume was *Digte af en dame* (Bergen: E. B. Giertsen, 1860).
16 *New York Times*, 5 January 1896.
17 *Meriden Daily Republican*, 5 October 1897.
18 C. Beach, *Staging Politics and Gender: French Women's Drama, 1880–1923* (New York: Palgrave Macmillan, 2005), pp. 19–23.
19 *Lewiston Daily Sun*, 14 April 1902, p. 3.
20 *New York Dramatic Mirror*, 26 April 1902, p. 17.
21 *Lincoln Evening News*, 15 January 1903, quoted in C. Del Valle, *The Brooklyn Theatre Index*, vol. I (New York: Theatre Talks, 2010), p. 325.
22 *Jus Suffragii*, 1 October 1913.
23 K. E. Kelly, 'The Actresses' Franchise League prepares for war: feminist theatre in camouflage', *Theatre Survey*, 35:1 (1994), 121–37, at p. 124; E. Marbury, *My Crystal Ball* (New York: Boni and Liveright, 1923), chapter 23.
24 *Boston Evening Transcript*, 18 March 1912.
25 Marbury, *My Crystal Ball*, chapter 30; *Boston Evening Transcript*, 18 March 1912.
26 *New York Times*, 18 April 1912.
27 T. L. Compton, *The Rise of the Woman Director on Broadway, 1920–1950* (Santa Barbara, CA: University of California, 1970), p. 60.
28 *New York Times*, 16 March 1909.
29 *New York Evening Post*, 10 May 1913, p. 1.
30 *Lewiston Daily Sun*, 14 April 1902, p. 3.
31 *New York Times*, 18 April 1912; *New York Clipper*, 22 February 1913, p. 8; *New York Evening Post*, 10 May 1913, p. 1; *New York Clipper*, 22 February 1913, p. 8.
32 *Star*, 12 December 1896, p. 3. This project became the Kvindernes Bygning, or Women's Building, which opened in Copenhagen in 1936.
33 AFL, *Accounts, June 1910–June 1911; June 1911–May 1912; June 1912–May 1913*.
34 *Votes for Women*, 17 April 1914, lists a number of large businesses in which supporters are urged to do their shopping, including Selfridges, Dickens & Jones, Heal & Son, Waring & Gillow, Debenhams, Harvey Nichols & Co, Jaeger's and Peter Robinson.

35 J. Bratton, *The Making of the West End Stage* (Cambridge: Cambridge University Press, 2011), p. 104.
36 Bratton, *The Making of the West End Stage*, p. 105.
37 Bratton, *The Making of the West End Stage*, p. 105.
38 Bratton, *The Making of the West End Stage*, p. 105.
39 G. B. Shaw, 'Preface', in *Three Plays by Brieux* (London: A. C. Fifield, 1911).
40 *Athenaeum*, 22 February 1913, p. 228.
41 M. Wallis, 'Social commitment and aesthetic experiment, 1895–1946', in B. Kershaw (ed.), *The Cambridge History of British Theatre* (Cambridge: Cambridge University Press, 2008), pp. 167–94, at p. 171.
42 Kelly, *The Actresses' Franchise League Prepares*, p. 125.
43 C. Hamilton, 'The woman's theatre: what it means', *Woman's Theatre Week Programme*, pp. 16–17.
44 Hamilton, 'The woman's theatre', p. 16.
45 F. A. Steel, 'An outside impression', *Woman's Theatre Week Programme*, pp. 20–1.
46 *Woman's Theatre Week Programme*, p. 29.
47 AFL, *Secretary's Report 1914*.
48 *Votes for Women*, 2 January 1914, p. 211.
49 Lena Ashwell was a committee member, and the vice presidents included Maud Arncliffe Sennett, Beatrice Harraden, Charlotte Shaw, Ben Webster, May Whitty, St John Ervine and Laurence Housman. *Votes for Women*, 6 February 1914, p. 281.
50 E. Crawford, *The Women's Suffrage Movement: A Reference Guide, 1866–1928* (London and New York: Routledge, 2001), p. 694.
51 *Votes for Women*, 23 January 1914, p. 255.
52 *Votes for Women*, 23 January 1914, p. 255.
53 *Daily News and Leader*, 19 January 1914, p. 3.
54 *Daily News and Leader*, 22 January 1914, p. 7.
55 *Votes for Women*, 30 January 1914, p. 275.
56 *Votes for Women*, 13 February 1914, p. 307; May Whitty Diaries, Margaret Webster Papers, Library of Congress; AFL, *Annual Report, June 1913–June 1914*, p. 9; *Votes for Women*, 6 February 1914, p. 291.
57 Programme for *Entertainment and Pageant of Famous Men and Women*, 29 June 1914, Bristol Theatre Collection.
58 *Votes for Women*, 17 July 1913, p. 650.
59 AFL, *Annual Report, June 1913–June 1914*, p. 11; *Votes for Women*, 10 July 1914, p. 638; 17 July 1914, p. 650.
60 May Whitty Diaries, Library of Congress.
61 *WEC Half Yearly Report*, January 1915, p. 3, British Library.
62 *Votes for Women*, 14 August 1914, p. 692.
63 *WEC Half Yearly Report*, p. 22.
64 *WEC Half Yearly Report*, p. 18.
65 *WEC Half Yearly Report*, p. 14.

66 *The Lancet*, 24 June 1916, p. 1282; leaflet advertising the WEC shop, c. 1914.
67 *The Times*, 3 October 1914, p. 11.
68 *Daily Chronicle*, 3 November 1914.
69 *The Ladies' Field Supplement*, 21 November 1914.
70 *The Ladies' Field Supplement*, 21 November 1914.
71 *Pall Mall*, 30 October 1914.
72 *WEC Half Yearly Report*, pp. 12–13.
73 *Games and Toys*, 1:9 (1915), p. 362.
74 *Games and Toys*, p. 374.
75 The *WEC Half Yearly Report* lists thirty societies including the Young Women's Christian Association, the AFL, the WWSL, the Women's Institute and the American Women's War Relief Fund. *Votes for Women*, 11 September 1914, p. 731.
76 L. Ashwell, *Myself a Player* (London: Michael Joseph, 1936), p. 183.
77 Leaflet for WEC Land Scheme, 1914, British Library.
78 *Daily News and Leader*, 24 December 1914.
79 E. Moore, *Exits and Entrances* (London: Chapman & Hall, 1923), p. 74; Moore was performing in her husband's play *Eliza Comes to Stay*, which had transferred from the Criterion Theatre to the Vaudeville on 6 July 1914; *Votes for Women*, 9 October 1914, p. 13.
80 *The Times*, 13 January 1915, p. 9.
81 *WEC Half Yearly Report*, 1915, p. 2.
82 K. Kelly, 'The Actresses' Franchise League prepares for war: feminist theatre in camouflage', *Theatre Survey*, 35:1 (1994), 121–37.
83 C. Collier, *Harlequinade* (London: John Lane, 1929), p. 231.
84 The Three Arts Club was founded by Lena Ashwell in 1911 to provide space for female performers. Many AFL members were on its management and advisory boards. For more, see C. Hindson, *London's West End Actresses and the Origins of Celebrity Charity, 1880–1920* (Iowa City, IA: University of Iowa Press, 2016).
85 May Whitty, unpublished autobiography, p. 74, Margaret Webster Papers, Library of Congress.
86 *The Era*, 7 July 1915, p. 12.
87 *Votes for Women*, 13 November 1914, p. 54.
88 *Votes for Women*, 30 October 1914, p. 34.
89 For more about Gertrude Elliott and the Shakespeare Hut, see A. Grant Ferguson, 'Lady Forbes-Robertson's war work: Gertrude Elliott and the Shakespeare Hut performances, 1916–1919', in G. McMullan, L. Cowen Orlin and V. Mason Vaughan (eds.), *Women Making Shakespeare* (London: Bloomsbury, 2013), pp. 233–42.
90 J. F. Geddes, 'Deeds *and* words in the suffrage military hospital in Endell Street', *Making History*, 51 (2007), 79–98, at p. 88.
91 Geddes, 'Deeds *and* words', p. 90; programmes for the Military Hospital pantomimes, 1915, 1916 and 1917, Bristol Theatre Collection.

92 B. Harraden, 'Women doctors in the war', *The Windsor Magazine*, 43 (1915), 179–93, at p. 191.
93 *The Times*, 13 May 1916, p. 3.
94 *Daily Mail*, 5 June 1916; M. Webster, *The Same Only Different* (London: Victor Gollancz, 1969), p. 260.
95 Hindson, *London's West End Actresses*, p. 186.
96 Letter from Squire Bancroft to Lord Chamberlain's office, 6 August 1914, British Library.
97 Lord Chamberlain's correspondence, 1914/2, British Library.
98 *Votes for Women*, 9 October 1914, p. 15; Kelly, 'The Actresses' Franchise League prepares', p. 130.
99 *Daily Express*, 24 October 1914.
100 *Votes for Women*, 13 November 1914, p. 55.
101 *Votes for Women*, 11 June 1915, p. 303.
102 Hirshfield, 'The Woman's Theatre', p. 133.
103 *The Era*, 23 June 1915, p. 12.
104 *The Era*, 23 June 1915, p. 21.
105 Woman's Theatre mission statement, war-relief matinee programme, 1915, Bristol Theatre Collection.
106 Woman's Theatre mission statement, p. 4.
107 *The Observer*, 5 November 1914.
108 *Votes for Women*, March 1916, p. 151.
109 *The Times*, 7 January 1915, p. 5.
110 *AFL Annual Play Department Report*, 20 October 1916, Women's Library.
111 *The Times*, 14 October 1915, p. 12.
112 *The Star*, 14 April 1917; *Evening Standard*, 7 April 1917.
113 Frances Wetherall produced *Caretaker Within* by Corton King with a cast that included League members Sydney Fairbrother and Jane Comfort. Janette Steer produced *Kitty's Catch* by Martha Myers and Patricia Murray, which included League member Eugenie Vernie among the cast. *The Stage*, 2 March 1916, p. 6.
114 Edith Anton Laing was business manager, Inez Bensusan the honorary organising secretary, and the stage managers were Edith Carter, Beatrice Wilson and Winifred Mayo. *The Stage*, 2 March 1916, p. 6.
115 *AFL Annual Play Department Report*, 1916; *The Stage*, 18 May 1916, p. 16.
116 *The Stage*, 22 June 1916, p. 16; E. Knoblock, *A War Committee* (London: S. French, 1915); R. Ganthony, *The Meeting: A Duologue* (London: S. French, 1903).
117 E. Knoblauch, *A War Committee* (London: Samuel French, 1915).
118 Minutes of the entertainment committee, 25 May 1916.
119 Programme for Woman's Theatre Camps Entertainments, 13 July 1917.
120 Kelly, 'The Actresses' Franchise League prepares', p. 128.
121 Hirshfield, 'The Woman's Theatre', p. 132.
122 Gertrude Elliott was the president of the advisory committee, upon which

also sat Lena Ashwell, Inez Bensusan, Gertrude Kingston, Auriol Lee, Winifred Mayo, Decima Moore, Eva Moore, Mary Moore, Madeleine Lucette Ryley, May Whitty, Lilian Braithwaite, Janette Steer and Miss Compton. Ashwell and Edyth Olive were joint honorary treasurers, the honorary secretary was Nina Boucicault, and the honorary organising secretary was Adeline Bourne.

123 Minutes of the subcommittee of the AFL, 20 August 1915, Wellcome Library.
124 Minutes of meeting of the hospital subcommittee, 10 September 1915, Wellcome Library.
125 *The People*, 26 September 1915; *The Standard*, 25 September 1915; *Daily News*, 25 September 1915; *Sunday Times and Sunday Special*, 26 September 1915; *Sunday Pictorial*, 26 September 1915; *Daily Graphic*, 27 September 1915. All clippings in the British Women's Hospital Fund scrapbook, Wellcome Library.
126 *Report of the British Women's Hospital Committee from the Commencement of Its Work, July 1015 to December 31st, 1919*, 1920, p. 4.
127 *Report of the British Women's Hospital Committee*, p. 25.
128 Letter from Adeline Bourne to Maud Arncliffe Sennett, 27 October 1915.
129 *Manchester Guardian*, 1 November 1915.
130 Programme for *Performance in Aid of Star and Garter Building Fund of British Women's Hospital*, 9 June 1916.
131 Programme for *Performance in Aid of Star and Garter Building Fund*.
132 J. M. Barrie, *Irene Vanbrugh's Pantomime*, British Library, LCP 1916/13.
133 *Report of the British Women's Hospital Committee*, p. 6.
134 *Daily Mail*, 24 March 1917, p. 3.
135 *The Times*, 31 March 1917, p. 9.
136 Programme for Playhouse, 18 April 1917, Wellcome Library.
137 *Votes for Women*, 12 March 1915, p. 199.
138 Ashwell, *Myself a Player*, p. 75.
139 *Times*, 8 June 1938, p. 13.
140 *Votes for Women*, 4 September 1914, p. 719.
141 *Daily Mail*, 1 January 1916, p. 3.
142 *Call Sign Magazine*, November 2002.
143 L. Whitelaw, *The Life and Rebellious Times of Cicely Hamilton* (London: The Women's Press, 1990), pp. 137–59; C. Law, *Women: A Modern Political Dictionary* (London: I. B. Tauris, 2000), p. 32; *Daily Mail*, 16 May 1919, p. 8.
144 May Whitty Diaries, p. 75, Margaret Webster Papers, Library of Congress.
145 Parliamentary Archives, LG/F/229/3.
146 For more about how suffrage societies responded to the limited franchise, see A. K. Smith, *Suffrage Discourse in Britain during the First Word War* (Aldershot: Ashgate, 2005).
147 Katharine Kelly draws attention to this paucity of scholarship, referring to

'fragmentary histories of the League' that exclude their wartime work but notes contributions to the debate about the league in wartime from Claire Hirshfield, Julie Holledge, Viv Gardner and Michael Sanderson, choosing to focus her own writing on the development of the Woman's Theatre and the Women's Theatre Camps Entertainments between 1913 and 1917. 'The Actresses' Franchise League prepares', p. 122.

148 *Era Annual*, 1919, p. 82.
149 *The Stage*, 26 June 1919, p. 16.
150 *The Stage*, 26 June 1919, p. 16.
151 *The Era*, 25 June 1919, p. 17.
152 *Time and Tide*, 5 January 1928, p. 21.
153 P. Thane, 'Impact of mass democracy on British political culture', in J. V. Gottlieb and R. Toye (eds.), *The Aftermath of Suffrage* (New York: Palgrave Macmillan, 2013), pp. 54–69, at p. 61.
154 Minutes of Fifth Annual Meeting of the Consultative Committee of Women's Organisations, July 1926, p. 3.
155 AFL birthday party notice card, 1926.
156 *The Stage*, 17 June 1926, p. 12.
157 *The Vote*, 9 July 1926, p. 210; *The Times*, 17 June 1926, p. 11; *The Vote*, 2 July 1926; *The Vote*, 9 July 1926, p. 210.
158 *The Vote*, 9 July 1926, p. 210. Applin had been in the cast of *Murder*, performed at the WSPU Women's Exhibition on 13 May 1909, and had also been part of an AFL reception for the Northern Men's Federation for Women's Suffrage on 6 February 1914.
159 *Manchester Guardian*, 5 July 1926.
160 Despite petitions in 1920 and 1948, bills in 1924, 1925, 1926, 1927 and 1928 and a vote in 1930, there was no official acceptance of the principle of admitting women to the Lords until 1949. Lady Rhondda did not live to see the admittance of women to the House of Lords. On the passing of the Life Peerages Act in October 1958, three months after her death, women became eligible to take their places in the Lords.
161 *The Times*, 4 February 1927, p. 10.
162 *The Vote*, 22 July 1927, p. 225.
163 *The Vote*, 22 July 1927, p. 227.
164 *Manchester Guardian*, 19 June 1928, p. 12.
165 Parliamentary Archives, HL/PO/PU/1/1928/18&19G5c12.
166 *Manchester Guardian*, 13 October 1928, p. 17.
167 *Glasgow Herald*, 7 September 1929, p. 7.

6
Legacy

It has been assumed that the passing of the Representation of the People (Equal Franchise) Act in 1928 marked the end of the campaigning of suffrage societies; however, the AFL, along with many other organisations, stayed active and continued to provide a means by which actresses could unite, collaborate, campaign and network in a politically active, professional organisation. Maggie B. Gale's study of women's professional theatre from 1918 to 1962 details the female playwrights who had their work put on in the West End – and shows how plays by well-known pre-war suffragist writers and actresses Gertrude Jennings, Cicely Hamilton and Emily Morse Symonds were still being produced alongside the work of the new generation of actresses and playwrights who had connections to the League such as Auriol Lee, Dorothy Massingham and Clemence Dane.[1] Careers of actresses, writers and producers that had started before the war and that had been nurtured by the League were shaping the future of the industry. Prominent men who had supported the League pre-war maintained their connection with the organisation, appearing at birthday parties and fundraising events. They were also useful to the League as employers – Nigel Playfair ran the Lyric Hammersmith from 1918 to 1933 and J. B. Fagan the Oxford Playhouse from 1923 to 1929. League members were also involved in the education of a new generation of performers, as the number of formal drama-training schools grew. The 1920s saw Constance Benson, May Whitty and Fay Compton opening dramatic schools and studios, Athene Seyler and Sybil Thorndike working with students at the Royal Academy of Dramatic Art and Johnston Forbes-Robertson, Henry Ainley and Lena Ashwell on the examination panel for the University of London diploma in dramatic art.[2] Many of the new, successful generation of stage stars had been taught by suffragist actors and actresses: John Gielgud attended Constance Benson's Dramatic School, and Italia Conti taught Noël Coward, Gertrude Lawrence and Hermione Gingold. There were therefore hundreds of young actresses and actors in theatre, musical comedy, revue, rep, film and radio that had had contact with suffragists at an early stage of their career. Of course it is impossible to know whether their performance education included an awareness of the suffrage campaign within the industry, but the new generation of theatre professionals starting their careers included children of League members already familiar with the work of the organisation, including director Margaret Webster, the daughter of May Whitty and Ben Webster, and Eva Moore and H. V. Esmond's daughter Jill Esmond, who was an actress. Reports of the League's annual birthday parties throughout the 1920s show that younger men and women were donating their time and talents alongside the previous generation of performers. In 1927, the birthday party saw Auriol Lee, May Whitty, Inez Bensusan, Fay Compton and Dame Madge Kendal celebrating with Tallulah Bankhead, Dorothy Massingham and Hilda Bayley, and three years later, Beatrice Lillie was among those who performed in the cabaret.[3]

The year 1930 saw the formation of British Actors' Equity, and its first two presidents, Godfrey Tearle (1932–40) and Lewis Casson (1940–45) had both been involved in performances given by the AFL and the Woman's Theatre. AFL networks developed further into the 1930s as new generations of performers created a link between the past and present of theatre. For example, League member Nancy Price, who had been part of the original cast for the 1913 Woman's Theatre season, launched the National People's Theatre with J. T. Grein in 1930, and would go on to mount seventy-three productions in the West End.[4] League members also maintained their political engagement with and connection to suffrage and feminist societies throughout the 1930s. Adeline Bourne became the organising secretary of the National Council of Girls' Clubs, which represented over 4,000 clubs with a membership of 250,000 girls, and lobbied local authorities and government for better educational and transport facilities.[5] Cicely Hamilton opened the first day of WFL's annual Green, White and Gold Fair – renamed the Universal Market – at Caxton Hall in November 1931, declaring that 'the Women's Freedom League was as necessary as ever … and its work must continue until women had equal freedom with men, politically and economically'.[6] The second day was opened by Lillah McCarthy, who reiterated Hamilton's theme: 'twenty years seemed a long time; but women had gained much during those years, and she could not help thinking that women's complete freedom could not be far off'.[7] The Old Vic's Lilian Baylis, who had not openly expressed her support for suffrage before the war, became more vocal about the issue throughout the 1930s, writing a New Year greeting for the *Vote* in January 1932 and adding her name to a petition drawn up in 1937 by Philippa Strachey of the London Society for Women's Service (previously the London Society for Women's Suffrage) for Emmeline Pethick-Lawrence to be on the Honours list.[8] Other signatories to the petition included Elizabeth Robins, Cicely Hamilton, Decima Moore, May Whitty and Sybil Thorndike.[9] Eva Moore represented the League in July 1934 at a deputation of twenty-six societies, including the National Union of Women Teachers, the National Council of Women and the Co-operative Women's Guild, to the London City Council to ask them to reconsider their policy of not employing married women.[10] In 1939, the League was listed among the supporters of the annual celebrations of Emmeline Pankhurst's birthday in July, consisting of a commemoration service in St John's Church, Smith Square, Westminster, followed by a procession to her statue.[11]

A second war: the Women's Adjustment Board

> Those who remember the hardships and distress suffered by the women war workers of 1914–18 ... feel that a strong group of women deeply interested in the welfare of women, should plan ahead so that the valuable contributions made by the women in the years of crises since September, 1939, should not be ignored, overlooked or undervalued, when the years of crises are over.[12]

Soon after the outbreak of the Second World War in September 1939, the AFL held an emergency committee meeting at which Decima Moore, Janette Steer and Adeline Bourne were present. Their first resolution was to restart the British Women's Hospital Fund, the second to form a national adjustment board to help find employment for women who needed it, and the third was that 10 per cent of any profits raised from charity entertainments in which artists donated their time should be divided among the theatrical charities.[13] At a second committee meeting held directly after the League's annual tea party a month later, it was resolved to use the entire profits from the event to support theatrical charities.[14] There had been swift progress made on plans for the adjustment board, and in order that there should be no party political bias, the board's presidents included both Labour and Conservative representatives, working alongside members of the League and representatives from the WFL and the London Women's Parliament, among other organisations. Like the WEC, the aim of the Women's Adjustment Board (WAB) was not to duplicate or undertake work that was already being done by the government or by other women's organisations.[15] The board issued the following objectives:

1. To explore and make effective ways and means to secure the social and economic status of women.
2. To promote the efficient training of women for domestic, professional and industrial vocations.
3. To secure the adequate participation of women in post-war planning.
4. To hold regular meetings each month as an active part of the WAB policy.[16]

In its promotional literature, the WAB stated it had been 'initiated by the Actresses' Franchise League', and by June 1940 a theatre committee had been formed 'to help unemployment through Repertory Companies'.[17] When the AFL committee met again in August 1940, the plans of the adjustment board and its subcommittees were discussed, and Geoffrey Whitworth, the first director of the British Drama League, was named as the deputy chairman of the newly formed Repertory Theatre Committee. The committee was made up of writers, actresses, performers and producers across a range of genres who had established their careers before 1914 as well as those who had come to prominence in the 1920s and 1930s, and included Peggy Ashcroft; Inez Bensusan; John Christie, the founder of Glyndebourne Opera House and Festival; Bertha Graham; Cicely Hamilton; Laurence Housman; Barry Jackson, founder of the Birmingham Repertory Theatre; Violent Loraine; J. B. Priestley; Gillian Scaife; Emlyn Williams; Mrs Howard Wyndham and Diana Wynyard.[18] There appears to be no record of the work of the Repertory Theatre Committee currently catalogued in archives, and it is difficult to follow this intriguing strand of the WAB in any detail. What can be gleaned from press releases is that the theatre committee remained active at least into the mid-1940s, as theatre and film tea parties to raise money for the WAB and the theatre committee were held at Grosvenor House in 1943 and the Dorchester in 1944.[19] The last known meeting of the theatre and film evening party committee was held on the 27 October 1944, and the last recorded theatre and film evening party took place on the 9 November that year.[20] The other committees in the WAB were: the roll of honour committee, to ask employers to re-employ women workers after they were discharged from war work; the ways and means committee, to 'explore and suggest ways and means to prepare work for the women who will be thrown out of work at the end of the war'; the daily domestic workers committee, to stabilise wages and 'secure adequate training with certificates'; the women's agricultural committee, to 'promote the placing of women in dairy, farming and market gardening'; and the meetings committee 'to secure adequate participation of women in post war planning'.[21]

The WAB held public monthly meetings between 1942 and 1958, inviting speakers to talk on a huge variety of topics. Many AFL members and supporters both spoke at and chaired these meetings, including Decima and Eva Moore, Lady Standing, Cicely Hamilton, Naomi Jacob, Adeline Bourne, Ruby Miller, Marie Lohr and Jill Esmond. In May 1944, the speakers included actress Julia Neilson on the subject of 'The Provincial Audience' and William Armstrong from the Liverpool Playhouse speaking on 'The Future of Repertory'.[22] Social and political causes were always opportunities for the AFL and the WAB to take action. At a board meeting in January 1944, the speakers included Nancy Adams of the National Union of Domestic Workers, who championed 'the prospects of raising the status of domestic workers', and the journalist, philanthropist and playwright Ada Chesterton who spoke about the treatment of domestic servants, calling for them to be retitled 'domestic assistants'.[23] The WAB subsequently created plans to form a new company that would provide training centres for young girls and women to learn domestic work.[24] With the experience of setting up the WEC and British Women's Hospital Committee already successfully behind them, one can assume that the logistics of such a project would not have been overwhelming for the League or the WAB. A leaflet printed c. 1946 briefly announced that the first training centre had opened in London in March 1946, but as there is no known WAB archive it is very possible that further documentation of the project lies elsewhere.[25] Records of the meetings of the WAB in the late 1940s and 1950s show a mix of topics including theatrical, charitable and political causes. December 1949 saw Beatrice Forbes-Robertson speaking about the modern theatre in a meeting entitled 'A Glance Back to the Theatre of Yesterday', and in January 1953 she spoke again at a meeting on the subject of 'The Trend in the Theatre of To-day' alongside the theatre critics Bill Boorne and Alan Dent, and Llewellyn Rees, who was honorary president of the International Theatre Institute at the time.

Connections with the suffrage societies were also maintained throughout the 1940s and 1950s. Frederick Pethick-Lawrence had spoken at the WAB's September 1943 meeting on the subject of the 'Silver Jubilee of Votes for Women', Beatrice Forbes-Robertson spoke on behalf of the AFL at a WAB meeting on the topic of 'Equal Pay for Equal Work' in January 1947, and the League made a formal donation to the Suffragette Fellowship in 1956. Along with other suffrage societies, including the WFL and the Suffragette Fellowship, the AFL was involved also in the Equal Pay Campaign from 1944 to 1955. The League appeared on the Advisory Council of the Campaign in 1949, 1953, and 1954, and the WAB was part of the Advisory Council in 1952 and 1954.²⁶ There were echoes of the non-violent direct action seen in the suffrage movement in plans put forward to the Equal Pay Campaign Committee – hardly surprising as so many of those involved had experience of activism. The committee was cautious when considering plans to demonstrate at the House of Commons by interrupting proceedings from the public galleries or plastering leaflets on the houses of MPs, but did urge members of its advisory council to consider 'Public propaganda' an important part of the campaign.²⁷

In a decision reminiscent of their redevelopment of the Star and Garter homes during the First World War, the AFL and the WAB started a number of projects to fund residential homes for elderly and infirm men and women. The Wayfarers' Trust was set up to support the foundation of the Alice Waddilove Residential Club in Clapham and to redevelop Gosfield Hall, an Elizabethan manor in Essex, for use as a nursing home and hospital for elderly people with limited means. It opened as the Princess Marie Louise Nursing Home in 1955, and the princess frequently attended AFL fundraising events to support the Home. The Alice Waddilove Club also attracted theatrical support – a gala performance of *Zip Goes a Million* was held at the Palace Theatre in 1951 in aid of the WAB Special Appeal for Residential Clubs for Elderly Gentlewomen.²⁸ It was announced that the gala proceeds would go to naming a room in memory of impresario Charles B. Cochran, and that one room in the Alice Waddilove Club was already named after Eva Moore.²⁹ In 1958, League members were still active: Winifred Mayo was president of the Suffragette Fellowship, and Una Duval (née Dugdale) the honorary treasurer, while Decima Moore and Sybil Thorndike were on the Christabel Pankhurst Memorial Fund Committee, alongside Nancy Astor and Emmeline Pethick-Lawrence. The WAB newsletter of September 1958 revealed that the financial pressures of running the Wayfarers' Trust and the board were becoming too much for Adeline Bourne who was in her eighty-sixth year and unable to continue to cover the basic costs of her work as secretary for both organisations, finding 'that the anxiety of trying to make two ends meet' was more than she could manage.³⁰ A year earlier, she had refused an OBE in the birthday honours list. She resigned her position, but the Wayfarers' Trust and the WAB continued.

A grand finale: 'Exit singing and dancing. Curtain!'³¹

The final event which bore the name of the AFL was the 'My Fair Lady Ball', given at the Savoy Hotel in December 1958 'to commemorate the 50th

Anniversary of the Actresses' Franchise League by giving a farewell gift to its founder, Miss Adeline Bourne'.[32] The list of vice presidents for the event glitters with the names of famous performers, including new generations of theatrical professionals. Original AFL members and supporters such as Gillian Scaife, Lewis Casson and Sybil Thorndike appear alongside stars of the 1950s including Margot Fonteyn, Hattie Jacques, Vivien Leigh, Beatrice Lillie, Laurence Olivier, Ralph Richardson, Norman Wisdom and Sheila Van Damm. The youngest vice president was actress Anna Massey, aged twenty-one. This eclectic group, drawn from many different branches of the theatrical profession, is reminiscent of the founding meeting of the League, held at the Criterion restaurant fifty years earlier – performers from all generations and genres joined together for one purpose. It has not previously been thought that the League as an organisation remained part of the theatrical community in which it had been founded, but the continuing professional careers of its members and their own sustained interest in campaigning for equal rights and social causes kept the League connected to the industry for half a century, a connection that is obvious from programme of the My Fair Lady Ball. The theatre community contributed gifts for the occasion, and the support of eleven West End theatres and at least two producers – H. M. Tennant Ltd and Moss Empires Ltd – was listed alongside some of the most exclusive retail outlets in London, including Aquascutum, Norman Hartnell, Pepsi-Cola, Doulton, Kodak, Jaeger and Yardley. Thanks were given to the many people and companies who gave their services for free, including all the cabaret performers and bands, four printing companies who provided the invitations, programmes and stationery for the event, two national newspapers for printing advertisements and an accounting firm for auditing. The AFL was clearly still an organisation that important individuals and companies recognised and wanted to be associated with.

In the heart of the West End, and close to the site of the League's former offices, the Savoy Hotel was easily reached after a show in any of the major London theatres. Considerable effort was made at the event to especially include working performers – although the main dinner service for the ball was at 8 p.m., there was an 'actresses' supper' with a different, lighter menu served at 11 p.m., to accommodate those who had been working in theatres earlier in the evening. This was certainly the case for Stanley Holloway, who was at the time playing in *My Fair Lady* at the nearby Theatre Royal, Drury Lane and presented the raffle prizes at 1 a.m., after the actresses' supper and two cabaret performances had taken place. There were three cabaret performances at the

My Fair Lady Ball, each in different rooms at the hotel. The first two were compèred by actress Harriette Johns and featured performances from young rock-and-roll sensation Marty Wilde, pianist and vocalist Harry Jacobson, who had recorded with Gracie Fields and was the uncle of Hollywood child star Sybil Jason; musical comedy actor Brian Reece; and actor Richard Murdoch, famous for his work in BBC radio comedy. The

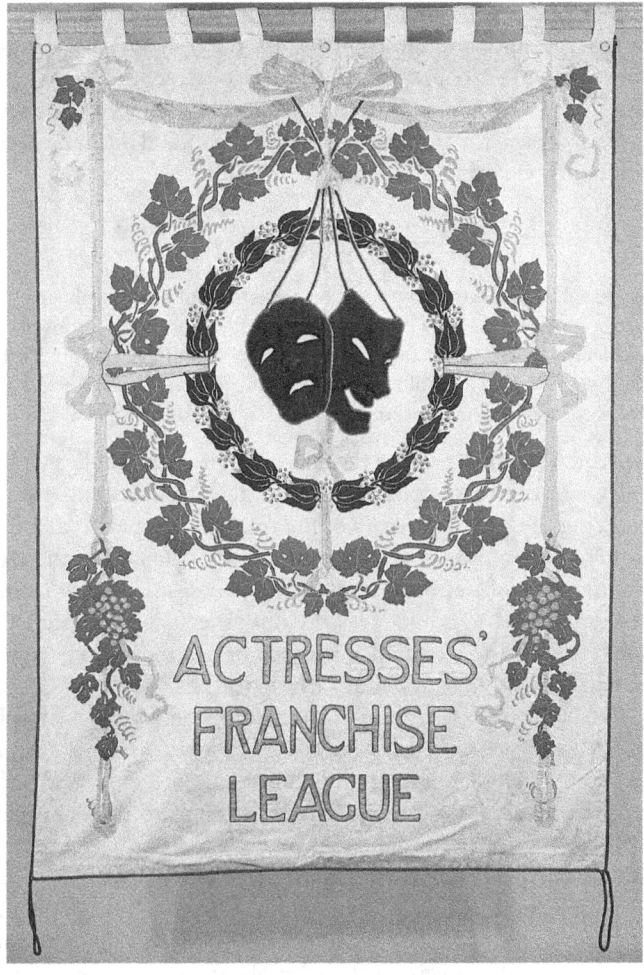

6.1 AFL banner, c. 1911
© Museum of London

third began at 2 a.m. and featured Joe Melia and Dudley Moore, while other entertainments across the evening included performances from stage astrologer and clairvoyant Maurice Woodruff, three bands playing for dancing in three different rooms, an auction and a raffle, with the evening ending at 3 a.m. with the singing of the National Anthem. Lady Cynthia Colville's dedication in the programme spoke of Adeline Bourne as being 'more of a national figure during these last 40 years than she herself realises', and it was due to the efforts, interest and determination of Bourne and the other founding members of the League that the organisation stayed active for so long and continued to attract the support of new generations of performers.[33] The ripple effect of their feminist activism had created a space for women in the profession and a legacy of openly and confidently claiming the right to that space.

A legacy to be proud of

> English suffrage theatre is a potent, brief example of a politically inspired theatre which leaves us with a legacy: it made new assumptions about theatrical space, domestic space and public space simultaneously; it catapulted women into the full range of roles in theatre; and it played a key role in women writers' conscriptions of dramatic form.[34]

Why did the AFL remain active for fifty years? The answer lies within the broad scope of the League's ambitions and talents, its essentially neutral stance during the turbulent years of the militant campaign, its extensive contribution to the theatrical profession as a whole and to the creation and maintenance of networks of training, work, creative collaboration and development. The League was the only specifically feminist theatre group that existed and operated at a highly professional level throughout the first half of the twentieth century. Theatrical charities and clubs existed through which actresses could network and become involved in philanthropy, but there was no other organisation for professional performers that had a politically feminist foundation. Members, allies and supporters altered their career trajectories and career opportunities permanently by becoming part of the League and by collaborating and experimenting with new plays and ventures that placed women, access and equality firmly at the centre. While suffrage plays were regularly performed in mainstream theatre spaces, they were also produced in unconventional venues – town halls, drawing rooms, small studio theatres, restaurants, exhibitions, immersive spaces, site-specific spaces and the equivalent of what we call today 'pop-up theatres'. Suffrage performances had flexibility in form and genre, meaning that writers and performers were able to quickly respond to changing political situations and to reflect the lives of women not often represented on stage. Suffragist actresses and actors took their experiences into all areas of their professional and personal lives, and the visibility of the suffrage sisterhood in public space engaged new audiences and opened up opportunities for performers, blurring the boundaries between on and off stage. However, of the AFL's fifty years of work, just the first six specifically involved the creation and production of suffrage plays and performances. Through the broad and varied spread of its work after 1914, the League retained an outward-looking and politically informed position within both the theatre industry and the women's movement that remained innovative and yet true to the founding tenets of the organisation.

Written out of their history

> To ignore their work, even if the ideological basis of that work is difficult to accept, is tantamount to writing *out* of history an important aspect of women's contribution.[35]

As scholars such as Maggie B. Gale have shown, the work of women playwrights, directors and producers in the twentieth century is less well documented and has not been given the same attention or importance as that of their male contemporaries. Scholarship that has predominantly defined the work of the League as suffrage theatre, without a nuanced understanding of the meaning of that term or the variety of content it encompasses, has placed the organisation outside of the wider theatrical and political space it inhabited. Because of a lack of understanding or appreciation of the complexities of the suffrage campaign, scholars have questioned the legitimacy and relevance of the League within its contemporary theatre scene and consequently under-represented its work in theatre histories and analyses of the Edwardian period and of political theatre. This is to fundamentally misunderstand the role of the League in the campaign for Votes for Women. Scholarly descriptions of the League as a 'subaltern group' perpetuate the fallacy that the organisation was not integrated and networked within both mainstream and experimental theatres and fail to acknowledge the influence of members on the development of key institutions and creative practices in the twentieth-century.[36] Other scholars have often failed to sufficiently challenge or interrogate this, thereby perpetuating the absence of the League from theatre histories and, by extension, the impression that this absence is indicative of the insignificance of the organisation. The breadth of male support for the League from theatre professionals has also not been acknowledged in previous research, further ensuring that the group have been sidelined. Limited published research data on the AFL has meant that contextualising the Woman's Theatre within a global feminist and suffragist movement and understanding the League's deliberate use of patriotism to further its agenda has been difficult, and consequently the work of the League in wartime has been both overlooked and dismissed. Pamela Cobrin introduces the term 'creationary mimesis' in her analysis of American suffragist actresses, stating that their political power lay in 'the act of imitating an absent subject' and their projection of an absent ideal – that is to say, the fully emancipated woman.[37] League members were not afraid of asserting their political presence in public, but, having developed networks of female and male support within their theatrical sphere, they were reduced to being seen, and treated, as *merely* female in their wartime ventures, particularly between 1914 and 1918. For an organisation and a movement that deliberately and publicly embraced and debated nuanced, analytical and challenging representations of women and womanhood, it is frustrating that this lazy gendered stereotyping remains dominant. For example, in his review of *The Same Only Different*, Margaret Webster's 1969 memoir, *The Times*'s Michael Ratcliffe dismissed the work of the Three Arts Women's Employment fund as 'elderly wardrobe mistresses running up soft toys', completely distorting the accounts given of their work in Webster's book.[38] Having had their work belittled at the time, the women of the Three Arts Women's Employment Fund are again rejected some fifty years later, and there is no recognition that perhaps these 'elderly wardrobe mistresses' instead had their professional skills respected at a time of extreme economic hardship by an organisation that understood how perilous freelance work in the industry could be. For those helped into employment by the WEC and WAB, and those cared for in rest homes in wartime and at the end of their lives, the League made a practical and vital contribution to their long-term economic and social well-being, although many may not have been aware of the theatrical origins of their benefactors.

Stretching forward, moving on

> The dominant reality in which women are diminished and in which their muteness and invisibility are constructed and maintained is still the prevailing reality, the one which is legitimated and generally accepted.[39]

Legacy 201

An understanding of the legacy of the AFL is important because it points towards a recognition of the range of its many spheres of influence and interest and includes an analysis of the potential of theatrical engagement with ideas of political activism in a wider social context, an intrinsic part of the historiography of the League. Continued activism – feminist, suffragist and political, for equal pay and the equal franchise – characterised the League throughout the post-1918 years. When actress Gertrude Kingston considered standing for Parliament in 1924, her experience of political mass meetings from over a decade beforehand prepared her for her performance in interviews and on public platforms, and she recalled that her appearance in front of the National Council of Women 'was not formidable after the gigantic congregations we had addressed during the contention for our suffrage'.[40] Despite their awareness of the importance of creating an atmosphere conducive to fundraising through events, parties, at homes and performances, the League did not become a social club or lecture club for actresses. Adeline Bourne was quoted in the *Daily Express* in 1951 urging women to engage with politics and articulate their views. 'Get on a soapbox, darlings. I don't care which side you're on, but for heaven's sake take this General Election seriously, and get up and speak.'[41] The multiple legacies of the AFL are not only in a record of their activities or satellite organisations but also among audiences and the general public. Winifred Mayo and Adeline Bourne gave interviews to the BBC in the 1960s about their memories of the suffrage campaign, and Bourne was interviewed on television in 1964 in *Something to Say*, produced by Associated Rediffusion.[42] This interview prompted a letter that provides a glimpse of the impact the work of the WAB had on one woman from Chichester:

> How I miss those W.A.B. meetings … when I first knew you … I had been left on my own with three children to bring up. Well, they are almost 'up'. I no longer moan, and steadily fight my way through … One always has to fight it seems, unfortunately … At a time when I needed the influence of someone like you, I met you, and I have never forgotten you.[43]

While this book closes with a consideration of the legacy of the AFL, there is still much to be explored in detail. This book introduces new research to the field of both theatre and suffrage histories, particularly around the intersections between performance, representation and visibility of suffragists within the performative propaganda of and inspired by the suffrage movement. The account of the work of the League in suffrage exhibitions and the relationship between the organisation and the issue of suffrage militancy is also new, as is the story of the League post-1928 and the description of the work of the WAB. It has been difficult thus far to find detailed recollections of the League after the Second World War, particularly as the autobiographies of many of the actresses involved were mostly written between the wars and so do not give an account of the later work of the organisation.[44] The most active and long-standing League members did not write autobiographies and do not have a known or accessible archive of papers – including Decima Moore, Gertrude Elliott, Inez Bensusan, Adeline Bourne, Winifred Mayo, Edyth Olive, Nina Boucicault and many others who might have written passionately and eloquently about the continuing political and social engagement of the AFL. The diversification of the League's portfolio after 1914 places its work alongside those running campaigns for political and social change, extending its professional and historical legacy far beyond the Edwardian period. The research that underpins this book suggests that there is still a great deal which might be done to track the League through networks of theatrical, social and political activism in the first half of the twentieth century and much that remains relevant about its work and the issues affection women in the professional theatre. Inez Bensusan's Woman's Theatre project was designed to both work with and challenge the institutionalised sexism pervading the industry as a whole, harnessing the energy, ambition and imagination of the League's membership and creating new opportunities for women in the performing arts that would have far-reaching consequences. Embracing ideas of patronage, networking, publicity and philanthropy, the League had more experience and ambition than has been acknowledged – and this new account of its work demands a more focused reflection on and re-evaluation of these elements. It is possible to map the work and the presence of the AFL onto scholarship surrounding the emergence of pre- and post-First and Second World War debates around the idea of a national theatre, as well as communist and socialist political theatre movements from the 1920s onwards. Indeed, many of the writers and performers involved with the AFL before 1913 became integral to progressive political theatre groups after the First World War. With professional links to prominent play-producing societies, regional repertory theatres and the commercial theatre business in both the UK and America, the League and its membership should be seen as not only facilitators and artistic collaborators but also as activists in their own right – with each performance a gesture of protest, each meeting a demonstration and each woman and man a political activist. Here I have introduced a fuller study of the AFL which is intended to contribute to the renewed interest in feminist theatre scholarship as well as more general theatre histories of the first half of the twentieth century.

Notes

1 M. B. Gale, *West End Women: Women and the London Stage, 1918–1962* (London and New York: Routledge, 1996).
2 M. Sanderson, *From Irving to Olivier: A Social History of the Acting Profession in England, 1880–1983* (London: Athlone Press, 1984), pp. 190–3.
3 *The Stage*, 17 November 1927, p. 18.
4 *The Vote*, 5 February 1932, p. 42; *Who's Who in the Theatre* (London: Pitman & Sons, 1947), p. 1163.
5 *Manchester Guardian*, 15 April 1930.
6 *The Vote*, 20 November 1931, p. 377.
7 *The Vote*, 20 November 1931, p. 377.
8 *The Vote*, 1 January 1932, p. 2.
9 Letter from Lilian Baylis to P. Strachey, 15 October 1938, Women's Library.
10 *Manchester Guardian*, 3 July 1934, p. 10.
11 The other supporters were the Suffragette Fellowship, the Women's Guild of Empire, the WFL, the Six Point Group, the British Commonwealth League and the National Union of Women Teachers. Papers of Emily Wilding Davison, Women's Library at LSE, 7EWD/E3/3.
12 WAB leaflet, c. 1945.
13 Minutes of *AFL Emergency Committee Meeting*, 8 November 1939.
14 *The Times*, 27 November 1939, p. 9; £100 was given to the Actors' Benevolent Fund, £40 to the Theatrical Ladies Guild and £10 to Lilian Braithwaite's Fund for Evacuated Hospitals.
15 Letter from WAB to National Council of Social Service, 29 September 1942.
16 WAB leaflet, c. 1946.
17 WAB leaflet, c. 1945.
18 WAB preliminary draft, c. 1942.
19 *The Times*, 24 June 1943, p. 7; 24 October 1944, p. 6.
20 *The Times*, 24 October 1944, p. 6.
21 WAB preliminary draft, c. 1942.
22 WAB booklet, p. 4.
23 *Glasgow Herald*, 8 January 1944, p. 4.
24 *Daily Mail*, 6 October 1945, p. 3.
25 WAB leaflet, c. 1945.
26 Equal Pay Campaign Committee, *Equal Pay for Equal Work: The Rate for the Job 1914–49: A Black Record* (London: Equal Pay Campaign Committee, 1949); letter from Equal Pay Campaign Committee, 7 December 1953; letter from Equal Pay Campaign Committee, 6 February 1954; Equal Pay Campaign Committee, *The Case for Equal Pay in Government Service Now* (London: Equal Pay Campaign Committee, 1952); Equal Pay Campaign Committee, *Equal Pay for Equal Work: Any Questions?* (London: Equal Pay Campaign Committee, 1954).

27 A. Potter, 'The Equal Pay Campaign Committee: a case study of a pressure group', *Political Studies*, 5:1 (1957), 49–64, at p. 62; letter from Equal Pay Council Campaign Committee, 5 May 1947.
28 *Yorkshire Post and Leeds Intelligencer*, 19 October 1951, p. 4.
29 *The Times*, 19 September 1951, p. 6.
30 *WAB Newsletter*, September 1958.
31 Handwritten addition by Adeline Bourne on the *WAB Newsletter*, September 1958.
32 Programme for My Fair Lady Ball, private collection.
33 Programme for My Fair Lady Ball, private collection.
34 S. Carlson, 'Suffrage theatre: community activism and political commitment', in M. Luckhurst (ed.), *A Companion to Modern British and Irish Drama* (Oxford: Blackwell, 2006), pp. 99–109, at p. 107.
35 M. B. Gale, *West End Women: Women and the London Stage, 1918–1962* (London and New York: Routledge, 1996), p. 62.
36 T. C. Davis, 'Private women and the public realm', *Theatre Survey*, 35:1 (1994), 65–71, p. 68.
37 P. Cobrin, *From Winning the Vote to Directing on Broadway: The Emergence of Women on the New York Stage, 1880–1927* (Newark, DE: University of Delaware Press, 2009), p. 18.
38 *The Times*, 13 December 1969, p. 4.
39 D. Spender, *Man Made Language* (London: Routledge & Kegan Paul, 1980), p. 229.
40 G. Kingston, *Curtsey While You're Thinking* (London: Williams & Norgate, 1937), p. 237.
41 *Daily Express*, 4 October 1951, p. 2.
42 BBC Archive LP 24386, LP 28834.
43 Letter from Margaret Batchel to Adeline Bourne, 9 January 1963, Bourne Family Archive.
44 Lena Ashwell and Eva Moore published theirs in 1923; Lillah McCarthy's was published in 1933 and Gertrude Kingston's in 1937.

Bibliography

Online newspaper and journal databases consulted

British Newspaper Archive
(www.britishnewspaperarchive.co.uk)

Daily Herald
Daily Telegraph
Yorkshire Post and Leeds Intelligencer
The Suffragette

Old Fulton NY Post Cards
(www.fultonhistory.com/Fulton)

New York Clipper
New York Dramatic Mirror
New York Evening Post
New York Press
New York Telegraph
New York Times
New York Tribune
Variety

Gale Databases (http://gale.cengage.co.uk/
product-highlights/general-reference/
gale-historical-newspapers.aspx)

British Newspapers 1600–1950
Daily Mail Historical Archive
Financial Times Historical Archive, 1888–2010
Illustrated London News Historical Archive, 1842–2003
19th Century British Newspapers
The Sunday Times Digital Archive, 1822–2006
The Times Digital Archive, 1785–2009

Google Newspapers (www.news.google.com/newspapers)

Boston Evening Transcript
Common Cause
Lewiston Daily Sun
Meriden Daily Republican
Star
Vote
Votes for Women

Hathi Trust Digital Library

McClure's Magazine – http://catalog.hathitrust.org/Record/000548741

The Internet Archive

Athenaeum – https://archive.org/details/p1athenaeum1913lond
The Stage Yearbook – https://archive.org/details/stageyearbo1910londuoft [example]

The Modernist Journals Project

www.modjourn.org
The Freewoman
The New Freewoman
The New Age
The 1910 Collection

Papers Past

Evening Times
www.paperspast.natlib.govt.nz
Poverty Bay Herald

ProQuest British Periodicals

www.proquest.com/products-services/british_periodicals.html
The Idler; an illustrated monthly magazine

ProQuest Historical Newspapers

Guardian (1821–2003)
Observer (1791–2003)
www.proquest.com/libraries/academic/news-newspapers/

Trove

Advertiser (Adelaide)
www.trove.nla.gov.au

UK Press Online

Daily Express 1900–
Daily Mirror 1903–
www.ukpressonline.co.uk

Library of Congress

Call Sign Magazine – online at www.dac-callsign.co.uk
Jus Suffragii – in the Miller National American Woman Suffrage Association Suffrage Scrapbooks, 1897–1911. http://memory.loc.gov/ammem/collections/suffrage/millerscrapbooks/index.html

Theatre Royal Margate Archive

Sketch – http://trm-archive.blogspot.co.uk/2012/04/interview-with-sarah-thorne.html

The *Stage* Archive

www.archive.thestage.co.uk

Online Databases

Find My Past (www.findmypast.co.uk)
Hansard (www.hansard.millbanksystems.com)
1911 Census (www.1911census.co.uk)
Old Bailey Online (www.oldbaileyonline.org)
The Orlando Project (www.orlando.cambridge.org)
Oxford Dictionary of National Biography (www.oxforddnb.com)

Newspaper archives consulted

British Library Newspaper Room

Daily Chronicle
Daily News and Leader
Evening Standard and St James' Gazette
Globe
London Standard
The Weekly Despatch
Westminster Gazette

Library of Congress – La Follette papers

Cleveland News
La Follette's Magazine
Woman Voter

Mitchell Library, Glasgow

Glasgow Herald

Swansea Central Library

Swansea Herald of Wales

Westminster Reference Library

The Era

Libraries and Archives

BFI Library, London

TV Times

BFI Library, Special Collections

Misc. items associated with the recording of *Something to Say*, Associated Rediffusion Network, 13 January 1964

Bibliography

BFI National Archive

Something to Say, Associated Rediffusion Network, 13 January 1964

BFI Reuben Library

The Bioscope

British Library, Manuscripts

Arncliffe Sennett Collection
Lord Chamberlain's Plays and Correspondence
Reports and Publications, Women's Emergency Corps – General Reference Collection 8416.k.17

British Library Sound Archive, BBC Radio Archive

Adeline Bourne, *Home This Afternoon*, 1964 – BBC ref 836067
Winifred Mayo, 1958, BBC ref 896383

John Rylands Library, University of Manchester

Papers of Madeleine Lucette Ryley – GB 133 MLR

Library of Congress, Manuscripts and Archives Reading Room

George Middleton Papers, Boxes 23–4, 48, 50–2, 67–8, 84
LaFollette Family Papers, Box 1
Margaret Webster Papers, Boxes 3 and 20

London Metropolitan Archives

Architectural drawings of the Aldwych Rinkeries, c. 1910

Mitchell Library, Glasgow

Glasgow and West of Scotland Association for Women's Suffrage Scrapbook

Museum of London

Suffragette Fellowship Collection
Woman's Theatre Inaugural Week programme – MoL, Z6099/4

New York Public Library, Schwarzman Building, Manuscripts and Archives Division

Kitty Marion Papers, Box 1
Swinburne Hale Papers, Series 1

New York Public Library for the Performing Arts, Dorothy and Lewis B Cullman Center

Locke Collection
Robinson Locke Scrapbooks
Vandamm Scrapbook

University of Bristol Theatre Collection

Mander and Mitchensen Collection
Papers of Johnston Forbes-Robertson and Gertrude Elliott – MM/B9/R4/S3–4
Woman's Theatre 1913–17

Vaughan Williams Memorial Library, Cecil Sharp House

Papers of Mary Neal and the Esperance Club
Unpublished autobiography of Mary Neal

Wellcome Library, Archives and Manuscripts

British Women's Hospital Committee cuttings books – SA/NFN/A/7
British Women's Hospital Committee minute books – SA/NFN/A/2–6
Programme of matinee in aid of the Star and Garter Building Fund, 1916 – SA/NFN/A/8

Westminster Archives, London

Kelly's Post Office Directories

Women's Library, London

Exhibition Programme for WSPU Christmas Fair and Fete (London: The Woman's Press, 1911)
Men's League for Women's Suffrage Annual Reports
Men's Political Union for Women's Enfranchisement Second Annual Report
Oral Evidence on the Suffragette and Suffragist Movements: the Brian Harrison Interviews – 8SUF
Papers of Elizabeth Impey – 7ELI
Papers of Ellen Isabel Jones – 7EIJ
Papers of Emily Wilding Davison – 7EWD
Papers of M. E. Roberts – 7MER
Papers of Kitty Marion – 7KMA
Papers of Teresa Billington-Greig – 7TBG
Papers of Vera (Jack) Holme – 7VJH
Records of the Actresses' Franchise League – 2AFL
Records of the Consultative Committee of Women's Organisations – 5CWO
Records of the Equal Pay Campaign Committee – 6EPC
Records of the Women's Forum and its Predecessors – 5WFM
Records of the Women's Freedom League – 2WFL
Six Point Group publications and press cuttings – 5SPG
The Suffragette
WSPU Women's Exhibition Programme (London: Women's Social and Political Union, 1909)

Printed books and journal articles

A. J. R. (ed.), *The Suffrage Annual and Women's Who's Who 1913* (London: Stanley Paul, 1913).
Abrams, F., *Freedom's Cause: Lives of the Suffragettes* (London: Profile, 2003).
Adickes, S., 'Sisters, not demons: the influence of British suffragists on the American suffrage movement', *Women's History Review*, 11:4 (2002), 675–90.
Adlard, E., *Edy: Recollections of Edith Craig* (London: Frederick Muller Ltd, 1949).
Ainger, M., *Gilbert and Sullivan: A Dual Biography* (Oxford: Oxford University Press, 2002).

Alltree, G. W., *Footlight Memories: Recollections of Music Hall and Stage Life* (London: S. Low, Marston, 1932).
Andrews, M. R. and M. Talbot, *All the World and Her Husband: Women in Twentieth Century Consumer Culture* (London: Cassell, 2000).
Arthur, M., *Lost Voices of the Edwardians* (London: Harper Press, 2006).
Asche, O., *Oscar Asche, His Life* (London: Hurst & Blackett, 1929).
Ashwell, L., 'Acting as a profession for women', in E. J. Morley (ed.), *Women Workers in Seven Professions: A Survey of Their Economic Conditions and Prospects* (London: George Routledge & Sons, 1914), pp. 298–313.
—— *Modern Troubadours, A Record of the Concerts at the Front* (London: Gyldendal, 1922).
—— *Myself a Player* (London: Michael Joseph, 1936).
—— *The Stage* (London: G. Bles, 1929).
Asquith, M., *The Autobiography of Margot Asquith, vol. II* (London: Thornton Butterworth, 1922).
Atkinson, B., *Broadway* (New York: Macmillan, 1970).
Atkinson, D., *Funny Girls* (London: Penguin, 1997).
—— *Mrs Broom's Suffragette Photographs* (London: Nishen Photography, 1989–).
—— *The Suffragettes in Pictures* (London: Museum of London, 1996).
Atkinson, D., and Gardner, V. (eds) *Kitty Marion, Actor and Activist* (Manchester: Manchester University Press, 2019).
Auerbach, N., *Ellen Terry: Player in Her Time* (New York: W. W. Norton, 1989).
Auster, A., *Actresses and Suffragists: Women in the American Theatre, 1890–1920* (New York: Praeger, 1984).
Barson, S., D. Kendall, P. Longman and J. Smith, *Scene/Unseen: London's West End Theatres* (Swindon: English Heritage, 2003).
Bartlett, G. B. and W. G. Benham, *Mrs Jarley's Far-Famed Collection of Waxworks, Vols. 1–4* (London and New York: Samuel French, 1873).
Bauer, C. and L. Ritt, *Free and Ennobled: Source Readings in the Development of Victorian Feminism* (Oxford: Pergamon Press, 1979).
Beach, C., *Staging Politics and Gender: French Women's Drama, 1880–1923* (New York: Palgrave Macmillan, 2005).
Bearman, C. J., 'An army without discipline? Suffragette militancy and the Budget Crisis of 1909', *The Historical Journal*, 50:4 (2007), 861–89.
Beecham, T., *A Mingled Chime: An Autobiography* (New York: G. P. Putnam, 1943).

Beerbohm, M., *And Even Now* (London: William Heinemann, 1920–).
—— *Around Theatres* (London: Rupert Hart-Davis, 1953).
Bennett, S., 'The making of theatre history', in C. Canning and T. Postlewait (eds.), *Representing the Past: Essays in Performance Historiography* (Iowa City, IA: University of Iowa Press, 2010), pp. 63–83.
—— 'Theatre history and women's dramatic writing', in M. B. Gale and V. Gardner (eds.), *Women, Theatre and Performance: New Histories, New Historiographies* (Manchester: Manchester University Press, 2000), pp. 46–59.
Benson, C., *Mainly Players: Bensonian Memories* (London: Thornton Butterworth, 1926).
Besas, P., *Inside 'Variety'* (Madrid and New York: Ars Millenii, 2000).
Birrer, D. F. and D. Gillespie (eds.), *Diana of Dobson's* (New York: Broad view Press, 2003).
Bland, L., *Banishing the Beast: Feminism, Sex and Morality* (London: Tauris Parke, 2001).
Boisseau, T. J., *Gendering the Fair: Histories of Women and Gender at World's Fairs* (Chicago, IL: University of Illinois Press, 2010).
Booth, M. R. and J. H. Kaplan, *The Edwardian Theatre: Essays on Performance and the Stage* (Cambridge: Cambridge University Press, 2008).
Bosanquet, T., *Henry James at Work* (London: L. and V. Woolf, 1924).
Brandon, R., *The New Women and the Old Men: Love, Sex and the Woman Question* (London: Secker & Warburg, 1990).
Bratton, J., *The Making of the West End Stage: Marriage, Management and the Mapping of Gender in London, 1830–1870* (Cambridge: Cambridge University Press, 2011).
—— 'Reading the intertheatrical, or, the mysterious disappearance of Susanna Centlivre', in M. B. Gale and V. Gardner (eds.), *Women, Theatre and Performance: New Histories, New Historiographies* (Manchester: Manchester University Press, 2000), pp. 7–24.
Bratton, J. and G. T. Peterson, 'The internet: history 2.0?' in D. Wiles and C. Dymkowski (eds.), *Cambridge Companion to Theatre History* (Cambridge: Cambridge University Press, 2012), pp. 299–313.
Breen, C., *Olga Nethersole, Her Life, Career, Family and the Peoples League of Health* (CreateSpace Independent Publishing Platform, 2012).
Brittain, V., *Testament of Youth* (London: Virago, 1979).
Brookes, P., *Women at Westminster* (London: Peter Davies, 1967).
Burns, M. U., 'Minnie Maddern Fiske', in A. M. Robinson, V. M. Roberts and M. S. Barranger (eds.), *Notable Women in the American Theatre* (New York: Greenwood Press, 1989), pp. 282–6.

Bush, J., *Women Against the Vote: Female Anti-Suffragism in Britain* (Oxford: Oxford University Press, 2007).
Byrne, O., *The Stage in Ulster* (Belfast: Linen Hall Library, 1997).
Cameron, R., 'From great women to top girls: pageants of sisterhood in feminist theater', *Comparative Drama*, 43:2 (2009), 143–66.
Campbell, T., *Women's Banners* (Ynyslas: Women for Life on Earth, 1984).
Canning, C. M. and T. Postlewait, *Representing the Past: Essays in Performance Historiography* (Iowa City, IA: University of Iowa Press, 2010).
Carlson, S., 'Comic militancy: the politics of suffrage drama', in M. B. Gale and V. Gardner (eds.), *Women, Theatre and Performance: New Histories, New Historiographies* (Manchester: Manchester University Press, 2000), pp. 198–215.
——'Suffrage theatre: community activism and political commitment', in M. Luckhurst (ed.), *A Companion to Modern British and Irish Drama* (Oxford: Blackwell, 2006), pp. 99–109.
Carter, Lady M., *A Living Soul in Holloway* (London: F. Miller, 1938).
Chapman, M. and A. Mills, *Treacherous Texts: US Suffrage Literature, 1846–1946* (New Brunswick, NJ: Rutgers University Press, 2011).
Cobrin, P., *From Winning the Vote to Directing on Broadway: The Emergence of Women on the New York Stage, 1880–1927* (Newark, DE: University of Delaware Press, 2009).
Cockin, K., 'Cicely Hamilton's warriors: dramatic reinventions of militancy in the British women's suffrage movement', *Women's History Review*, 14:3–4 (2005): 527–42.
——*Edith Craig (1869–1947)* (London: Cassell, 1998).
——'Women's suffrage drama', in M. Joannou and June Purvis (eds.), *The Women's Suffrage Movement: New Feminist Perspectives* (Manchester: Manchester University Press, 1998), pp. 127–39.
——*Women and Theatre in the Age of Suffrage* (Basingstoke: Palgrave, 2001).
Cockin, K., G. Norquay and S. Park, *Women's Suffrage Literature*, vol. III (London: Routledge, 2007).
Cockroft, I., *New Dawn Women* (Compton: Watts Gallery, 2005).
Cockroft, I. and S. Croft, *Art, Theatre and Women's Suffrage* (London: Aurora Metro, 2010).
Collier, C., *Harlequinade: The Story of My Life* (London: John Lane, 1929).
Compton, T. L., *The Rise of the Woman Director on Broadway, 1920–1950* (Santa Barbara, CA: University of California, 1970).
Corbett, M. J., *Representing Femininity: Middle Class Subjectivity in*

Victorian and Edwardian Women's Autobiographies (Oxford: Oxford University Press, 1992).
Cory-Wright, S., *Lady Tree: A Theatrical Life in Letters* (Raleigh, NC: Lulu, 2012).
Courtney, W. L., *The Soul of a Suffragette, and Other Stories* (London: Chapman & Hall, 1913).
Coward, N., *Present Indicative* (London: Heinemann, 1974).
Cowman, K., *Mrs Brown Is a Man and a Brother: Women in Merseyside's Political Organisations, 1890–1920* (Liverpool: Liverpool University Press, 2004).
—— *Women of the Right Spirit: Paid Organisers of the WSPU, 1904–1918* (Manchester: Manchester University Press, 2007).
Crawford, E., *Campaigning for the Vote: Kate Parry Frye's Suffrage Diary* (London: Francis Boutle, 2013).
—— 'Police, prisons and prisoners: the view from the Home Office', *Women's History Review*, 14:3–4 (2005), 487–506.
—— *The Women's Suffrage Movement: A Reference Guide, 1866–1928* (London: Routledge, 2001).
—— *The Women's Suffrage Movement in Britain and Ireland* (London: Routledge, 2006).
Crew, D. O., *Suffragist Sheet Music* (Jefferson, NC: McFarland, 2002).
Croft, S. (ed.), *Votes for Women and Other Plays* (Twickenham: Aurora Metro, 2009).
Cosgrove, S., E. MacColl, and R. Samuel, *Theatres of the Left, 1880–1935* (London: Routledge & Kegan Paul, 1985).
Davies, A., *Other Theatres: The Development of Alternative and Experimental Theatre in Britain* (London: Macmillan Education, 1987).
Davies, P., *Lost London, 1870–1945* (Amersham: Trans Atlantic, 2009).
Davis, J., and V. Emaljanow, '"Wistful remembrancer": the historiographical problem of Macqueen-Popery', *New Theatre Quarterly*, 17:4 (2001), 299–309.
Davis, T. C., *Actresses as Working Women: Their Social Identity in Victorian Culture* (London and New York: Routledge, 1991).
—— 'Edwardian management and the structures of industrial capitalism', in M. R. Booth and J. H. Kaplan, *The Edwardian Theatre: Essays on Performance and the Stage* (Cambridge: Cambridge University Press, 2008), pp. 111–29.
—— 'A feminist methodology in theatre history', in B. A. McConachie and T. Postlewait (eds.), *Interpreting the Theatrical Past* (Iowa City, IA: University of Iowa Press, 1989), pp. 59–81.

—— *George Bernard Shaw and the Socialist Theatre* (Westport, CT: Greenwood Press, 1994).
—— 'Private women and the public realm', *Theatre Survey*, 35:1 (1994), 65–71.
Dean-Myatt, W., *Scottish Vernacular Discography, 1888–1960* (Hailsham: City of London Phonograph and Gramophone Society, 2013).
Dee, R., *Sweet Peas, Suffragettes and Showmen: Events that Changed the World in the RHS Halls* (London: Phillimore & Co., 2011).
Del Valle, C., *The Brooklyn Theatre Index*, vol. I (New York: Theatre Talks, 2010).
Delap, L., M. DiCenzo and L. Ryan, *Feminism and the Periodical Press*, vol. III (London and New York: Routledge, 2006).
—— *Feminist Media History: Suffrage, Periodicals and the Public Sphere* (Basingstoke: Palgrave Macmillan, 2011).
Demastes, W. W., *British Playwrights, 1880–1956* (Westport, CT: Greenwood Press, 1996).
de Jongh, N., *Politics, Prudery and Perversions: The Censoring of the English Stage, 1901–1968* (London: Methuen, 2000).
Diamond, M. J., 'Olympe De Gouges and the French Revolution: the construction of gender as critique', *Dialectical Anthropology*, 15:2–3 (1990), 95–105.
Dodge, J., and S. Forward, 'Miss Agnes Rebury (1858–1943): the memoirs of a warder at Holloway', *Women's History Review*, 15:5 (2006), 783–804.
Duff, C., *The Lost Summer: The Heyday of the West End Theatre* (London: Hern Books, 1995).
Dunn, K., *Exit through the Fireplace: The Great Days of the Rep* (London: John Murray, 1998).
Dyhouse, C., *Girls Growing Up in Late Victorian and Edwardian England* (London: Routledge & Kegan Paul, 1981).
Eltis, S., *Acts of Desire: Women and Sex on Stage, 1800–1930* (Oxford: Oxford University Press, 2013).
Engle, S., *New Women Dramatists in America, 1890–1920* (New York: Palgrave Macmillan, 2007).
Ervine, St.-J., *The Organised Theatre* (London: Allen & Unwin, 1924).
—— *The Theatre in My Time* (London: Rich & Cowan, 1933).
Eustance, C., 'Meanings of militancy: the ideas and practice of political resistance in the Women's Freedom League, 1907–14', M. Joannou and J. Purvis (eds.), *Women's Suffrage Movement: New Feminist Perspectives* (Manchester: Manchester University Press, 2009), pp. 51–64.

Eustance, C., J. Ryan and L. Ugolini, *A Suffrage Reader* (New York: Leicester University Press, 2000).
Fairbrother, S., *Through an Old Stage Door* (London: Frederick Muller Ltd., 1939).
Ferguson, N., *Lost Empires: The Phenomenon of Theatres Past, Present and Future* (London: Cassell Illustrated, 2005).
Ferris, L., 'The female self and performance: the case of *The First Actress*', in K. Laughlin and C. Schuler (eds.), *Theatre and Feminist Aesthetics* (Madison, WI: Fairleigh Dickinson University Press, 1995), pp. 242–57.
Filippi, R., *Hints to Speakers and Players* (London: Edward Arnold, 1911).
Finnegan, M., *Selling Suffrage: Consumer Culture and Votes for Women* (New York: Columbia University Press, 1999).
Fitzgerald, A., and C. McPhee, *The Non-violent Militant: Selected Writings of Teresa Billington-Greig* (London: Routledge & Kegan Paul, 1987).
Florence, M. S., M. Kamester, C. Marshall, C. K. Ogden and J. Vellacott, *Militarism versus Feminism* (London: Virago, 1987).
Florey, K., *Women's Suffrage Memorabilia: An Illustrated Historical Study* (Jefferson, NC: McFarland & Company, Inc., 2013).
Forbes-Robertson, D., *My Aunt Maxine: The Story of Maxine Elliott* (New York: Viking Press, 1964).
Forbes-Robertson, Sir J., *A Player under Three Reigns* (London: T. Fisher Unwin, 1925).
Forbes-Robertson Hale, B., *What Women Want: An Interpretation of the Feminist Movement* (New York: Frederick A. Stokes, 1914).
Freeman, L., S. La Follette, G. A. Zabriskie, *Belle: The Biography of Bell Case La Follette* (New York: Beaufort Books, 1986).
Friedl, B., *On to Victory: Propaganda Plays of the Woman Suffrage Movement* (Boston, MA: Northeastern University Press, 1987).
Gale, M. B., 'Lena Ashwell and auto/biographical negotiations of the professional self', in M. B. Gale and V. Gardner (eds.), *Auto/biography and Identity: Women, Theatre and Performance* (Manchester: Manchester University Press, 2004), pp. 99–125.
—— *West End Women: Women and the London Stage, 1918–1962* (London and New York: Routledge, 1996).
Gale, M. B. and C. Barker, *British Theatre between the Wars, 1918–1939* (Cambridge: Cambridge University Press, 2000).
Gale, M. B. and G. Bush-Bailey, *Plays and Performance Texts by Women, 1880–1930* (Manchester: Manchester University Press, 2012).

Gale, M. B. and V. Gardner, *Auto/biography and Identity: Women, Theatre and Performance* (Manchester: Manchester University Press, 2004).
——*Women, Theatre and Performance: New Histories, New Historiographies* (Manchester: Manchester University Press, 2000).
Gamble, S., *Routledge Critical Dictionary of Feminism and Postfeminism* (London and New York: Routledge, 2000).
Garb, T., *Sisters of the Brush: Women's Artistic Culture in Late Nineteenth-Century Paris* (New Haven, CT: Yale University Press, 1994).
Gardner, V., 'Provincial stages, 1900–1934: touring and repertory theatre', in B. Kershaw (ed.), *The Cambridge History of British Theatre* (Cambridge: Cambridge University Press, 2008), pp. 60–85.
——*Sketches from the Actresses' Franchise League* (Nottingham: University of Nottingham, 1985).
Gardner, V. and S. Rutherford, *The New Woman and Her Sisters* (Ann Arbor, MI: University of Michigan Press, 1992).
Garner, L., *Stepping Stones to Women's Liberty: Feminist Ideas in the Women's Suffrage Movement, 1900–1918* (London: Heinemann, 1984).
Gates, J. E., *Elizabeth Robins, 1862–1952, Actress, Novelist, Feminist* (Tuscaloosa, AL: University of Alabama Press, 1994).
Geddes, J. F., 'Deeds *and* words in the suffrage military hospital in Endell Street', *Making History*, 51 (2007), 79–98.
Gillett, P., *Musical Women in England, 1870–1914: 'Encroaching on All Man's Privileges'* (New York: St Martin's Press, 2000).
Glenn, S. A., *Female Spectacle: The Theatrical Roots of Modern Feminism* (Cambridge, MA: Harvard University Press, 2000).
Glover, E., *Cats and My Camera* (London: M. Joseph Ltd, 1938).
Godfrey, E., *Femininity, Crime and Self-Defence in Victorian Literature and Society: From Dagger-Fans to Suffragettes* (London: Palgrave Macmillan, 2012).
Gooddie, S., *Annie Horniman: A Pioneer in the Theatre* (London: Methuen London, 1990).
Gottleib, J. V., and R. Toye (eds.), *The Aftermath of Suffrage: Women, Gender and Politics in Britain, 1918–1945* (London: Palgrave Macmillan, 2013).
Grant Ferguson, A., *The Shakespeare Hut: A Story of Memory, Performance and Identity, 1916–1923* (London: The Arden Shakespeare, 2018).
——'Lady Forbes-Robertson's war work: Gertrude Elliott and the Shakespeare Hut performances, 1916–1919', in G. McMullan, L. Cowen Orlin and V. Mason Vaughan (eds.), *Women Making Shakespeare* (London: Bloomsbury, 2013), pp. 233–42.

Green, B., 'From visible flâneuse to spectacular suffragette? The prison, the street and the sites of suffrage', *Discourse*, 17:2 (1994-5), 67-97.
—— *Spectacular Confessions: Autobiography, Performance Activism and the Sites of Suffrage* (New York: St Martin's Press, 1997).
Haggard, S. and A. Seyler, *The Craft of Comedy* (London: F. Muller, 1944).
Hamilton, C., *How the Vote Was Won* (London: Women Writers' Suffrage League, 1909).
—— *Marriage as a Trade* (London: The Women's Press, 1981).
—— *Triumphant Women*, in E. Adlard (ed.), *Edy: Recollections of Edith Craig* (London: Frederick Muller, 1949).
Hammill, F., E. Miskimmin and A. Sponenberg, *Encyclopedia of British Women's Writing, 1900-1950* (London: Palgrave Macmillan, 2009).
Hannam, J. and K. Hunt, 'Towards an archaeology of interwar women's politics: the local and the everyday', in J. V. Gottleib and R. Toye (eds.), *The Aftermath of Suffrage* (London: Palgrave Macmillan, 2013), pp. 124-41.
Harrison, B., 'The militant suffragettes by Antonia Raeburn', *Oral History*, 2:1 (1974), 73-6.
—— *Prudent Revolutionaries: Portraits of British Feminists between the Wars* (London: Clarendon Press, 1987).
—— *Separate Spheres: The Opposition to Women's Suffrage in Britain* (London: Croom Helm, 1978).
Harrison, P. G., *Connecting Links: The British and American Woman Suffrage Movements, 1900-1914* (Westport, CT: Greenwood Press, 2000).
Hartman, K., 'What made me a suffragette: the new woman and the new (?) conversion narrative', *Women's History Review*, 12:1 (2003), 35-50.
Hayman, C. and D. Spender, *How the Vote Was Won, and Other Suffragette Plays* (London: Methuen, 1985).
Him, G. and M. W. Preston, *How It Feels to Be the Husband of a Suffragette* (New York: George H. Doran, 1915).
Higham, C., *Dark Lady: Winston Churchill's Mother and Her World* (London: Virgin, 2007).
Hindson, C., *Female Performance Practice on the Fin-de-Siècle Popular Stages of London and Paris* (Manchester: Manchester University Press, 2007).
Hirshfield, C., 'The Actresses' Franchise League and the campaign for women's suffrage, 1908-1914', *Theatre Research International*, 10:2 (1985), 129-53.
—— 'Suffragettes onstage: women's political theatre in Edwardian England', *New England Theatre Journal*, 2 (1991), 13-26.

—— 'The suffragist as playwright in Edwardian England', *Frontiers: A Journal of Women Studies*, 9:2 (1987), 1–6.
—— 'The woman's theatre in England, 1913–1918', *Theatre History Studies*, 15 (1995), 121–37.
Hoare, P., *Wilde's Last Stand* (London: Duckworth, 1997).
Holledge, J., *Innocent Flowers: Women in the Edwardian Theatre* (London: Virago Press, 1981).
—— 'Innocent flowers no more: the changing status of women in theatre', in L. Goodman (ed.), *The Routledge Reader in Gender and Performance* (London and New York: Routledge, 1998), pp. 92–6.
—— 'Women's theatre – women's rights', Ph.D., University of Bristol, 1985.
Holloway, D., *Playing the Empire: The Acts of the Holloway Touring Theatre Company* (London: George G. Harrap, 1979).
Holroyd, M., *A Strange Eventful History: The Dramatic Lives of Ellen Terry and Henry Irving* (London: Vintage, 2009).
Holton, S. S., *Suffrage Days: Stories from the Women's Suffrage Movement* (London and New York: Routledge, 1996).
—— 'The suffragist and the "average woman"', *Women's History Review*, 1:1 (1992), 9–24.
—— 'Women and the vote', in J. Purvis (ed.), *Women's History: Britain, 1850–1945* (London and New York: Routledge, 1998), pp. 277–306.
Housman, L., *Alice in Ganderland* (London: The Woman's Press, 1911).
—— *The Unexpected Years* (London: Jonathan Cape, 1937).
Howard, D., *London Theatres and Music Halls, 1850–1950* (London: Library Association, 1970).
Hynes, S., *The Edwardian Turn of Mind* (London: Pimlico, 1968).
Jeffreys, S., *The Spinster and Her Enemies: Feminism and Sexuality, 1880–1930* (London: Pandora Press, 1987).
Joannou, M. and J. Purvis, *The Women's Suffrage Movement: New Feminist Perspectives*, Manchester: Manchester University Press, 1998.
John, A. V., *Elizabeth Robins: Staging a Life* (Stroud: Tempus, 2007).
—— 'Men, manners and militancy: literary men and women's suffrage', in A. V. John and C. Eustance (eds.), *The Men's Share? Masculinities, Male Support and Women's Suffrage in Britain, 1890–1920* (London and New York: Routledge, 1997), pp. 88–109.
—— 'The privilege of power: suffrage women and the issue of men's support', in A. Vickery (ed.), *Women, Privilege and Power: British Politics, 1750 to the Present* (Stanford, CA: Stanford University Press, 2001), pp. 227–52.

John, N. A., *Holloway Jingles: Written in Holloway Prison during March and April 1912* (Glasgow: Glasgow WSPU, c.1912).
Kaplan, J. H. and S. Stowell, *Theatre and Fashion: Oscar Wilde to the Suffragettes* (Cambridge: Cambridge University Press, 1994).
Kelly, Katherine E., 'The Actresses' Franchise League prepares for war: feminist theatre in camouflage', *Theatre Survey*, 35:1 (1994), 121–37.
—— *Modern Drama by Women, 1880s–1930s* (London and New York: Routledge, 1996).
—— 'Seeing through spectacles: the woman suffrage movement and London newspapers, 1906–13', *European Journal of Women's Studies*, 11:3 (2004), 327–53.
Kemp, T., *Birmingham Repertory Theatre: The Playhouse and the Man* (Birmingham: Cornish Bros., 1943).
Kenney, A., *Memories of a Militant* (London: Edward Arnold & Co., 1924).
Kershaw, B., *Research Methods in Theatre and Performance* (Edinburgh: Edinburgh University Press, 2011).
Keyssar, H., *Feminist Theatre* (London: Macmillan, 1984).
Kinchin, P., *Glasgow's Great Exhibitions* (Wendlebury: White Cockade Publishing, 1988).
Kingston, G., *Curtsey While You're Thinking* (London: Williams & Norgate, 1937).
Kohn, M., *Dope Girls: The Birth of the British Drug Underground* (London: Granta Books, 2001).
Lansbury, G., *My Life* (London: Constable & Co., 1928).
Lathan, P., *It's Behind You! The Story of Panto* (London: New Holland, 2004).
Law, C., *Suffrage and Power: The Women's Movement, 1918–1928* (London and New York: I. B. Tauris, 1997).
—— *Women: A Modern Political Dictionary* (London: I. B. Tauris, 2000).
Lawrence, G., *A Star Danced* (London: W. H. Allen, 1945).
Lawrence, J., 'Contesting the male polity: the suffragettes and the politics of disruption in Edwardian Britain', in A. Vickery (ed.), *Women, Privilege and Power: British Politics, 1750 to the Present* (Stanford, CA: Stanford University Press, 2001), pp. 201–26.
Lee, E., *Folksong and Music Hall* (London and New York: Routledge & Paul, 1982).
Leneman, L., *'A Guid Cause': The Women's Suffrage Movement in Scotland* (Aberdeen: Aberdeen University Press, 1991).
Leslie, H., *More Ha'pence than Kicks: Being Some Things Remembered* (London: Macdonald, 1943).

Lewis, J. (ed.), *Before the Vote Was Won: Arguments for and against Women's Suffrage* (London and New York: Routledge, 1987).

Liddington, J., *Rebel Girls: Their Fight for the Vote* (London: Virago, 2006).

—— *Vanishing for the Vote: Suffrage, Citizenship and the Battle for the Census* (Manchester: Manchester University Press, 2014).

Liddington, J. and J. Norris, *One Hand Tied Behind Us* (London: Virago, 1978).

London, J., *The People of the Abyss* (London: Isbister & Co., 1903).

Looser, D., 'Radical bodies and dangerous ladies: martial arts and women's performance, 1900–1918', *Theatre Research International*, 36:1 (2011), 3–19.

Lysack, K., *Come Buy, Come Buy: Shopping and the Culture of Consumption in Victorian Women's Writing* (Athens, OH: Ohio University Press, 2008).

Lytton, C., *Prison and Prisoners* (London: Heinemann, 1914).

McCarthy, L., *Myself and My Friends* (London: Thornton Butterworth, 1933).

Mackenzie, M., *Shoulder to Shoulder* (New York: Knopf, 1975).

MacQueen-Pope, W., *Carriages at Eleven: The Story of the Edwardian Theatre* (London: Robert Hale & Co., 1947).

—— *An Indiscreet Guide to Theatreland* (London: Muse Arts, 1947).

—— *Ladies First* (London: W. H. Allen, 1952).

Maitland, S., *Vesta Tilley* (London: Virago Press, 1986).

Maloney, P., *Scotland and the Music Hall, 1850–1914* (Manchester: Manchester University Press, 2003).

Marbury, E., *My Crystal Ball* (New York: Boni & Liveright, 1923).

Marston, E., *Prison: Five Hundred Years of Life behind Bars* (Kew: National Archives, 2009).

Martin-Harvey, Sir J., *The Autobiography of Sir John Martin-Harvey* (London: Sampson Low, Marston & Co., 1933).

May, R., *Theatremania* (London: Vernon & Yates, 1967).

Mayhall, L. N., 'Creating the 'suffragette spirit': British feminism and the historical imagination', *Women's History Review*, 4:3 (1995), 319–44.

—— 'Defining militancy: radical protest, the constitutional idiom, and women's suffrage in Britain, 1908–1909', *Journal of British Studies*, 39:3 (2000), 340–71.

—— 'Domesticating Emmeline: representing the suffragette, 1930–1993', *NWSA Journal*, 11:2 (1999), 1–24.

Mayhew, H., *London Labour and the London Poor* (London: Cass, 1851).

Mayo, W., 'Prison experiences of a suffragette', *The Idler* (April 1908), 85–99.

Melville, J., *Ellen and Edy* (London: Pandora Press, 1987).
Mercer, J., 'Media and militancy: propaganda in the Women's Social and Political Union's campaign', *Women's History Review*, 14:3-4 (2005), 471-86.
Metcalfe, C., *Peeresses of the Stage* (London: Andrew Melrose, 1913).
Middleton, G., *These Things Are Mine: The Autobiography of a Journeyman Playwright* (New York: The Macmillan Company, 1947).
Miller, J. E., *Rebel Women: Feminism, Modernism and the Edwardian Novel* (London: Virago, 1994).
Miller, R., *Champagne from My Slipper* (London: Herbert Jenkins, 1962).
Mitchell, H., *The Hard Way Up: The Autobiography of Hannah Mitchell Suffragette and Rebel* (London: Faber & Faber, 1968).
Moffat, G., *Join Me in Remembering: The Life and Reminiscences of the Author of 'Bunty Pulls the Strings'* (Camps Bay: W. L. Moffat, 1955).
Moore, E., *Exits and Entrances* (London: Chapman & Hall, 1923).
Moran, S., *The Stage Career of Cicely Hamilton (1895-1914)* (Frankfurt: Peter Lang, 2017).
Morell, C., *'Black Friday' and Violence Against Women in the Suffragette Movement* (London: Women's Research and Resources Centre Publications Collective, 1981).
Morley, M., *Margate and Its Theatres, 1730-1965* (London: Museum Press, 1966).
Mullin, D. C., *Victorian Actors and Actresses in Review* (Westport, CT: Greenwood Press, 1983).
Naylor, S., *Gaiety and George Grossmith* (London: Stanley Paul & Co., 1913).
Nead, L., *Victorian Babylon: People, Streets and Images in Nineteenth Century London* (New Haven, CT: Yale University Press, 2000).
Neal, M., *As a Tale That Is Told*, unpublished autobiography, 1937, held in the English Song and Dance Society Library and Archive, Cecil Sharp House, London.
Nelson, C. C., *Literature of the Women's Suffrage Campaign in England* (Peterborough: Broadview Press, 2004).
—— *A New Woman Reader: Fiction, Articles and Drama of the 1890s* (New York: Broadview Press, 2001).
Newton, H. C., *Cues and Curtain Calls* (London: John Lane The Bodley Head, 1927).
Nicholson, S., *British Theatre and the Red Peril: The Portrayal of Communism, 1917-1945* (Exeter: University of Exeter Press, 1999).

—— *The Censorship of British Drama, 1900–1968* (Exeter: Exeter University Press, 2003).
Nicoll, A., *English Drama, 1900–1930: The Beginnings of the Modern Period* (Cambridge: Cambridge University Press, 1973).
Norquay, G., *Voices and Votes: A Literary Anthology of the Women's Suffrage Campaign* (Manchester: Manchester University Press, 1995).
Oldfield, S., *Spinsters of This Parish: The Life and Times of F. M. Mayor and Mary Sheepshanks* (London: Virago, 1984).
Ovenden, G., *The Illustrators of Alice* (New York: St Martin's Press, 1972).
Owens, R. C., *Smashing Times: A History of the Irish Women's Suffrage Movement, 1889–1922* (Dublin: Attic Press, 1984).
Pankhurst, E. S., *The Suffragette Movement* (London: Longmans, 1932).
Parker, L., *But – What Do You Do in the Winter? 100 Years of the CAA* (London: Concert Artistes' Association, 1996).
Paxton, N. 'Suffragette Judy: Punch and Judy at suffrage fairs and exhibitions in Edwardian London' in Astles, C., Mello, A,. and Orenstein, C, (eds) *Women and Puppetry: Critical and Historical Investigations* (London: Routledge, 2019), 126–40.
—— 'Will you, won't you, will you, won't you join the Suffrage Dance' in Riley, C., and Rose, L,. (eds) *Women's Suffrage in Word, Image, Music and Drama* (London: Routledge, 2020).
—— (ed.), *The Methuen Drama Book of Suffrage Plays* (London: Bloomsbury, 2013).
—— (ed.), *The Methuen Drama Book of Suffrage Plays: Taking the Stage* (London: Bloomsbury, 2018).
—— (ed.), 'Very much alive and kicking: the Actresses' Franchise League from 1914–1928', in M. B. Gale and K. Dorney (eds.), *Stage Women, 1900–1950. Female theatre workers and professional practice* (Manchester: Manchester University Press, 2019).
Paxton, S., *Stage See-Saws* (London: Mills & Boon, 1917).
Pearson, H., *The Last Actor-Managers* (London: Methuen & Co., 1950).
Pethick-Lawrence, F., *Fate Has Been Kind* (London: Hutchinson, 1943).
Pfisterer, S. and C. Pickett, *Playing with Ideas: Australian Women Playwrights from the Suffragettes to the Sixties* (Sydney: Currency Press, 1999).
Phillips, A., *Divided Loyalties: Dilemmas of Sex and Class* (London: Virago, 1987).
Phillips, M., *The Militant Suffrage Campaign in Perspective* (London: M. Phillips, 1957).

Phillips, T., *We Are the People* (London: National Portrait Gallery, 2004).
Pollock, D., *Exceptional Spaces: Essays in Performance and History* (Chapel Hill, NC: University of North Carolina Press, 1998).
Potter, A., 'The Equal Pay Campaign Committee: a case-study of a pressure group', *Political Studies*, 5:1 (1957), 49–64.
Powell, K., *Women and Victorian Theatre* (Cambridge: Cambridge University Press, 1997).
Price, N., *Into an Hour Glass* (London: Museum Press, 1953).
Pugh, M., *Women and the Women's Movement in Britain, 1914–1959* (London: Palgrave Macmillan, 2000).
Purvis, J., 'Deeds, not words: the daily lives of militant suffragettes in Edwardian Britain', *Women's Studies International Forum*, 18:2 (1995), 91–101.
—— *Emmeline Pankhurst: A Biography* (London and New York: Routledge, 2002).
—— 'A lost dimension? The political education of women in the suffragette movement in Edwardian Britain', *Gender and Education*, 6:3 (1994), 319–27.
—— 'The prison experiences of the suffragettes in Edwardian Britain', *Women's History Review*, 4:1 (1995), 103–33.
—— 'The suffragette and women's history', *Women's History Review*, 14:3–5 (2005), 357–64.
Rachlin, A., *Edy Was a Lady* (London: Matador, 2011).
Raeburn, A., *Militant Suffragettes* (London: Michael Joseph, 1973).
—— *The Suffragette View* (New York: St Martin's Press, 1976).
Ramelson, M., *The Petticoat Rebellion* (London: Lawrence & Wishart, 1976).
Rees, T. and D. Wilmore (eds.), *British Theatrical Patents, 1901–1950* (London: The Society for Theatre Research, 2010).
Reynolds, F., *'Punch' Pictures* (London: Cassell & Company, 1922).
Richardson, M. R., *Laugh a Defiance* (London: George Weidenfield & Nicolson, 1953).
Robertson, U. A., *Coming Out of the Kitchen: Women beyond the Home* (Stroud: Sutton Publishers, 2000).
Robins, E., *Both Sides of the Curtain* (London: William Heinemann, 1940).
—— *Way Stations* (London: Hodder & Stoughton, 1913).
Rollyson, C. E., *To Be a Woman: The Life of Jill Craigie* (London: Aurum, 2005).
Rosen, A., *Rise Up, Women! The Militant Campaign of the Women's Social and Political Union, 1903–1914* (Aldershot: Gregg Revivals, 1993).

Rover, C., *Love, Morals and the Feminists* (London and New York: Routledge & Kegan Paul, 1970).
—— *The 'Punch' Book of Women's Rights* (London: Hutchinson, 1967).
Rowbotham, S., *A Century of Women: The History of Women in Britain and the United States* (London: Viking, 1997).
—— *Dreamers of a New Day: Women Who Invented the Twentieth Century* (London: Verso, 2010).
—— *Women, Resistance and Revolution* (London: Allen Lane, 1972).
Rowell, G., *The Old Vic Theatre: A History* (Cambridge: Cambridge University Press, 1995).
Royden, M., *Downward Paths: An Inquiry into the Causes Which Contribute to the Making of the Prostitute* (London: G. Bell & Sons Ltd, 1916).
Ryan, L. and M. Ward, *Irish Women and the Vote: Becoming Citizens* (Dublin: Irish Academic Press, 2007).
St John, C., *Ellen Terry and Bernard Shaw: A Correspondence* (London: Constable & Co., 1931).
—— *Ethel Smyth: A Biography* (London: Longmans, 1959).
Sanderson, M., *From Irving to Olivier: A Social History of the Acting Profession in England, 1880-1983* (London: Athlone Press, 1984).
Schafer, E., *Lilian Baylis: A Biography* (Hatfield: University of Hertfordshire Press: Society for Theatre Research, 2006).
Schouvaloff, A., *The Theatre Museum, London* (London: Scala Publications, 1987).
Shanley, M. L., *Feminism, Marriage and Law in Victorian England* (London: I. B. Tauris, 1989).
Sharp, R. F., *A Short History of the English Stage from Its Beginnings to the Summer of the Year 1908* (London: Walter Scott, 1909).
Sheppard, A., *Cartooning for Suffrage* (Albuquerque, NM: University of New Mexico Press, 1994).
Short, E., *Sixty Years of Theatre* (London: Eyre & Spottiswoode, 1951).
Showalter, E., *The Female Malady: Women, Madness and English Culture, 1830-1980* (London: Virago, 1987).
Smith, A. K., *Suffrage Discourse in Britain during the First World War* (Aldershot: Ashgate Publishing Limited, 2005).
Smith, S. and J. Watson, *Reading Autobiography: A Guide for Interpreting Life Narratives* (Minneapolis, MN: University of Minnesota Press, 2010).
Speaight, G., *Bawdy Songs of the Early Music Hall* (Newton Abbot: David & Charles, 1975).

Spender, D., *The Education Papers: Women's Quest for Equality in Britain, 1850–1912* (London: Routledge & Kegan Paul, 1987).
—— *Feminist Theorists* (London: The Women's Press Ltd, 1983).
—— *Man Made Language* (London and New York: Routledge & Kegan Paul, 1980).
—— *There's Always Been a Women's Movement This Century* (London: Pandora Press, 1983).
Stowell, S., *A Stage of Their Own: Feminist Playwrights of the Suffrage Era* (Ann Arbor, MI: University of Michigan Press, 1992).
——'Drama as a trade', in V. Gardner and S. Rutherford (eds.), *The New Woman and Her Sisters* (London: Harvester Wheatsheaf, 1992), pp. 187–200.
Strachey, R., *Our Freedom and Its Results* (London: L. Woolf and Virginia Woolf at the Hogarth Press, 1936).
Stratman, C. J., *Britain's Theatrical Periodicals, 1720–1967: A Bibliography* (New York: The New York Public Library, 1972).
Striezheff Lewis, M. and J. Lewis, *Costume: The Performing Partner* (Colorado Springs, CO: Meriwether, 1990).
Sutcliffe, D., *The Keys of Heaven* (Nottingham: Cockasnook Books, 2010).
Sutherland, J., *Mrs Humphrey Ward: Eminent Victorian, Pre-eminent Edwardian* (Oxford: Clarendon Press, 1990).
Taylor, A., *'Down with the Crown': British Anti-monarchism and Debates about Royalty since 1790* (London: Reaktion, 1999).
Templeton, J., *Ibsen's Women* (Cambridge: Cambridge University Press, 1997).
Thane, P., 'Impact of mass democracy on British political culture', in J. V. Gottlieb and R. Toye (eds.), *The Aftermath of Suffrage* (New York: Palgrave Macmillan, 2013), pp. 54–69.
Thomas, S., 'Crying "the horror" of prostitution: Elizabeth Robins's "Where Are You Going To … ?" and the moral crusade of the Women's Social and Political Union', *Women: A Cultural Review*, 16:2 (2005), 203–21.
Tickner, L., *The Spectacle of Women: Imagery of the Suffrage Campaign, 1907–14* (London: Chatto & Windus, 1987).
Tucker, S., *Some of These Days: An Autobiography* (London: Hammond & Hammond, 1948).
Tusan, M. E., *Women Making News: Gender and Journalism in Modern Britain* (Chicago, IL: University of Illinois Press, 2005).
Tylee, C. M., '"A better world for both": men, cultural transformation and the suffragettes', in M. Joanou and J. Purvis (eds.), *The Women's Suffrage*

Movement: New Feminist Perspectives (Manchester: Manchester University Press, 2009), pp. 140–56.

Tynan, K., *Kenneth Tynan Letters* (London: Random House, 1998).

Vanbrugh, I., *To Tell My Story* (London: Hutchinson and Co., 1948).

Vicinus, M., *Independent Women: Work and Community for Single Women, 1850–1920* (London: Virago Press, 1985).

Vickery, A. (ed.), *Women, Privilege and Power: British Politics, 1750 to the Present* (Stanford, CA: Stanford University Press, 2001).

Vining, M. and B. C. Hacker, 'From camp follower to lady in uniform: women, social class and military institutions before 1920', *Contemporary European History*, 10:3 (2001), 353–73.

Wagner, L., *How to Get on the Stage and How to Succeed There* (London: Chatto & Windus, 1899).

Walkowitz, J., *Cities of Dreadful Delight* (Chicago, IL: University of Chicago Press, 1992).

—— 'The "Vision of Salome": cosmopolitanism and erotic dancing in central London, 1908–1918', *The American Historical Review*, 108:2 (2003), 337–76.

Wallis, M., 'Social commitment and aesthetic experiment, 1895–1946', in B. Kershaw (ed.), *The Cambridge History of British Theatre* (Cambridge: Cambridge University Press, 2008), pp. 167–94.

Webster, M., *The Same Only Different* (London: Victor Gollancz, 1969).

White, C. L., *Women's Magazines, 1693–1968* (London: Michael Joseph, 1970).

Whitelaw, L., *The Life and Rebellious Times of Cicely Hamilton* (London: The Women's Press, 1990).

Wilberforce, O., *Backsettown and Elizabeth Robins* (Nijemen: private circulation, 1952).

Wiles, D. and C. Dymkowski (eds.), *Cambridge Companion to Theatre History* (Cambridge: Cambridge University Press, 2012).

Wilkinson, L. R., 'Feminism, modernism, and the morality debate: Anne Charlotte Leffler's "Tre Komedier"', *Scandinavian Studies*, 76:1 (2004), 47–70.

Williams, G., *British Theatre in the Great War: A Revaluation* (London: Continuum, 2005).

Wilson, G., *With All Her Might: The Life of Gertrude Harding Militant Suffragette* (Canada: Goose Lane, 1996).

Winsten, S., *Days with Bernard Shaw* (London: Hutchinson & Co., 1948).

Wolf, T., *Edith Garrud: The Suffragette Who Knew Jujutsu* (Raleigh, NC: Lulu, 2009).

Woodfield, J., *English Theatre in Transition, 1881–1914* (London: Croom Helm, 1984).
Woodrough, E., *Women in European Theatre* (Oxford: Intellect Books, 1995).
Woods, L., '"The Golden Calf": noted English actresses in American vaudeville, 1904–1916', *Journal of American Culture*, 15:3 (1992), 61–71.

Index

Note: 'n.' after a page reference indicates the number of a note on that page

Albert Hall 17, 39, 82, 127
Andrews, Gertrude 152, 154–5
Arncliffe Sennett, Maud 53, 68, 103, 112–14, 123–6, 132–4, 181–2
Ashwell, Lena 31, 56–7, 68, 73, 85–6, 127, 134, 149, 165–6, 172, 187n.122, 190
Astor, Nancy 181, 195

Barrie, J. M. 5, 153, 168, 176
Baylis, Lilian 191
Bensusan, Inez 41–2, 44, 55, 68, 72–3, 149–54, 155, 158, 168–70, 172, 187n.122, 191, 193
  Apple, The 55, 139
Bewicke, Hilda 71, 170
Bioscope, The 72
Bjornson, Bjornstiern 114, 152–7
  Gauntlet, A 114, 156–7
'Black Friday' 112–13, 123
Bonstelle, Jessie 153–5
Boucicault, Nina 57, 178, 181, 187n.122, 202
Bourne, Adeline 11–12, 31, 32, 51, 55, 57, 68, 101, 114, 174, 179, 181, 187n.122, 191–2, 195–6, 198, 201
Bratton, J. 2, 9, 154–5
Brieux, Eugène 155–7
  Woman on Her Own (La Femme seule) 155–7

British Actors' Equity 191
British Women's Hospital 168, 173–6, 179, 192, 194

Carlson, Susan 7–8, 88, 92
Casson, Lewis 55, 191, 196
Cavell, Edith 174–5
Caxton Hall 17, 70, 88, 118, 123, 161, 167, 182, 191
censorship 31, 61, 140, 169
Census Boycott 66–9
Chapin, Alice 88
  At the Gates 88
Chapman Catt, Carrie 74, 128–9
Cheliga, Marya 152, 155
Cockin, Katherine 8, 10, 64
Common Cause, The 9
Consultative Committee of Women's Organisations 181
Conti, Italia 71, 190
Coronation Procession 82–7
Coronet Theatre 156, 169
Craig, Edith 30, 31, 38–9, 62, 68, 89–91, 117, 122, 132–3, 161, 174
Crawford, Elizabeth 26
Criterion restaurant 50, 55, 59, 74, 108, 126, 196
Croft, Susan 6–7, 88

Daily Chronicle 18, 129, 164
Daily Mail 125, 168, 177
Daily Telegraph 18, 66, 129–30, 137

INDEX 231

dance 14, 31–2, 39, 42, 71, 74, 76, 135, 170
Davis, Tracy C. 52, 149–50
Davison, Emily Wilding 13, 132–3
Despard, Charlotte 93, 128, 151
Drum and Fife band 19–20, 43, 91
Dugdale, Joan 20, 59–61, 83, 90, 110, 112
  10 Clowning Street 44, 59–61, 66
Duval, Una (née Dugdale) 60–1, 112, 195

East London Federation of Suffragettes 59
Elliott, Gertrude (Lady Forbes-Robertson) 52, 54–5, 86, 98, 128, 167, 187n.122
Elliott, Maxine 73, 75
Endell Street Hospital 168, 174
entertainments
  Anti Suffrage Waxworks 34–7
  Punch and Judy 41–2
Equal Pay Campaign 194–5
Equity *see* British Actors' Equity
Era, The 70, 95–103, 139, 135, 166, 180
Eustance, Claire 64
Evening Standard 66, 113, 172
exhibitions
  Anglo-American 162
  National Union of Women's Suffrage Societies (NUWSS) 38
  United Suffragists 38, 167
  Women and Army Work 38
  Women's Freedom League (WFL) 38–9, 70, 191
  Women's Social and Political Union (WSPU) 17–45, 37, 38–40, 45, 126

Women Writers' Suffrage League (WWSL) and Men's League for Women's Suffrage (MLWS) Sweated Labour 38

Fawcett, Millicent Garrett 128, 130–1, 151
Forbes-Robertson, Beatrice 34, 73–5, 85, 194
Forbes-Robertson, Johnston 5, 31, 54–5, 75, 96, 168, 172, 176, 190
forcible feeding 27–8, 96, 108, 115, 132–3, 135, 141

Gale, Maggie B. 11, 190, 199
Games and Toys 164
Gardener, Viv 141, 188n.146
Garrud, Edith 37–8, 41
Glasgow 27, 39, 89, 118, 125
Glover, Evelyn 34, 44, 168
Gibb, Ellison 112, 124
Granville-Barker, Harley 51, 53, 68
Guilbert, Yvette 71

Hamilton, Cicely 20, 34–6, 44–5, 62, 64, 69, 114, 117, 137, 157–8, 161, 169, 178, 181, 190–2
  Anti Suffrage Waxworks 34–7
  How The Vote Was Won 34, 65–6, 86–7, 183
  Pageant of Great Women 36, 64, 73, 132
  Pot and Kettle 23, 34, 117
  Where Are You Going To? 62, 169
Harraden, Beatrice 59, 168
  Lady Geraldine's Speech 34, 93–4
Harrison, Brian 110
Harwood, H. M. 62
  Honour Thy Father 62–3

Hatton, Bessie 58, 168
Hirshfield, Claire 50, 188n.146
Holledge, Julie 4–5, 7, 115, 188n.146
Holloway prison 24, 27–8, 29, 60, 97, 118, 133
Holme, Vera 89, 121, 125
Housman, Laurence 31, 56, 66–7
  Alice in Ganderland 87
  Woman's Cause 66–7
  Woman This and Woman That 66
Hyde Park 25, 113, 127, 162, 181

Illustrated London News 24

Jennings, Gertrude 68, 168, 190
  Woman's Influence, A 34, 44, 53, 75
Ju-jitsu 37–8
  see also Garrud, Edith
Jus Suffragii 152

Kelly, K. E. 83–4, 170, 173, 188n.146
Kendal, Madge 51, 181, 191
Kenney, Annie 70, 109
Kingston, Gertrude 50–1, 56, 119, 149, 168, 176, 187n.122, 201
Kingsway Theatre 75, 172
Knoblock (also Knoblauch), Edward 172–3
  War Committee, A 172–3

La Follette, Fola 73–5
Lawrence, Mabel 94
  Salvation of Her Sex, The 94–5
Liddington, Jill 68–9
Little Theatre 56, 119, 163
Lloyd, Marie 70–1
Lloyd George, David 42, 165
London Budget 131

Lucette Ryley, Madeleine 52, 97, 162, 187n.122
Lytton, Constance 132–3

McCarthy, Lillah 53, 68, 123, 172, 176, 181, 191
MacLachlan, Helen 93
  Mad Hatter's Tea Party Up to Date, The 93
McLeod, Irene Rutherford 138
  Reforming of Augustus, The 138–9
Manchester Guardian 18, 103, 129–31, 181
Marbury, Elisabeth 153, 155
march 18, 20, 58, 66, 76, 82–7, 89, 91, 103, 113, 116, 118, 132, 134, 141, 181
  see also procession
Marion, Kitty 20, 33, 57, 68, 71, 91, 99, 110, 112, 124
Matters, Muriel 68, 114–16, 126, 141
Maxine Elliott's Theatre 75
Mayo, Winifred 68, 83, 101, 110, 112, 114, 118–20, 122, 124–6, 156, 187n.122, 195
Mendl, Gladys 92
  Su' L' Pave 92–4
Men's League for Women's Suffrage (MLWS) 39, 55, 60, 97
Men's Political Union for Women's Enfranchisement (MPU) 40–1, 42, 60
Middleton, George 74
MLWS see Men's League for Women's Suffrage
Moffat, Graham 39, 118
  Maid and the Magistrate, The 44, 118
Moffat, Maggie 118

INDEX

Moncure Parker, Mary 153–5
Moore, Decima 51, 66–7, 69–70,
    83–4, 163, 165, 177–9, 187n.122,
    192, 195
Moore, Emily *see* Pertwee, Emily
Moore, Eva 53, 54, 58, 114–15,
    117, 127, 163, 165–6,
    187n.122, 191
Morning Post 18, 129
Morris, Margaret 71, 172
MPU *see* Men's Political Union for
    Women's Enfranchisement

National Union of Women's
    Suffrage Societies (NUWSS)
    75, 128, 133, 141, 182
    see also exhibitions
Nethersole, Olga 51, 70, 179
NUWSS *see* National Union of
    Women's Suffrage Societies

Olive, Edyth 182, 187n.122, 202

Pankhurst, Christabel 66, 85–6,
    109, 126, 139, 195
Pankhurst, Emmeline 38, 59, 66,
    117, 122, 129, 182, 192
Pankhurst, Sylvia 20, 43, 59
Parliament 23, 61, 88, 112–16, 118,
    160, 180–1, 201
Parry Frye, Kate 112–13
Paull, Harry Major (H. M.) 34, 163
    An Anti-Suffragist; or, The Other
    Side 163
Performer, The 96, 99
Pertwee, Emily 68, 71, 83, 166
Pethick Lawrence, Emmeline
    18–20, 66, 119, 123, 151, 165,
    192, 195

Pethick Lawrence, Frederick
    119, 194
petitions 54, 59, 114, 181, 191–2
Political Peepshows 23, 37
Price, Nancy 191
prison and prisoners 20, 24–30, 39,
    42–3, 60, 63, 70, 82, 107–11,
    113–14, 115, 118–20, 125–6, 128,
    132–7, 139–42
    see also forcible feeding;
    Holloway Prison
procession 12, 66, 82–8, 103, 132–3,
    141, 181, 192
    see also march
Purvis, June 108, 111

Richardson, Mary 71
Robins, Elizabeth 54, 62, 95, 153, 168
    Votes for Women 153
    Where Are You Going To?
    62, 169
Robson, Marie 140
    Suffragette, The; or, A Woman's
    Vote 140
Royal Academy of Dramatic
    Art 190

Sanderson, Michael 52, 101,
    188n.146
Savoy Hotel 195–6
Scottish Women's Hospitals
    176, 179
Seruya, Sime 29, 38–9, 117, 120,
    122, 141
Shakespeare Hut 167
Shaw, Charlotte 53, 89, 155
Shaw, George Bernard 5, 53, 62, 74,
    89, 153, 155, 157, 169
    Press Cuttings 39, 74

Shaw, Mary 62, 73, 153–4
Six Point Group 181
Smyth, Ethel 20, 180
   March of the Women 20
Stage, The 96, 102–3, 126
Star and Garter Home 168, 174–6, 179, 195
Steele, Flora Annie 157
Steer, Janette 98, 124–5, 187n.122, 192
St John, Christopher 62, 64–5, 117, 120–2, 181
   Defence of the Fighting Spirit, A 121–2
   First Actress, The 64–5, 97
   Her Will 132–3
   How The Vote Was Won 34, 65–6, 86–7, 182
   Pot and Kettle 23, 34, 117
Suffragette Fellowship 12, 110, 194–5
Syrett, Netta 137
   Might is Right 23, 137–40

Theatre Royal, Drury Lane 55, 127–30
Theatre Royal, Margate 51
Thorndike, Sybil 26, 55, 183, 190, 192, 195–6
Thorne, Sarah 51
Time and Tide 181
Times, The 24, 115, 164–6, 172, 177, 200
True Womanhood (film) 72

United Suffragists 158, 163, 167

Vanbrugh, Irene 50, 57, 68, 129, 130–2

Vanbrugh, Violet 51, 131, 166
vegetarian restaurants
   Eustace Miles 89–91, 167
   Gardenia 67, 127
Vote, The 39, 54, 93, 98–9
Votes for Women 31, 60, 94, 121–2, 127, 158–60

WAB *see* Women's Adjustment Board
WEC *see* Women's Emergency Corps
Wedekind, Frank 152–3
Westminster Gazette 113, 129
WFL *see* Women's Freedom League
Whitty, May 50–1, 68, 168, 179–81, 182, 187n.122, 191
Wilding Davison, Emily 13, 132–3
woman's theatre 149–52, 155–8, 172–3
   Camps Entertainments 170–3
   during World War One 169–73
   projects in Europe and America 152–5
Women Writers' Suffrage League (WWSL) 38, 43, 53–4, 66, 82, 132, 161, 164, 181
Women's Adjustment Board (WAB) 192–5, 200–2
Women's Emergency Corps (WEC) 163–6, 170, 177, 179, 192
Women's Freedom League (WFL) 12, 39, 45, 115–16, 118, 123, 127–8, 182, 191
   see also exhibitions

Women's Social and Political Union (WSPU) 12, 28, 60, 66, 70, 89, 91, 108–11, 118–19, 121–4, 126, 132–3, 139, 168
  see also exhibitions
WSPU *see* Women's Social and Political Union

WWSL *see* Women Writers' Suffrage League

YMCA 167
  see also Shakespeare Hut

Zangwill, Israel 53, 54–5, 68, 98, 134
  Prologue for a Women's Theatre 56

EU authorised representative for GPSR:
Easy Access System Europe, Mustamäe tee 50,
10621 Tallinn, Estonia
gpsr.requests@easproject.com

www.ingramcontent.com/pod-product-compliance
Lightning Source LLC
Chambersburg PA
CBHW070237240426
43673CB00044B/1825